T0354316

One Vision, Many Voices
A Multicultural and Multigenerational Collection of Scenes and Monologues

Gail Noppe-Brandon

Foreword by
Dr. Robert A. Neimeyer, Narrative Therapist

iUniverse, Inc.
Bloomington

One Vision, Many Voices
A Multicultural and Multigenerational Collection of Scenes and
Monologues

iUniverse books may be ordered through booksellers or by contacting:

*iUniverse
1663 Liberty Drive
Bloomington, IN 47403
www.iuniverse.com
1-800-Authors (1-800-288-4677)*

*Because of the dynamic nature of the Internet, any web addresses or links contained in this
book may have changed since publication and may no longer be valid. The views expressed
in this work are solely those of the author and do not necessarily reflect the views of the
publisher, and the publisher hereby disclaims any responsibility for them.*

ISBN: 978-1-4401-3591-0 (sc)
ISBN: 978-1-4401-3592-7 (ebook)

Printed in the United States of America

iUniverse rev. date: 5/2/2011

*"The Night Light" from THE POETRY OF ROBERT FROST edited by Edward Connery
Lathem. Copyright 1947, 1969 by Henry Holt and Company. Copyright 1975 by Lesley
Frost Ballantine. Reprinted by permission of Henry Holt and Company, LLC.*

The cover image is a photograph taken by Andrea Sperling. I selected this photo from the
thousands I was shown at a photo stock house because it was so "storyful." Little did I know
that the photographer was also a writer. It has inspired dozens of amazing plays over the years,
many of which are featured in this collection.

This book is dedicated to my students, colleagues, and teachers—
you are all one and the same.
And to my son, Jesse, who urged me to embrace this legacy.

Table of Contents

Girls

(1 Scene: Two males, teens — serio-comic) A teenage boy confronts the loss of a best friend who has fallen love.

Father, Me

(Monologue: Latina, teen—serious) A young woman explores the genesis of her bulimia.

Unspoken Words

(1 Scene: African-American male, 20s/African-American female 20s—serious) A young couple confront an unexpected pregnancy.

Etude

(1 Scene: Two males, 11 and 40s—serious) A father and son confront their relationship, following the death of the mother.

Loca

(1 Scene: Latino, 28/Latina, 25—serious) A young couple find themselves wanting different furtures.

Third Generation

(1 Scene: Two females, 40s, 20s—serio-comic) A mother is forced to accept her daughter on her own terms.

Foreward

As a theorist and a clinician, I have always believed that the meanings that people attribute to their experience shape that experience, and in so doing shape who they become. Leading them toward the articulation of these meanings is an art, and an act of love. The Find Your Voice process is just that: a loving act of art making, and an artful act of love. Theatre, like therapy, entails a quest for an authentic voice, one that articulates with power and clarity some facet of the experience of the writer or client in a way that speaks to a relevant listener. And like therapy, the work of finding that voice, honing it, and bringing it into meaningful and sometimes moving dialogue with others draws on a common pool of tools and proclivities, which entail a mix of active listening, improvisation, mutual orientation and risk taking. Artist and clinician, Gail Noppe-Brandon, the editor of this anthology, recognizes this crossover, and with originality and discipline has crafted a method to help contain the inevitable anxiety of both new and experienced writers as they construct a fresh way of seeing life, and the possibilities inherent for protagonists in their own stories.

This book conveys that method. It offers a systematic exposition of the Find Your Voice (FYV) process, through which participants as diverse as high school students trying to construct an identity in the social world, seniors hoping to harvest and depict the lessons of a long life, and professional playwrights confronting the white page can find self-expression, at the same time that they build community. The results—amply depicted in the words and works of participants—demonstrate beyond question the capacity of the method to allow people to step over the obstacles that separate them from who they want to be and what they wish to portray in the appreciative presence of others. The kind of coaching that makes this possible, much like transformative therapy, fosters an interaction fueled by curiosity, compassion and connectedness. It requires mutual respect among workshop participants, and the joint commitment to in-dwell the experience of the 'other.' And the result of such work in crafting and performing an emotionally "true" scene generalizes well beyond the studio, whether the participant is a student asked to answer a single question in the classroom, a client invited to tell his life story in the privacy of a therapy session, or a playwright preparing to go public with some aspect of her view of the world.

Reading the testimonials of these representative participants, some as much as ten to fifteen years down the road, is proof positive that the impact of the work is profound. The plays themselves, authentic articulations of the ways in which our human wants and needs can come in to conflict and then resolve, are a vivid and lively map of the human drama, one that validates and often extends the horizons of both speaker and listener. As an appreciative witness to this work from the kindred domain of narrative therapy, I have long encouraged Gail to establish an Institute for Creative Clinicians with the FYV method as a central feature; with this anthology, the door swings open. I am confident that this book and the thoughtful, artistic approach to coaching that it so cogently conveys will usher the reader into an *avant-garde* theatre of possibility, in which both author and audience will be engaged, enlivened, and enlarged by the experience.

Robert A. Neimeyer, PhD, Narrative Therapist & Poet
Author of *Constructivist Psychology* and *The Art of Longing*

Preface

This collection of dramatic literature is unique and very special to me, in several ways. All of the scenes and monologues that follow, written over a period of about twenty years, were developed within my Find Your Voice Workshops, using a very particular method of dramaturgy. They were each performed before a live audience and staged under my directorial vision. The settings in which the pieces were developed ranged from schools to social service agencies to professional theatres. The workshop participants, spanning ages from eight to eighty, included public school students, teachers, seniors, and professional playwrights; each writer was held to the same standards and process within their respective levels.

There was much hard work, joy, and pain involved in the creation of the thousands of plays that grew out of the Find Your Voice method—the very best of which I have collected for this anthology. None of the student or teacher plays, particularly those written by *first time* playwrights— and there are many in the collection—came easily. However, the plays were so substantial and powerful by the time they were performed that no one would recognize the first drafts, in which various degrees of poor grammar, unfocused plot, lack of conflict, wordiness, and low stakes rendered many of them almost impenetrable.

If you are moved, enlightened, or inspired by something you read in this collection, it is the truest testament to the power of revision and a credit to the playwright's tolerance for hard work. For the new writers, it is a testament to their ability to risk "not already knowing" how to write a play. It takes a lot of courage to learn how to do something, and it takes a lot of courage to put your imaginings down on paper and share them with the world. It is my fervent hope that other coaches, teachers, students, and writers will be inspired by these plays. If so, I hope you will read the Method chapters within and possibly even seek out my *Find Your Voice* (Heinemann, 2004) book in order to learn how to lead your own classes through the exercise. You can use the plays, scenes, and monologues in this collection as assignments for the recommended acting study. If you are an acting teacher perusing this collection, I trust that you will find ample selections for diverse students who often struggle to find themselves represented in published dramatic literature. Above all, you will find material that will not only challenge and satisfy, but will provide the opportunity for actors of all ages to 'fight for' rather than fight 'with' one another.

The work from the professional stage writers, some of whom had not yet been produced in theatres outside of the realms of their particular cultural heritages, represents the powerful voices of artists who were courageous enough to engage in a method that took them down a different path from writing alone in their own studios. I believe that every piece we developed and produced demonstrated craft and integrity, and that is why I have chosen to mix the work of the new writers together with that of the professionals. And, in deference to the universality of the captured human experiences, I have only indicated the ethnicity of the characters if the playwrights themselves felt that that was important to the realization of the story. Because every piece in this book was presented before an audience, I have also chosen to retain the original stage directions recorded by the stage manager, so that they can be envisioned as well as read.

These presentation technicalities bring me to the part of this Preface that must deal with the discussion of what constitutes, in my mind, a good play. Probably ten different writing teachers would give you ten different answers, so the subjectivity of this assessment must be acknowledged up front. I, for one, want to *feel* something when I encounter a story, whether on stage or in a book; if I *learn* something too, that's even better. So, first and foremost, I have to care about the characters and their struggles. To my mind, that caring grows out of a sense that the experience being represented on stage is authentic, that something important is at stake, and that the characters are being treated with respect and even affection by their creator. Because all of this feeling is being carried by language, I also have to understand what is being said in a way that doesn't make me feel that I am working too hard to feel *anything*. And I want to sense that I am hearing a unique voice, not one that I heard on a sitcom last night or at a different theatre last week. It is my belief that such uniqueness grows out of the *specificity* with which characters are drawn.

While the qualities listed above might seem terribly old-fashioned in this post-post-post-modern age, in which the "well-built" play is often seen as an outmoded edifice, to my mind good plays need not necessarily be either realistic or linear. In fact, this collection features works about an airplane that stops in mid-air, a young woman who plays her violin in a steam room, and a teddy bear that magically appears in a young man's home after his teenaged girlfriend announces her pregnancy. I believe a good play *does* have to engage the audience ... to my mind, that is what having a voice is for.

You may not all be comfortable with all aspects of the Find Your Voice pedagogy, but I hope you will agree that the results are poignant. Not only do these short works appear "simple"—which is always the greatest testament to craft—but so many of the featured writers remain connected to the voice-finding experiences they had and are still using that voice to express themselves and to generatively cultivate the voices of others. It is indeed a gift that keeps on giving.

In order to clarify the Find Your Voice process, I offer a brief history in the Introduction, which follows the Acknowledgments.

Acknowledgments

First and foremost, I want to acknowledge all of the writers who trusted me with their stories and gave me permission to include them in this text. I am honored by that sharing.

Laura Castro, Jeannette Horn, Emily Morse, Amatullah King, and Victoria Abrash, who lent their dramaturgical gifts to the development of many of the works herein.

Rose Olivito, who served as stage manager for most of our productions and who diligently recorded the stage directions.

Milan Stit and Charles Kakatsakis, two extraordinary coaches who shaped my own craft.

New York University, The Children's Aid Society, and The New York City Department of Education, where the seeds of this project were planted, nurtured, grown, and disseminated.

The Find Your Voice Board of Directors and our funders, past, present and future.

Linda Faigao-Hall and Natasha Marco, both of whom worked tirelessly to help me compile and transcribe this collection.

Evelyne Chemouny and Amy Fox, who helped me condense a method book into a single chapter.

And my husband, Scott, who showed up for every opening night.

Introduction

The Backstory

Drawing Students Toward a Love of Their Own Voices

I first developed what became the Find Your Voice method sort of by accident. While serving as assistant dean of Arts and Sciences at New York University, I was invited to teach a freshman English course. This was during the late 1980s, when colleges were working to redress the poor skills with which many students were leaving high school. Most of the students in my class professed a disinterest in writing, and because I was a playwright/director, I tried a creative approach to writing in order to draw them toward a love of their own voices.

Photographs Trigger Even the Most Reluctant Writers

As a starting point, I decided to have my students write in response to a picture—an illustrative Rorschach ink-blot of sorts. I asked that first group of students to write freely (to free associate) about what they thought had happened, or might happen, in that picture. After a moment of shock, they were *all* able to do so. Some wrote in dialogue, some in prose, some in poetry; some only wrote a few descriptive words ... but they all wrote something. The photographic "trigger" proved to be a wonderful can-opener for even the most reluctant of writers.

After providing much reassurance about the intended result, I helped them share their initial writings aloud. Through a series of thought-provoking questions, I then led each student toward the development of a story, which then became a treatment for a play. The initial response to almost all of my questions was, "I don't know." To which I kept replying, "You don't have to *know,* just *imagine.*" It became clear that they had not used their imaginations in that way for a very long time, and they were all quite concerned about not providing the "correct answer"—that is, the one that *I* was waiting to hear. Once underway, they all began to give over to the exercise to some degree, especially after seeing that the students who shared their responses before them were being treated in a very respectful and patient manner, which was key to the result.

As was the case with every workshop I would lead for the next two decades, the stories that emerged, while not strictly autobiographical, reflected the hopes, fears, and dreams that were most pressing, or most unresolved, in each writer's mind. The exercise presented the opportunity for participants to examine those issues through the emotional distance of another character, in concert with a dramaturge who was asking challenging questions about the character's motivation. I also highlighted the consequences of the character's actions, providing the writers with a perspective and clarity that enabled them to explore different choices for, and interpretations of, their own lives. That freshman English course was my first experience with helping to draw stories from reticent speakers and writers, and it required me to learn how to create the kind of "safe space" needed to do so. It became apparent that if the desire to tell our stories is one of our most basic human needs, then fear and desire are opposite sides of the same coin. It was essential that I managed their fear, at the same time encouraging their human desire for self-expression. In so doing, I placed equal emphasis on instilling craft and instilling comfort.

Having once been a reluctant communicator myself, one whose voice had been unearthed by a band of extremely talented acting, writing, and singing coaches, I was excited and curious about how this coaching might be applied in a more academic setting. I didn't yet realize it, but those tools and that coaching style would become part and parcel of my work.

Unlocking the Imagination
For several terms after that initial class, I kept using the free-writing approach as an entry point for unlocking the imaginations of my

college-aged students. I always followed up the initial free write and development of a story idea with a workshop-style approach to the more difficult task of *re*-writing. That is, after the initial free write, which spawned the treatments for their plays, the students went on to complete at least five rewrites. These rewrites were done in response to very specific questions about what the writer intended and why it might not be paying off yet, which yielded final polished versions of their plays many weeks later.

During this process, I discovered that having their work read aloud by others enabled the less confident writers to hear the ways in which poor grammar and usage leads to a *mis*-reading. Conversely, it enabled the overly confident writers to hear when their stilted language sat awkwardly in the air or when an unoriginal idea felt embarrassingly familiar to every one. These perceptions were further affirmed by my sensitive feedback.

Leveling the Playing Field Between Introverts and Extroverts

I discovered, too, that this kind of interactive style of learning—hearing your own work read aloud and also responding to the work of others, if facilitated with sensitivity—was very engaging for both the outgoing as well as the reluctant participants. When a shy writer's play was being discussed, that writer simply had to sit and listen and could later risk being more vocal when someone else's play was in the spotlight. Conversely, when a poor listener's play was being discussed, he or she could *only* sit and listen, and, over time, such listeners actually became eager and willing to hear what the others thought.

It was clear that writing short plays, which are highly compressed stories in which every word must count *and* which must sound natural when spoken aloud, was a wonderful exercise for focusing analytical thinking, authenticating voices, and leveling the playing field between introverts and extroverts. I was consistently amazed by how capable every student, even those who were not native English speakers and those with learning challenges, could be at expressing their thoughts when given clear tools and lots of encouragement.

Reading One Another Is Different from
Reading Text: A Method Is Born

I proceeded to teach this way for several terms, bringing my professional actor friends in at the conclusion of each term to rehearse the finished plays with me and then reading them aloud before the student writers and their invited guests. This approach was very successful—and popular—with the students. Over time, I was asked to consider preparing the students to *enact* each other's plays too, as a way of further improving their speaking, listening, and social skills. Because most of the students had never acted publicly, or even studied acting privately, this presented quite a challenge! *The primary goal of the expended training was not to create actors, but to instill in participants the ability to fully "engage" with another person.* By *engage*, I mean that the students were assigned monologues to learn and encouraged to actively pursue a particular response from listeners—to really *read* the listeners to see if they were getting it. Reading a person requires a different kind of literacy than reading a text, one that is both visual and emotional, and this can be a tremendous challenge to those who have chosen to be either inscrutable or indifferent to others. The potential benefit of this training, for learners of every age, is that *improving social skills opens the way for improving cognitive skills.*

Once they were able to move from a position of *self*-consciousness to one of *other*-consciousness, participants were on their way to becoming communicators. This is not an easy transition to make, but after coaching many professional and aspiring actors, I was amazed to see how quickly people with no preconceived notions or bad acting habits could be led to work well as actors and, more importantly, as *inter-actors*. Over the weeks—during which their monologues deepened in meaning and became increasingly physical—their comfort with seeing and being seen, hearing and being heard, grew exponentially. After participants mastered their assigned monologues, they applied their newfound ability to engage to the public reading of one another's original work. These final presentations before an invited audience were always transformative and empowering. The Find Your Voice method was born.

Embracing My Destiny as a Coach

After several successful terms, I was invited to bring this Find Your Voice approach to the inner-city teenagers who came to the after-school program at the Children's Aid Society, around the corner from NYU; we called these young communicators the Sullivan Street Players. Although I had not yet embraced my destiny as a coach, I was tantalized by the idea of testing out the conservatory-style approach on younger and less broadly educated communicators. It was similarly transformative for these younger participants, as well as their guests. Ultimately, we began to offer matinee performances for public school groups, and the students were amazed to see the spellbound reactions of their peers. It was a far cry from the kind of youth-oriented work that adults wrote when attempting to approximate the voice of a teenager. It was grippingly honest yet highly crafted writing and acting work, and the student audiences recognized it as such—as did their teachers. I was soon inundated with requests from classroom teachers who wanted to lead their own students toward the creation and presentation of this kind of writing. In response to these requests, the Children's Aid Society allowed me to offer a workshop for New York City public school English teachers as a pilot. Being a believer in experiential learning, I decided to lead the teachers through the exact same process the younger learners had undertaken. I was surprised to see all of the same fears and resistances in this older population, particularly because they had opted into a profession in which they had to speak before a group all day.

I learned over time that speaking publicly as the authority in charge of one's own room is very different than speaking publicly to one's potentially judgmental peers out in the wider world. It is also a lot easier to encourage someone else to write than it is to complete a piece of writing yourself. Sadly, neither of these crucial communication skills were emphasized in graduate education training programs, nor was the sensitive coaching that is required to enable the teacher's future students to practice them with comfort.

Multiple Facets of the Same Jewel

During the late eighties, the Sullivan Street Players was the only New York City youth company I knew of that was dedicated to cultivating excellence in written and oral expression, rather than simply showcasing talent where it already existed. The company's work created a new genre, doubly unique in that it featured cultural diversity not only on the stage but in the audience as well. Because the plays from any given workshop always grew from a shared "trigger," the final performances offered multiple facets of the same jewel, all presented in a common setting and under the direction of the artist who had served as midwife to the stories. I called this approach *clustering*, and my artistic challenge as director was to take the multiple stories and styles and find commonalities that would bring flow to the evening of theatre. The connection between the pieces could be highlighted by the set, which often mirrored the triggering photograph; the costumes; the music, much of it composed by Bobby Lopez, composer and lyricist of *Avenue Q*, a former student whose work is featured in this collection; as well as the subject matter. It was an exciting and challenging process, one made even more exciting by the post-show dialogues with the diverse audience members. Everyone present found some character to relate to, and often these identifications crossed cultural and generational lines. That was a time when professional theatre companies were largely ghettoized into telling the stories of only one kind of people, to an audience of predominantly the same kind of people. During that time on Sullivan Street, I learned vividly that we often mistakenly assume that people who look alike are alike and that people who look different from one another have little in common. The seeds of my desire to cultivate universality in the world of professional theatre-making were being sown.

Find Your Voice, Inc. *(FYV)* was incorporated in the early 1990s, and several hundred additional teenagers were trained, along with teachers from over one hundred New York City schools. These teachers were led through the identical process of developing and performing plays. Along the way, they not only became more communicative themselves, they developed the empathy required to lead their students through the risk-taking exercise of publicly sharing their thoughts, both aloud and on paper. It became very apparent to me that *everyone* could benefit from being coached toward excellent self-expression and that everyone could get there if coached well. Though the goal was never to turn students into professional playwrights or actors, because plays are such compressed and heightened communiqués and because acting requires such intense concentration and connectedness, using those pursuits as the conduit for social and cognitive skill development was clearly effective.

Crystallizing the Human Experience

After establishing a professional main-stage arm for the new company, I also discovered that even working writers welcomed a different way of getting started with their writing and therefore appreciated a triggering photograph from which to generate an idea. They also appreciated receiving ongoing and supportive dramaturgical feedback on their work, in concert with other writers who were undergoing the same process. The fact that the process always culminated in a full production, not just a reading, was further assurance that their voices would be heard.

We always made a concerted effort to bring together playwrights of diverse cultures, ages, and genders in each "cluster," and the participants, in turn, brought similarly diverse followings. Taking a cue from our educational program, we facilitated post-show discussions with those audiences as well, discovering similar universally held responses to the stories they had just viewed. The process also yielded the same kind of overlapping story elements that we had seen among the students. In fact, there are two scenes in this collection from a cluster entitled "Four Views with a Room:" one written by Charles Watson and one written by me, in response to Andrea Sperling's photograph of the chair in front of a door that is featured on the cover, a setting that could suggest an infinite number of situations or characters. This is the trigger image that I have used most often in my years of cultivating stories, in keeping with the Gestalt therapeutic notion of placing a character from your life into an empty chair and imagining the dialogue you would have with them, if you could. Interestingly, both of our plays dealt with a woman stubbornly seated in her last piece of furniture before being moved out of her home against her will. Although Charles is a black man and I am a white woman, and the textures and language of the two pieces reflect very different sensibilities, there were a few almost identical lines of dialogue in our first drafts—which were written in isolation. When my piece, which featured an aging Jewish woman and her daughter, was read in the workshop, one of the other participating writers featured in this collection, Linda Faigao-Hall, a Filipina-American, expressed amazement at how much my older character sounded like her own Asian grandmother. Countless moments like those not only crystallized the human experience that we all share, they underscored the joy of sharing them. When *I* participated as a playwright in many of the clusters, one of our guest dramaturges, most notably Laura Castro, Emily Morse, and Victoria Abrash, would serve as midwife to *my* play. What a joy it was to sit on that side of the play-making table as well.

Becoming Comfortable In the Spotlight ... and Out of It

I was also pleased that many of the fine artists who were produced on our main stage went on to teach in our educational program with me, and many of our former students went on to write and act on the main stage. Alongside both of those groups were the scores of public school teachers who came to study with me in the hope of bringing improved writing, listening, speaking, and social skills back to their own classrooms. I am particularly pleased that, twenty years later, those aforementioned skills are now central to the national literacy standards—and that the teachers we trained were able to widen the reach of this approach to hundreds of other inner-city students. I have also led workshops for college professors and graduate students, and I have yet to meet any individuals who were not struggling with some anxiety level about expressing themselves to others—whether before a crowd or just one other person—and who did not voice remorse that they had not been coached in this manner throughout their own education. This was expressed so consistently, in fact, that my board of directors urged me to write up the method in a book and then create a video to accompany it. The book, *Find Your Voice*, which has been condensed and summarized in the method chapters of this book, was published by Heinemann in 2004, and a documentary film, written by screenwriter Amy Fox, was completed in 2007. Thirty minutes of this film, which features a Find Your Voice training with ten inner-city teenagers, airs on PBS, and the feature-length version *(Listening With Their Eyes)* received a Chris Award at the Columbus International Film Festival in 2008. The film tracks the transformations of young people struggling with such common obstacles as shyness, second-language interference, ADD, social awkwardness, depression, and academic challenges. Emblematic of the hundreds of participants who took the training before and after them, these students each came to feel comfortable in a realm that was previously beyond their reach—either because they were shy and finally came to be comfortable in the spotlight or they were perhaps too intrusive and came to be comfortable out of the spotlight.

Since completing that film and more widely disseminating the FYV method, I have seen it work successfully with an even wider variety of learners across the lifespan. Twenty pre-readers and pre-writers in a kindergarten class learned to orally shape and imagine play ideas and dialogue, as well as master monologues, in order to learn how to maintain eye contact when another child or an adult was speaking to them. A group of eight-year-olds learned to listen to their classmates as respectfully as they listened to their teacher. There were ten octogenarians at a community agency, including one with dementia, whose stories helped them to review aspects of their past lives through clear and less jaundiced eyes and who emerged with greater social skills and less depression. Twenty graduate students attaining their masters degrees in fund-raising and philanthropy discovered that they needed a real "voice" with which to ask potential funders for support. The bottom line is that every human interaction requires that we communicate, and the better we are able to do so, the better the chances are that we will *know* what we want and *get* what we want.

The Human Need To Voice

1. What the Method Accomplishes

The Find Your Voice (FYV) method *helps people to articulate their true selves and to effectively receive the articulations of others.* It is precisely because self-expression places us in a very vulnerable position that public speaking is the number-one fear of Americans. We all shy away from certain situations, and this shyness is largely a fear of negative responses. To avoid a negative response, many of us learn to keep silent in certain situations, thus becoming partially voiceless. Others have a fuller voice, but it may be an inauthentic one. Additionally, people who have never really been listened to are often incapable of listening to others well; at bottom, they share the same fear of connection as those who listen well but are hesitant to speak. *Communication is a loop.*

Everyone I know feels unheard or inarticulate in some situations, but they also have the need to articulate their experiences. For many of the people I coach, I am the first person in their lives who has really listened to what they had to say and then encouraged them to say it in their own authentic voices. Toward that end, I engage them in the study of acting, which involves speaking, listening, and connecting in the hope of getting the response you want. Good acting actually requires us to *remove* our masks and to employ our own true emotions on behalf of the character we are portraying. When we "act" in a way that may have been previously verboten for us, we grow increasingly more comfortable speaking publicly; after receiving kudos for allowing ourselves to be seen and heard more fully, we begin to drop our defenses.

I augment this verbal articulation with the study of playwriting, because it invites the commitment of our original thoughts to paper, with the intention that those thoughts will eventually be read and then spoken by and for others.

This method can work with learners of every age, as long as it includes the elements most crucial for finding a voice: establishing a trusting relationship between coach and participant, setting high standards for revision, and encouraging engagement and the pursuit of positive wants.

2. How the Method Works

The complete Find Your Voice training requires about thirty hours and can be conducted in a variety of ways, ranging from a week of day-long sessions or three biweekly meetings culminating in a rehearsed reading, to a twelve- or twenty-four week course with fully produced presentations. Each session usually lasts three hours, with equal parts assigned to acting and writing if there is only one facilitator; the acting and writing sessions can run simultaneously with two. It is a flexible model, but all options start with an orientation, which can be completed in one session or spread over several.

Orientation

1. Establishing Trust

The goal of Orientation is to help the participants feel safe, professional, connected, and excited.

1a. The Circle

This begins with the chairs being placed in a circle for maximum engagement, and the door being closed for maximum privacy. A quiet environment conducive to listening gives participants confidence that their risk-taking will be contained. *The ultimate level of trust and sharing is strongest if it's established right at the beginning.*

1b. The Welcome

The coach must begin to manage fear from the moment the participants walk through the door. When everyone and everything is new, discomfort with public sharing can be as basic as having to speak one's name before the group. I welcome every participant with a reassuring smile, and then, by name, I invite each person in. This simple gesture sends the message that their experience with me will be relationship-based.

1c. The Golden Rule

I begin by telling the group members that they will all learn to communicate ideas that are original and well-crafted and that all members will address their own challenges at their own pace. I explain that I will be their guide through this experience, that I well know how scary public sharing can be, and that they will also learn much from being keen observers of one another. That is why the workshop must be a place where they can concentrate, take risks, and be vulnerable to each other. Toward that end, we will uphold an unalterable Golden Rule: *no one may laugh at anyone's attempt to communicate—ever.* I make eye contact with each participant and speak in a warm professional tone. I continually stop to ask for questions and comments and encourage them to respond.

2. Becoming Professional: The Map

Next, I go over the schedule for the work we will do together, including the final presentations of the plays, number of drafts to be written, and due dates for the "final polish" of the scripts. The schedule orients the participants about what is expected of them and allows them to begin to take ownership of the process. Participants have been most successful when the journey toward their own voices was laid out for them in knowable and manageable steps. Below is an example of how this might look.

Sample Schedule
Six 3-hour Sessions with a Rehearsed Reading
(20–25 Students)

Sessions	Acting	Writing
1	Read 1st monologue (Orientation)	Free-write
2	Monologue memorized	Treatment
3	Monologue with flow	1st Draft
4	Monologue with movement	2nd Draft
5	Final monologue	3rd Draft
	Play Selection and Casting	
6	Rehearsal/Table Work	Polish
7	Dress rehearsal/Presentation of rehearsed reading and Q&A	

3. Getting Connected: The Name Game

Now the participants can begin to learn one another. Having shared their given names, I invite them to choose a descriptive Native American-style name for themselves, one that will highlight an authentic attribute about which they feel proud. I explain that they should attach the new name to their old first name. Then, after emphatically evoking the Golden Rule, I always go first. I try to offer an example that is both honest and reassuring: "I'm 'Gail-Listens-With-Her-Eyes'." The choice of a name is difficult for many. I try to articulate their potential resistance to the exercise before they can even demonstrate it, stating that we all worry about the way other people might react to us. Some of us might be tempted to say something goofy or to not answer at all. I tell them that it will take courage and ask them to assume that they will get a positive response; that's what they're all here to learn: how to offer and receive positive responses.

This exercise requires vigilant listening and much encouragement on the part of the coach. As we go around the circle, most of the participants play by the rules. If someone has nothing to say, I ask him or her a nonthreatening question: "What is your favorite color?" Then I dub that person something like, "Jasmin-loves-yellow." By the end of the circle, with the pressure off, the previously mute participants often ask me for another chance to choose a name for themselves. I always grant it. The responses to the Name-Game reveal a great deal about the participants' personalities, interests, and fears. *Their new names can provide the surest paths to important anxieties and dreams*, so I always jot them down beside the real names on my roster. When participants dub themselves as funny, at some point we will undoubtedly need to relieve them of the need to always be the class clown!

4. Generating Excitement

By this time, the participants have all survived a taste of seeing-and-being-seen, from my initial greeting through to the Name Game, so their public sharing can now deepen.

4a. The Trigger

I briefly explain the purpose of a triggered free-write and then circulate copies of an image that inspires a story. I've found that close-up shots of interesting objects *(*a broken umbrella lying in the street, a used tea bag, etc.*)* or moody rooms work best.

I tell the participants:
- There are no wrong answers and no grades.
- Not to worry about grammar or spelling, just to think out loud on paper and write whatever comes into their heads, even if it doesn't seem to make sense.
- To keep the pen moving, not to cross anything out, and to stop when I ask them to ... in five minutes.
- That this will be a little awkward for those not used to writing their thoughts down on paper, but it is not so different from describing feelings or situations out loud to a friend.
- Attempts to make fun of the exercise by writing something silly, or by not writing at all, are just symptoms of the fear of communicating, precisely what we are there to master. I've found that *naming those reactions in advance makes them less tempting to enact.*

While the group is writing, I take in more information about the members and jot down my observations. For many it is tough to get started; if they stare at me, I simply telegraph encouragement to them by nodding or smiling. If they are still not writing, I approach and invite them to begin by simply describing what they see and what it reminds them of.

4b. Sharing the Free-Write
After five minutes, I ask them to put down their pens and tell them that we'll go around the circle and share the pieces aloud. This causes a tidal wave of anxiety, which I normalize by reassuring them that *everyone* feels nervous and that I will treat their writing with the utmost respect. I also explain that sometimes one single phrase in the shortest of free-writes can be the catalyst for the most powerful of plays. I instruct them to read everything they wrote because *the greatest jewel is often the very phrase that the writer feels least comfortable sharing.*

After each participant reads a piece aloud, I praise each for his or her courage and thank the students for their trust. With no criticism whatsoever, I might gently ask participants to reread certain lines aloud because they may have read much of it fairly quickly and inaudibly. *Managing the anticipatory anxiety is half the battle*, so I start with the participants who were comfortable sharing in the Name Game. Working respectfully and enthusiastically with the raw material, I try to highlight something of value in each: descriptive language, keen observations, a lovely sense of humor, originality, or simplicity.

4c. The Dramaturgical Interplay

The process following the reading of each free-write, the Dramaturgical Interplay, allows the participants to enter into a dialogue with someone who takes them seriously, asks them hard questions, and can help them find their own answers. They need to sense that I have a great desire to learn about them and that they are worth all the time and effort that the learning will entail. The coach's task is to enter the poetic window that the free-write created. They can then use it to tap into the writer's imagination in order to find an idea for a play.

The Interplay is one of the most challenging aspects of this method, but it is also great fun. It can be a little scary because the coach cannot really prepare for it (for an example of an Interplay, please see p. 19). Some participants will be very uncomfortable "playing" with me and may give only a literal description of the picture. I remind myself that the participant's fears of the unknown are even greater than mine and that *I am the best role model for trusting and risk-taking in my own classroom*. I listen with three ears for a story idea and respond with both my head and heart, as best I can.

As students read their free-writes aloud, I wait for a key line that could lead to a dialogue, and I approach the entire piece as a potential scene. I ask a series of questions to which the participants will have to improvise the answers. For the coach, as well as the group members, there are no right answers, only right questions with an infinite number of possible responses.

Sample Questions

- I ask them to consider who is in the story, who else could enter the scene to interact with them, what they each might want, and how their wants are in conflict.
- I ask them to consider where their characters are, what they're doing, and how their conflict might resolve itself.
- I also ask them the Passover question: why is this day different from all other days for the characters, and what is at stake for each.
- After the Interplay, I repeat the participant's story back to each person and ask if this is one that they want to tell. If so, their homework will be to write it as a treatment—that is, a single paragraph about the story of the play.

My questions serve the sole purpose of drawing out *two characters and one conflict;* the participants should all end up with the underpinnings of a play. Once we've all agreed on play ideas, I collect the free-writes and refer back to them many times over the course of the workshop. It is crucial that the coach reiterate the agreed-upon story idea each time, to ensure that the participants remain true to their original story. The habit of rejecting the idea and beginning again is one of the most common ways in which participants undermine their ability to bring their articulations to completion. I compliment them again on their courage and thank them for listening respectfully to one another: they are now on their way to becoming writers—and a community.

5. The Monologue
If possible, I interview the participants before the workshop begins to tell them about the training, assess what their public and private communication experience is, and discover what they hope to gain and what they feel they could bring to a group. This encounter gives me an opportunity to get a sense of them physically and emotionally. Based on my observations, I select a monologue from a published play that would be appropriate for each. If there is no opportunity to meet them in advance, I select material for the second meeting (you can find a plethora of good material in this collection or get recommendations from the *FYV* book).

5a. Priming the Monologue

Before I distribute clean and legible copies of all the monologues in class, I explain the difference between a monologue and a dialogue (one speaker versus two), that the monologues are from published plays available in the library, and that they will memorize them and speak the words to a partner, who will represent the other character in the scene (a listener). I also reassure them that they will eventually feel comfortable in their roles. After the monologues are read silently, I answer all immediate text comprehension questions.

5b. Reading the Monologue

Each participant is then invited up to the front of the circle with a listener and directed to read the monologue aloud. This is a chance to hear each other's material and to practice public speaking in a safe environment, without the pressure of memorization. When they're finished, I compliment them on their courage and any other apparent strength, such as clear articulation, expressiveness, comprehension, or a nice pace.

5c. Comprehending the Monologue

I then ask them to describe in their own words what they think the piece is about, and I fill in around the edges. At the next meeting, they will be able to answer *three key questions*: who their character is, who the listener might be, and what their character wants from that listener.

I close the orientation by encouraging participants to think of themselves as professionals-in-training and to try and trust the process. Following the orientation, the coach continues to solidify this trust. I refer to the coaches I train as *guiding voices* because they must show empathy in understanding how scary it is to share spoken or written words before others. They must acknowledge every small step forward and lead with positive feedback, gently help the participants take risks, offer their loving and consistent presence; set high standards, know their subject matter, and clarify repeatedly to the participants that the goal of this work is to become better communicators. Trust in the classroom comes through the coaches' earnest desire to see and hear the participants, their ability to respond to them, and to get participants to respond to each other with authenticity.

What follows is an overview of the sequence of events in the acting part of the workshop, which is followed by the sequence of events in the writing part of the workshop.

The Methodology:
Acting and Reacting

Acting is the greatest agent of engagement, because it requires that you take the focus off of yourself and put it on the person from whom you are seeking a response; that's why I call it *re-acting*. Acting is also a noncompetitive team sport, and anyone can be taught to do it. I teach the craft of re-acting through the study of exciting, well-written published plays. With beginning participants, I start with a monologue rather than a dialogue, so that I can focus all of my listening skills on only them. I assure the group that they will tackle their own challenges in their own time; they primarily struggle with connecting, which involves *admitting that they want something from the person who is listening.*

In order to learn to act, the participants must become *act-ive* learners, be willing to pursue what they want with great energy, and take ownership of their own craft. This is essential for their *acting craft* as well as their *self-confidence* to grow. Acting is a study of human behavior that asks participants to explore and reveal their own behavior. If a character is angry because they can't get what they want, then the actor chooses how to help them get it by yelling, threatening, shoving, etc. That physical choice is called acting, which is why *I emphasize the behavior, not the emotion.* With permission to funnel the wants of another character through their own bodies and personalities, participants actually become more themselves than they have ever been. Acting also heightens their listening skills, because re-actors must constantly

11

assess the effect of their behavior on other characters to see whether it has elicited the desired response. They must be open to knowing others better and to becoming vigilant at listening, with all five senses, for their responses, so they can re-act appropriately to that response. This focus and full engagement with someone else demands tremendous trust and also *offers the antidote to self-consciousness.*

1. The First Step

When participants are at the point of committing the material to memory, which induces anxiety in almost everyone, I reassure them that another group member will always be "on book" for them. That is, another participant in the circle will hold the script and follow along, so that if the actor goes blank, he or she can simply say "line" and will be given the words they need. Early memorization is crucial so that participants can let go of the words and focus on the reactions of the listener, the person with whom they are connecting. *The best way to facilitate memorization is to cultivate comprehension of the material, which can be done by having participants paraphrase the piece.* While the text is the vehicle for creating and recreating human connections, the subtext—the motivation behind the words—provides the means for making these connections. Eventually, the participants' focus on getting what they want will supersede their focus on remembering lines. The second participant who functions as their listener will, in fact, become the focus of the scene. This dynamic takes the pressure off of speakers who are reluctant to be the centers of attention.

After they get up to work for the first time, I praise participants lavishly for having had the courage to get up in front of the group at all. Then I offer an "adjustment," a direction that will strengthen their physical behavior or want. I also gently make them aware of any of their own personal habits that are getting in their character's way, such as mumbling, avoiding eye contact, fidgeting, etc., in order to help them to better connect.

2. Coaching Introverts

What follows is an example of how the participant's fear and the coach's fear-management skills can interact productively. I ask Grace, an extremely shy participant, to begin by explaining the context of her monologue—who she is talking to, what she wants, and why she wants it. When I'm sure she understands her purpose, I gently invite her to begin. Grace is nervous and calls for many lines. She talks too quickly and focuses on the floor; her only "want" at this point is to finish as soon as possible so that she can return to the safety of her seat.

When she finishes, I first praise her for her courage in getting up in front of us and for the time she spent trying to learn the material. I reassure her that each time she goes up, she will remember more and that everyone, even professional actors, calls for lines when they're first getting off-book (memorizing their material). I try to ease her anxiety by acknowledging that it exists and by demonstrating that I'm not bothered by it. I do this through a humorous statement that is directed at her demon: "Don't leave, I'm not finished torturing you yet!" She laughs because it is true; it has felt like torture to her. She also likes the feeling that I, her soon-to-be-trusted coach, might actually be stronger than the demon that has hampered her freedom. I believe that this is how a trusting relationship is created.

I then ask her to reiterate what she wants from her partner. When she does, I ask how important it is to achieve this want. *It is crucial for reluctant communicators to understand the high stakes involved in dramatic situations, so that they can then pursue their wants with energy.* As Grace hesitantly explains the motivations of her character (to get permission to move back home), I continue to affirm and gently probe her, with questions such as, "Yes, but why?" (Because she has nowhere else to go.) I have found that tapping into people's natural curiosity is the key to teaching the crafts of re-acting and rewriting—perhaps to all teaching.

After a tortured silence, Grace will be able to verbalize the deeper motivation behind what the character is saying. I smile and praise her for her keen insight into the play. I then ask Grace if she sensed what response her partner was having toward her during her previous attempt. Grace shrugs: she doesn't know, because she never looked at her partner. I tell her that all of the answers are on her partner's face, and if the listener does not respond at all, then Grace must *pull for the response she wants*—that is acting. I ask her to try again and to really watch her partner this time, to try and listen for a response and to speak slowly enough to give herself the time to scrutinize the listener.

Once participants can control their own pace, they will discover that the rhythm of the fuller scene is determined by the heartbeat of the characters; the more adrenaline a situation induces, the faster the heartbeat. But the participants must always take the time to wait for a response or to consider something. For example, if Grace's scene partner was willing to grant what she wants but only under certain conditions, Grace would need a moment or two to consider her decision before she answers.

While I offer feedback to Grace, the other participants feel very much a part of her learning experience. Because they all share so many of the same issues, it is often easier for participants to watch how a problem is solved when it is vividly demonstrated on someone else. Once they see the problem and can anticipate the solution, they have begun to achieve mastery of the craft.

Chances are, Grace will not yet be able to sustain the connection I am helping her to establish. She will start out looking at her partner, and then her glance will drift back to the floor. Each time, I will softly urge her to watch her partner's reaction. Each time she connects to her partner, I will acknowledge her genuine success. When Grace finishes her next effort, she will immediately look out to me; I will meet her anxious gaze with my own calm and reassuring one. I will telegraph to her that she is on the right course and that she is safe. As our bond deepens, she will begin to feel increasingly better about communicating. Eventually this adjustment will be sustained over the course of the entire monologue, and I will then suggest several approaches to further Grace's connection to her partner, such as asking her to physically stop the listener from leaving his or her seat.

3. Coaching Extraverts

Unlike Grace, Shahita is a participant too eager to perform. Her keen desire for the attention of the group distracts her from the true focus of her words: her scene partner. She is animated and energetic but no more connected than the introvert. She's proud of her exhibitionism, which also impresses the rest of the class and makes it all the more challenging to have to dismantle her misguided notion of what re-acting is.

When asked what her character's want is, she describes a feeling, rather than an action: "She's angry." She is led to articulate the want: for the other character to stop stalking her. Again, she is asked to watch her partner, to read him and assess his responses, to wait for his responses through facial and body language as she is speaking. But during several more tries, she never looks at her listener for more than a second. She even begins to close her eyes while she talks, which is a common symptom when disconnecters are asked to connect. She begins to lose her carefully memorized words and gestures, also a typical reaction to the new adjustment to connect. Most over-actors told to do nothing but talk and listen become visibly and audibly depressed. Their energy is gone because their want—to show off—has been short-circuited. Now that the experience has to include someone other than herself, Shahita is completely thrown.

I focus only on the first few lines and begin to address her over-acting, praising her first: "You have such a rich and wonderful instrument: less is much, much more. You're working much harder than you have to." I ask Shahita to trust me, and I assure her that she can become a very good actress, but she's going to have to learn to share the spotlight. I explain that this discomfort is only a temporary setback. Shahita eventually emerges with a craft that is authentic and her own—one that others admire. It is difficult to give up an old idea of how something is done, but, fortunately, participants who are cut off from other people in some way all relish the sensation of total engagement once they finally achieve it. Shahita's ability to listen to others soon begins to alter off-stage as well. She eventually becomes a fully present and attentive member of the group.

All of the above learning happened through a dialogue with the participants. *Coaching is about creating a relationship with a learner.* Coaches don't lecture; they respond to what their participants do and say. If they talk less, the participants will talk more. Coaches must allow enough time and silence to read their group's response, be prepared to be vulnerable in not always knowing what to do, and confess mistakes. If I nonjudgmentally tell them about the feelings they're inducing in me, whether frustration or confusion, the truth will help to free them of their own need to hide their feelings from me.

4. Crossing the Bridge

At each session, when the participants get up to work I have them reiterate their character's want and articulate what problem in their work was identified last time. I ask this same question in the writing workshop. *This process of metacognition is crucial for giving participants ownership of their learning.* By the end of the second showing, the piece should be more fully memorized and have some flow, because the actors will be "in the flow" of pursuing something they want from their partners—wants that should now be completely clear to them. Again, the coach's critiques must always be prefaced by some positive feedback, and resistant behavior must be viewed as fearful, not naughty.

Although this method is all about connection, dramatic tension relies on conflict and disconnection. This is why it is so crucial for participants to learn that *fighting for* is different than *fighting with*, so that they can maintain the kind of connections they need. I encourage them to use their full physical and vocal ranges to try and get what they want. People who don't communicate well can't stay engaged, but good craft requires good engagement skills. Again, this is why re-acting is so helpful to reluctant communicators.

Acting is a complex art form, and connecting is the bedrock of good acting. When this way of working is consistently applied, participants will inevitably become more present, less lethargic, more articulate, and more communicative in their lives in general. Once this is embodied, participants will be more comfortable sharing in public.

The Methodology:
Writing and Rewriting

An integrated approach to the study of re-acting and rewriting proves successful because these crafts share many basic principles. Actors must articulate *who* their characters are, *what* they want, *why* they want it, and *how* to overcome obstacles that might prevent them from getting it. Answers to these questions will also provide the underpinnings for writing a play.

1. Establishing Trust with New Writers

Writing is a scary process to undertake publicly, as both the form and content of a participant's writing reveal much about them. Our imaginings reveal a window into our soul: they reflect our hopes, fears, and prejudices. However, for the purpose of finding voices, coaches should respond to the participant's text strictly in terms of its potential for good play-making and never as autobiography. This takes the focus off a participant who is afraid of being seen and reminds the participant who tries to cling to the exact details of her own life event that her purpose is only to craft a literate and dramatic piece of writing. When writers explore their character's behavior and motivations, they inherently explore their own. Putting the focus on the character makes it safe for a participant to discover his own voice, without being overexposed.

While we aim to make this experience safe for participants, their fears will elicit any number of protective behaviors: a total inability to write anything at all; imitation of another participant's style or story;

use of a false and melodramatic voice; overuse of jargon; perfectionism that keeps them starting over so that their writing never advances; or an absence of grammar that renders their writing incomprehensible. Interestingly, when participants are finally ready to communicate, they learn the proper use of grammar very quickly.

2. Writing Guidelines for New Writers

These are some basic guidelines that are useful for both the coach and the participants to keep in mind throughout the writing and rewriting process:

- Write free-writes quickly to avoid self-censoring.
- Keep the plays, and the speeches within them, short *(5–10 pages)* to ensure flow.
- Explore something you feel passionately about—the trigger will help ensure that!
- Plays must have conflict and urgency in them—crisis—to motivate action.
- Stay with contemporary people and activities for authenticity of voice.
- Limit the number of central characters to two; it is hard to create fleshed-out people in five pages.
- Limit settings and time frames and keep exposition to an absolute minimum, for focus.
- The people, places, and things in the play should be specific and detailed.

3. Coaching New Writers

It takes practice to help develop a play well; you have to be detective, psychologist, and labor-coach. Most importantly, you need a burning desire to really see and hear your participants. *Nothing is more empowering to them than your time and attention to their story,* thus showing your belief in its worth. The quality of your attention also demonstrates and models the craft of listening.

An example of how a script for a play is developed following the basic steps of the Find Your Voice method follows. As has been discussed, the first steps of the process take place during the orientation. The free-write below was penned by a high school student in five minutes, in response to a surrealistic photograph of a clock:

Time goes by too fast—much too fast. The sun travels overhead at a tremendous speed. The days are too short. We're forced to live as if each day is our last. One day the clock will stop, on a significant moment in our life. We won't know if it will keep ticking, if it will tick forward or backward. Are we in that moment now? Is time standing still? Is it going forward or backward? There is really no such thing as time, only a series of moments.

Dan Missale

While the participant reads his free-write aloud, I listen for a key line that might invite a play idea. The key line in this free-write was, "Are we in that moment now?" A question inherently begs a response, and his use of the plural "we" implies a potential second character. I share these insights with the writer, which naturally leads us into the dramaturgical interplay, of which the following is an excerpt:

a. *Sample Interplay*

Coach (C): Clearly the character who is speaking is very anxious about time. Who might they be talking to?
Participant (P): I don't know.
C: There are no wrong answers, give it a try.
P: (After a long silence) Maybe it's an older brother.
C: Okay. Why is he feeling anxious?
P: I don't know.
C: Take a guess.
P: (Silence) Maybe he doesn't approve of his brother's lifestyle.
C: What lifestyle would that be?
P: I don't know.
C: You don't have to know, we're just playing. Think out loud.
P: Maybe the older one thinks that the younger one should mind his own business.
C: What might happen if he does, or doesn't, mind his own business? What's at stake?

19

By the end of this interaction, Dan has the underpinnings of a play. His next assignment is to write the treatment, a paragraph about the story of his play.

b. Sample Treatment

The Perfect Day

This is a play about two brothers: Alan (seventeen) and Andrew (twenty-nine). They spend a lot of time together. Andrew thinks this is his last chance to really live. Alan wants Andrew to stop drugging and drinking and to settle down; he's afraid of being sucked into Andrew's lifestyle.

Now that he has a sturdy outline, the next step is to allow the characters to begin to speak to one another in dialogue form, which Dan has never done before. This first effort is brief and lacked some grammar, but it shows *great* potential. Notice he has already revised the title to better accommodate his emerging story.

c. Sample First Draft

The Perfect Drug

ANDRE
What are you doing?

ANDREW
I'm having another one.

ANDRE
Why? Aren't we going to the pub later?

ANDREW
Okay, Dad.

ANDRE
Shut up. I'm just concerned. You got pretty plastered last night—

ANDREW

Why are you being so antagonistic? I think I can
control myself.

ANDRE

Can you? Last night you told me you could barely
walk up the stairs because you drank so much.

ANDREW

There is nothing wrong with being too drunk to
fuck every now and then. You do the same thing
sometimes anyway; I don't get on your back about it.

ANDRE

I'm still a kid though; I'm allowed to behave that way.

Dan is now ready for the next stage of our work: rewriting. He has
established the character and the conflict, but we need to see one brother
who is getting wasted, *why* the other brother objects, *how* this conflict
plays out, and in *what* way it will resolve. With specific questions and
encouragement from me and the group, Dan will write multiple drafts
over many sessions to develop and resolve his story and ultimately
taste the triumph of connecting and communicating. The final play is
included on p. 154. For all of the drafts of this play, see the *Find Your
Voice* book.

4. Rewriting

Plays aren't written; they're rewritten. While participants reluctantly
accept that they can't get it right on the first try, their eventual realization
that they can address unresolved problems in subsequent drafts is very
liberating to them. *Vision can only be accessed through revision*, and this
is a lesson in flexibility that can be applied to their lives in general.

The coach can facilitate the rewriting process through the following
steps.

A. Establish a workshop approach: a supportive group where
   members listen to one another tell their stories in their own

21

way and share the struggle as they try to do the same. This gives reluctant participants the opportunity to practice their public sharing skills: *when they help someone else, they develop more confidence in their own ideas.* As the participants witness the delicate birth of each play, they should always refer their feedback, mostly in the form of questions, to the play, not to the writer, who, in turn, is encouraged not to respond by arguing. *Everyone should be reminded that unjustified likes and dislikes are irrelevant.*

B. Ask two other participants in the group to read the revised drafts aloud, which enables the writers to hear what their writing *sounds like* and helps them keep it authentic.

C. Once the play is complete, cast it for a public reading with other members of the group who have watched it develop. You can then do some table work, where participants and coach sit at a table to clarify character motivation, background story, and plot with the actors who will read them. This usually leads to further rewriting and eventually results in an authentic and credible drama reflecting the writer's own beliefs.

5. Questions for Table Work

No matter how long the table work session is, I always ask, "What is this play about?" We check to see if the actor's take on the play is supported by the text. I proceed with my next questions:

- Who is this play about, and how do you know?
- What do the characters want and why?
- Why does this present a conflict, and where is that seen in the play?
- How and why is the conflict resolved?
- Why is this conflict erupting today?

If the answers aren't clear, we ask the writer to enlighten us. The goal is to work out all of the glitches that reveal themselves when readers attempt to bring a new play to life, not to critique or dramatically rewrite the play.

During table work, the coach must be vigilant that writers don't lose their plays in the process of honing them, which can happen if they introduce new plot lines, change character profiles, or add major new events. We must help the participants keep the best and lose the rest by restraining them from over-correcting. We must also take great pains to ensure that all of the feedback is forwarded in the spirit of helping the writer tell the story most clearly and effectively, as opposed to suggesting solutions. When anyone in the room, coach or participant, offers solutions rather than questions, it immediately limits the creative potential of the writers to find a solution for themselves, in their own voices. Some writers will remain resistant to change throughout table work. They may have felt misunderstood in life for so long that they can't tolerate being questioned at all. For those who are phobic about feedback, it is better to pencil in the suggested changes and then ask them to just listen to the actors read them. If they like them, they can keep them. If not, they can leave the script unchanged, understanding that the audience may be confused. They nearly always agree to make the changes if given a choice, if they fully understand the reasons for the changes.

The tough questions asked during the table work session inevitably raise the quality of the texts significantly, and subtexts will deepen even further during the acting rehearsals that follow. The trusting relationship between participant and coach, plus the helpful feedback of the group, supports the exploration. During this process the participant learns much about flow, grammar, logic, clarity, persistence, and the art of rewriting. A piece has achieved a state of completion when:

- Two characters with fleshed out, clear wants, resolve their conflict—not necessarily happily.
- The characters' behavior can be realized on a real stage, in real time.
- The language is clear, and there is logic and flow to the behaviors.

- The Passover question of why this play had to happen *today* is answerable.
- There is some clear relationship to the triggering image.
- Something important to the characters is at stake.

Ending On a High Note: Going Public

Because all of the developing plays are read aloud and discussed in the group every week, the participants have addressed specific problems in each of their drafts. Simultaneously, in the acting class, everyone has brought at least one monologue to fruition as an actor. By the end of the workshop, all group members have achieved a basic level of craft in re-acting and rewriting, which is evident in their improved abilities to read, write, speak, and listen to one another with authenticity. At the same time, they have grown vulnerable to and respectful of one another, in the privacy of their studio. It's time to exercise their voices in a public forum. The final presentation of their own plays offers them this opportunity while it celebrates them for their hard work.

When instilling new communication skills, less is much more. A simple approach will set off a well-told story just as magnificently as a big-budget production if the story is well-told. Even a minimal seated reading in folding chairs and under fluorescent lights can allow participants to go public with pride.

The opportunity to have work witnessed is a privilege; one must earn the right to have an audience. The FYV method engenders a professional caliber of art, brought about by an emphasis on the cultivation of real craft, rigorous preparation, and respect for the process. This process includes attendance at each session of the workshops; attentive listening while fellow participants work, and the offering of supportive feedback. Because participants are coached to behave professionally all along the journey, no great adjustment is needed for going public. It is not easy, however, to be energetic in the face of terror: anxiety is very distracting and draining. The best antidote to this stage fright is for participants to remain fully engaged with one another as they rehearse the completed plays.

I try to match the right participant to the right role based on the work they've done in the acting workshop and the playwright's descriptions of the characters. I then give participants a few minutes to read through the plays they've been cast in, to familiarize themselves with the language and get a sense of the story. For most this is a cold reading, so the nervous energy in the room is great. It is crucial that participants all acknowledge the tension and the fact that it arises out of the collective desire to create something of excellence. I urge everyone not to be afraid of the anxiety; it can actually be very uniting.

I instruct the participants to simply read slowly and intelligently, and I ask the writers to listen carefully and take notes when their language doesn't "feel" right. If readers misconstrue the writer's intention, the writing might need clarification. I also read any salient setting or stage directions as we go, which allows the group to make sense of what they are hearing and to envision what they would see in a full production.

1. Preparing the Presentation

The coach leads the rehearsal process by guiding the participants through the following steps:

    A. Prepare for a quick and intense polish of the play by studying the script in advance, annotating all problem areas and considering potential solutions. Everyone involved in bringing this story to life needs to tell the same story. This is the time to answer any remaining questions about the story. Writers should focus on eliminating repetitious language, filling in any plot holes, replacing language with gestures, and cleaning up clunky dialogue.

    B. Help the actors explicate the plot and the character's wants. Scripts with greater flow, more clarity, and higher stakes will emerge out of table work. Everyone should now be able to explain the meanings of the play. I begin by asking each actor to once again summarize the story from their own character's point of view and to reiterate their wants.

C. Make sure the actors take the time to listen to what is said before they respond, especially because we all speed up when reading from the page.

D. Although they will need to periodically consult their scripts, participants should maintain eye contact in order to ensure a connected and meaningful performance. They must only have eyes for their scene partner; that will steady their nerves and ensure the quality of work.

E. When actors are comfortable with the text and have had ample opportunity to delve in to the behavior of their characters, the rehearsals can focus on the pursuit of their wants, which should easily translate to modest action: taking someone's hand, rising, turning away, etc. The addition of minor physical movement serves to further fulfill the play. *Actors should take the time to establish behavior,* rather than rushing in to speak their lines. Watching someone behave is very compelling, so reassure participants that it won't be boring. As a rule, at the top of the play I ask the actors to take a moment to connect with one another before even beginning to speak.

F. Higher production values can simply mean that the participants will be off-book or will include some minimal elements of design, such as: character-appropriate dress, lights coming up and down, music, and furniture. Good preparation and organization are most essential for the company to seem like a well-oiled machine.

G. All of this must be done with energy. Remind the participants what's at stake for their characters.

After rehearsing the plays individually, run them in sequence. The goal for this run-through of the cluster of plays is to lay a foundation for achieving flow. I have found that participants of all ages are remarkably supportive and proud of one another as they witness the presentation take shape. I try to get them on and off the stage (which can mean the front of the classroom) quickly and neatly, and I have them carry on their own hand-held props. Delegating this responsibility to the actors increases their sense of ownership of the presentation. We all have to trust the homework that has prepared us for the next moment. To help ensure flow on my end, I create a presentation Book: a binder with the plays in their proper running order and tabs indicating the name of the writer. This book is assembled for both seated and staged readings (moving with scripts in hand), as well as fully memorized presentations. Although it is certainly not necessary, I also like to work with music between the pieces, because the sound relaxes both the participants and the audience. The exact placement of the music is also indicated in the presentation book.

It is easy to become punitive with resistant participants when the presentation is approaching. This may be a time of increased absenteeism, lateness, and unpreparedness, which can threaten the viability of a positive outcome for everyone. However, *avoidant behavior is usually due to rising terror*, and it is important to maintain a proper balance of toughness and love. To reduce the growing anxiety, the most effective method is to simply acknowledge its presence. Like all good coaches, I give the team a pep talk. When I've named the anxiety for them, I can also admit my own. I might say, "We're all nervous. We've worked hard, and we want this to go well. We also don't want to let each other down. The most important thing that we can all do is to stay focused on the work itself. We'll all be scared, but we'll survive—together. We'll probably even enjoy it. And when we're finished, we'll all be proud—and sad—that it's over."

On the day of the presentation, we begin when most of the seats in the house (or room) are filled and the actors are in their places. If possible, I then have the lights dim; the actors for the first piece come on to the stage (up front), the music slowly fades out, and the light slowly comes back up. Lights come down again at the end of the scene, while music comes up and actors exit. The next cast immediately enters and gets their furniture in place; lights come back up while the music fades out. The less abruptly this pattern is followed from play to play, the more graceful the presentation will be. My goal is always seamlessness. Directing requires an organic weave of language, actions, images, sounds, and feeling tones.

I have another tradition for all levels of public presentation: I write an opening card to each participant, to encourage them as they battle their last-minute jitters. I praise them for their accomplishments in the workshop and articulate specific growth that I've witnessed. I mean this private communiqué from me to them to be a kind of love letter—not a report card. The purpose is to seal the trust between coach and presenter and to remind them of how good it can feel to be seen, heard, and known.

2. Wrapping Up

For the bow, all the participants return to the stage in a line, as a team. I then ask them to be seated on the stage to talk with the audience. I always invite the audience to share their thoughts during a question-and-answer (Q&A) session. This gives the participants another opportunity to use their newly strengthened voices in a public dialogue, as well as providing ultimate ownership of their accomplishment. It also keeps the emphasis on process and allows others in the audience to understand that although the actors and writers seemed highly accomplished, this level of communication skill is well within their own grasp as well.

During the Q&A, the coach must attempt to cull a productive dialogue from an unpredictable and unknown group of people. I explain to the audience that what the participants need to hear from them are questions about the process: how the plays were written or how the participants prepared for their roles, as well as questions about the stories themselves and comments on particular aspects of the work with which they identified. I usually limit the Q&A to five minutes, as the participants and the audience are all fatigued after a presentation of multiple works. Audiences presented with authentic and well-prepared material are usually helpful and appreciative. And the participants, high on the victory of having gone public and mellowed by the relief that it's over, are gracious and articulate.

Gaining the courage to find your voice and the craft to use your voice well are two of the most difficult things I know. Leading others through that process also takes tremendous courage. When formerly reluctant participants are clear and connected, they have learned how to speak. When they listen and re-act with intelligence and energy, they have fully comprehended what they read. When their stories are concise and impactful, they have learned how to rewrite. And when they articulate how they acquired these skills cogently and respectfully, they own their newfound craft.

It is almost impossible not to worry over every aspect of this public event, but in the end I find myself enchanted by the audience's amazement at all that just happened on stage. I am also often moved to tears by comments made by even the shyest participants during the Q&A. At one presentation, someone asked why the plays were all so serious. A stiff and humorless boy in that teenaged group surprised us all when he answered, "A comic moment is not usually a turning point in someone's life. We only had five pages to establish two people and the conflict they share. In a longer play, there would be room for lighter moments too. Besides, we're teenagers … everything is a crisis!" His graceful response allowed everyone in the audience to laugh and made the deep feelings stirred up in each of us easier to bear.

About seventy of the most memorable scenes and monologues that emerged from the various workshops follow. They are prefaced by a brief playwright biography and a look back at what was experienced.

Susan Peters & June Squibb in *Double Cross* by Gail Noppe-Brandon
Photograph by Carol Rosegg

Kate Sanderson & Sarah Goldstein in *Basement* by Tova Friedman
Photograph by Carol Rosegg

James Rich in *Building* by Gail Noppe-Brandon
Photograph by Carol Rosegg

Marcus Ho and Karen Lee in *Duet* by Linda Faigao-Hall
Photograph by Carol Rosegg

Alex Abell in *Ode to Joy* by Andre Zucker
Photograph by Carol Rosegg

Ron Trenouth & Lydia Gaston in *Pusong Babae (*The Female Heart*)*
by Linda Faigao-Hall Photograph by Carol Rosegg

Jo Twiss & Susan Peters in *Simulating Emily* by Gail Noppe-Brandon
Photograph by Carol Rosegg

Jeanette Horn & Tom Bozell in *The Last Chair* by Gail Noppe-Brandon Photograph by Carol Rosegg

Felix Cosme & Shadeed Elliott in *The Sandbox* by Dante Williams
Photograph by Daisy Taylor

Sarah Paulson & Bobby Lopez in *Ashes* by Nora Scott Simpson
Photograph by Daisy Taylor

Rosa Soto & Jason Torres in *Hidden Child* by Jan Kodadek
Photograph by Daisy Taylor

Mio Takada & Susan Gordon-Clark in *On A Plane* by Shawn
Hirabayashi Photograph Courtesy of Find Your Voice

Cathleen Wiggins in *Safety Net* by Lucy Matos
Photograph by Jerry Lacay

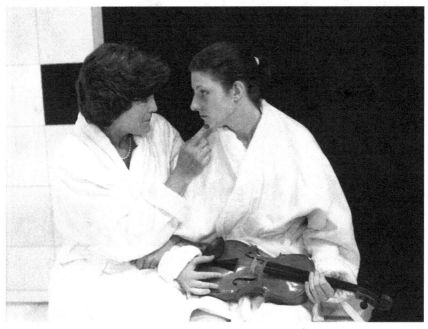

Susan Gordon-Clark & Liz Brown in *Laura & Wendy* by Lucy
Thurber Photograph by Susan Cook

Trigger image for the *Letters* Cluster Photograph by Andrea Sperling

Trigger image for the *St. Nicola* and *Into the Light* Clusters
Photograph by Andrea Sperling

Plays and Monologues

Omar Aguilar

Omar took the FYV training for one year, when he was a senior and I was leading an after school workshop at his high school. He was initially hesitant to enroll. He described himself as more of a "math head" than a writer. In his disarmingly honest and self-depricating way, he actually encouraged me to select another "more worthy" student in his place. Once he enrolled, he hid behind his long hair during the acting work and avoided beginning his writing for many weeks. When he finally began to write this play, in response to a photo of a broken window, it actually came very easily to him. Because he was such an authentic human being, he was a natural! As you read the play, notice how the dialogue on paper sounds exactly as it would when spoken—that is one of the goals of the method. It was performed at the Clark Studio Theatre at Lincoln Center that year. No one was more surprised than he when I subsequently chose to include it in my Find Your Voice *book, as an example of the kind of excellent work that reluctant writers can be encouraged to develop in a very short time once an environment is created in which they feel safe to be seen. Omar performed in another student's play at the launch of that book, which was held at the Four Seasons in NYC before a hundred people. He is also featured as an alumni performer in* Listening with Their Eyes, *the documentary film about the FYV work. At the time of this writing, he was serving in the Navy as a Field Med Corpsman and an EMT Basic. He remembered that this program was, "A blast. I can't believe I tried to let someone replace me! It was a very important step into who I developed into, because it gave me the chance to express myself freely. It's been about six years since I wrote this piece, and it still brings a smile to my face. I was a mediocre English student, yet Gail still believed in me. Pride isn't a great quality, but I believe this is more along the lines of accomplishment and just flat out feeling good. If only I'd enrolled at the beginning of high school, I can imagine what other potential I would have unlocked." Omar hoped to become a teacher someday.*

This was the first play that Omar ever wrote. It was inspired by a photograph of a broken window, for a cluster entitled Windows.

Girls
Omar Aguilar

Characters: CHRIS   Male, late teens
            STEVE   Male, late teens

AT RISE: In front of a warehouse in Hell's Kitchen. CHRIS and STEVE are throwing rocks at a factory window offstage.

CHRIS: Yes! You see that? Perfect aim, baby.

STEVE: Yeah! Nice shot. Now watch a pro. *(He throws … clank)*

CHRIS: Look at that; you missed. You suck.

STEVE: Whatever, I'm just distracted.

CHRIS: Distracted? *(CHRIS looks around.)* By what?

STEVE: Madeline. I wonder what she's doing right now.

CHRIS: Come on, man! This is *our* time. We're supposed to have fun.

STEVE: Yeah, you're right. Let me try again. *(He picks up a rock.)*

CHRIS: Good luck, because remember I'm great and you ain't.

STEVE: *(He throws ... clank)* Ah, man. I guess I'm off today, so I'll call it a night.

CHRIS: What! Already? *(Looks at his watch)* It's only ten thirty. *(Pause)* I know what you're trying to do! You're trying to ditch me, so you can spend time with *her.*

STEVE: No. Today's just not my day.

CHRIS: Bullshit. I can't believe you're trying to get rid of me by saying your throw is off. You got better aim than me.

STEVE: So what. I wanna spend time with my girl. Is that too much to ask?

CHRIS: Is it too much to ask to hang out with my best friend? I'm always hoping you don't already have plans. And when we do hang out, you seem bored.

STEVE: That's not true. Remember when we chilled that whole week, without once mentioning her name? *(No response)* C'mon, remember? We got twisted!

CHRIS: Wasn't that the week Madeline was being punished?

STEVE: So what, man; I'm in love.

CHRIS: How can you be in love at such a young age?

STEVE: I think I'm gonna marry this girl in a couple of years.

CHRIS: Shut up.

STEVE: You've got no idea what it means to be in love. Man, remember when Madeline and I tried to hook you up with her friend? What was wrong with ... um? What was her name again? Um, Amy.

CHRIS: Amy? That girl was a ditz. My thirteen-year-old brother was smarter than she was. I mean she was easy, but we had nothing in common. She liked Britney Spears and NSYNC; I like Linkin Park and Slipknot. *(Pause)* And what do you mean I don't know what it means to be in love? Remember when I fell for Michelle? She was perfect.

STEVE: So whatever happened to that?

CHRIS: She was too perfect. We had nothing to talk about because we were too much alike.

STEVE: So what do you want? You want us to hook you up with a girl again? This time we'll make sure that she's your type, but with some differences?

CHRIS: I don't need your help; I can do shit on my own. That's not the point. *(Pause)* How long have you known me?

STEVE: Around fifteen years.

CHRIS: How long have you known Madeline?

STEVE: *(Looks at his watch)* Three weeks, five days, four hours, and thirty-two minutes.

CHRIS: Loser.

STEVE: What do you want me to do, make a schedule? You're driving me crazy.

CHRIS: You have to start making choices. *(Pulls out a cigarette)*

STEVE: Choices? I already made choices. You're my best friend, and Madeline is my girlfriend. When are you going to make some choices of your own? I been beggin' you to quit smokin'.

CHRIS: Nah, see you caused this. Stressin' me out all the time.

STEVE: Whatever.

CHRIS: And stop trying to change the subject. I wanna know who's it gonna be, me or Madeline?

STEVE: Why can't you be like before? You never had a problem with any of my other girls; you used to understand. What happened?

CHRIS: You weren't as obsessed.

STEVE: Yo man, you have to give me some time to think on this.

CHRIS: You need time to think on this? Come on, man, girls come and go but boys stay together forever.

STEVE: Very heartfelt.

CHRIS: I can't believe you're choosing this trick over me.

STEVE: Watch your mouth; that's my wifey you talking about.

CHRIS: Come on. She's been around, the neighborhood knows about her.

STEVE: Man, you're just sayin' that cause you're jealous.

CHRIS: If that's what you wanna believe. *(Silence)* So … choose already! *(Silence)* This isn't a very hard choice.

STEVE: Damn, man, it's gotta come down to this?

CHRIS: Yep.

STEVE: All right, fine.

CHRIS: So have you come up with your decision? *(STEVE nods his head.)* So spit it.

STEVE: Sorry man. *(Starts to walk away)*

CHRIS: What!! I can't believe you!

STEVE: High school's over. You need to grow up and get on with your life. *(He exits.)*

CHRIS: Nah. Fuck you!! *(Throws a rock, hits target)*

BLACKOUT

Sherisse Alvarez

Sherisse began her FYV training when she was a freshman in high school, and she studied with me for many years. She was always a very intense and creative young woman, but her sweetness belied a turbulent inner life. As she grew more comfortable expressing her anger, in the guise of the characters she was portraying in the acting class, she became an increasingly crafted, courageous, and powerful actor and writer. This monologue is from a play that reflected some of the internal drama that she was dealing with during her adolescence. Because the feelings and images evoked were so raw and disturbing, it took many rewrites for Sherisse to shape something that caught the character's rage, while also sustaining her vulnerability. "I was interested in exploring the ways in which girls develop a sense of self/family/body image as they come of age. Had I not had a vehicle, the tool of writing, I would not have found my voice. This experience paved the way for me as a writer, and as a woman artist and thinker." Mature beyond her years, Sherisse went on to assist me on- and back-stage for many years as a paid intern. At the time of this writing, she was in graduate school pursuing a degree in creative nonfiction.

This monologue was taken from a play that was written for a cluster of plays entitled Seeing the Light, *which dealt with breakdowns in communication.*

Father, Me
Sherisse Alvarez

(NADINE, a Latina teenager, is struggling with bulimia and reaches out to her estranged sister for help.)

NADINE

He looks at me with such disgust and rage. He tells me that no man will ever want to marry me: "You're a fat whore with a body no man will want." *(She closes her eyes.)* When he yells, I can smell the liquor on his breath. I can almost taste it. *(Inhales deeply)* After, I run and kneel in front of the toilet; I feel nothing but numb. I want to scream. I want to scream so loud that the whole fucking deaf world will hear me. *(Looks at her sister)* But all I can do is sit there with my fingers down my throat, forcing them until they can't go any further, trying hard not to make any noise so Daddy won't hear me. *(Her sister takes her hand.)* Remember this sweater? *(Pause)* It was Mom's. It reminds me of her when I wear it. *(She smells it.)* It still smells like her; that strong, sweet perfume she wore. *(Silence)* After she left, at first the throwing up only happened once in a while; then it became constant. Every day, three times a day. Each time after it happened I felt desperate—like Daddy. I'm like *him* now … empty. *(Looks at her sister)* I keep praying that he'll come in and tell me that it doesn't have to happen anymore, but he never comes. So I just rock myself to sleep, hoping that I'll never wake up. *(Closes her eyes)* I wish I could just sleep forever.

Tanya Butler Holder

Tanya began her FYV training when she started high school; she was an exceptionally pretty fourteen-year-old girl who struggled to take her intellect seriously. As you read this play, note the strength of character and voice that Fay exudes. Tanya went on to study for several terms, and eventually she returned to take a master class after she graduated from college. This play, her first truly complete work, was written during that summer, immediately following the birth of her son. "Writing this piece was wonderful for me; I was new to marriage and motherhood, and developing these characters allowed me to express many issues that aren't spoken about when it comes to relationships. In hindsight, I should have taken part in the writing aspect of the training sooner. I didn't write as I went through the training in high school, and when I finally did, it was such a relief to get all the ideas on paper. I regret not using the tool earlier." Tanya went on to teach alongside me for many years and to assist in the ongoing work of the company. At the time of this writing, Tanya was working as a jewelry designer and an assistant at a children's museum. She had a third child in the spring of 2008.

This play was written in response to an image of an open drawer full of old letters, for a cluster entitled Letters *(p. 38).*

Unspoken Words
Tanya Butler Holder

Characters: ROMAN   Male, African-American, 20s

                 FAY   Female, African-American, 20s

AT RISE: ROMAN and FAY are seated on the couch, having "a talk"; she is holding a letter he wrote to her.

ROMAN: Ever since we moved in together things have been ... different; no, they've been *whack* between us. We come home from work, we eat, and then we go to sleep. We don't *do* anything anymore.

FAY: What do you mean we don't *do* anything?

ROMAN: We don't talk; we don't hold hands; we don't laugh. It's like once you officially moved in, all the affection in our relationship went out the door.

FAY: I don't have time for affection! I have to cook, make sure the dishes are done—

ROMAN: I never asked you to do those things.

FAY: Yeah, well ... if I don't do them, who will? Not you.

ROMAN: I don't need another mother.

FAY: You could have fooled me.

ROMAN: Well, I don't.

FAY: *(Pause)* I'm still affectionate.

ROMAN: Not like before. You used to write me letters and cards, for no special reason other than just to say you loved me. I liked it. All of a sudden that just stopped. How do you expect me to be secure anymore?

FAY: I don't have time to stroke your ego.

ROMAN: Don't be a smartass; I don't want you to stroke my ego. But I'm human. *(Takes her hand)* Don't you remember what it was like before? Now I have to make an appointment just to get a hug. Moving in together wasn't supposed to become a *responsibility*.

FAY: *(Frees her hand)* Well, it has. *(Pause)* Y'know, you haven't taken the time to see that maybe something more is going on with *me*. All you see is what I'm not doing for *you*.

ROMAN: That's not true—

FAY: Maybe, just maybe, you don't know everything. *(Long pause)* Maybe I might be pregnant.

ROMAN: *(Looks at her in disbelief)* Why didn't you say anything?

FAY: I wanted to be sure first.

ROMAN: Why would you choose to go through that alone?

FAY: Why didn't you *talk* to me? *(Waves letter)* Why did I have to read everything in a letter?

ROMAN: Your planner was always filled.

FAY: Now who's being a smartass?

ROMAN: Okay, I guess I have to learn to express myself better. But I'm not the only one. *(Awkward silence)* So—

FAY: So, what?

ROMAN: So when did you find out?

FAY: The doctor confirmed it today; I'm over a month late.

ROMAN: You suspected it for that long and you never said anything?

FAY: I tried to … it doesn't matter now anyway.

ROMAN: Of course it matters.

FAY: How could it matter if you're planning to be out?

ROMAN: Be out? Fay, don't you get what I've been saying all this time? *(No response)* I love you. I want the old *us* back.

FAY: How do we do that?

ROMAN: Well … *(Puts his arms around her and then pauses.)* Is it okay if I do this without an appointment? *(Pulls her close)*

FAY: Yes, stupid. *(Hugs him back)*

ROMAN: We could start by choosing names.

FAY: We don't need to pick out names.

ROMAN: Why not? I know you must have something in mind; girls plan this type of thing from birth!

FAY: *(Pulls away from him)* Okay, so now all women live for is to pick names for their children?

ROMAN: Whoa! It really wasn't that deep—

FAY: Well, it sounded to me like you were trying to insinuate something.

ROMAN: I really wasn't. Don't turn all feminist on me. I just wondered why we shouldn't pick out names. *(Pause, trying to change the mood)* If it's a boy, I think we should name him after me! *(He smiles at her.)*

FAY: It's pointless to pick out names.

ROMAN: *(Pause)* And what's that supposed to mean?

FAY: It means not now, I can't go through with this now.

ROMAN: What do you mean *can't*. Of course you can—

FAY: Well, I *won't*.

ROMAN: Oh, it's like that? You make this kind of decision and don't even consult me?

FAY: I'm not ready for a child yet … it's too soon. So don't make such a big deal over it.

ROMAN: Don't make a big deal? I think the chance to bring another human being into this world is a *very big deal*! I don't know how you could *not* see it as a big deal.

FAY: Like I said, I don't think I'm ready to raise a child.

ROMAN: Why do you keep talking about only *you*? Don't you think I'll be there to help you?

FAY: Let's be realistic—

ROMAN: I *am* being realistic. Actually, I'm being damn serious.

FAY: Well, whatever—

ROMAN: *(In sudden outburst, rising)* No, dammit, *not* whatever! We have been blessed with a child, and that's what I want. I want to have this baby.

FAY: In a perfect world, we *would* have this baby. We would get married and have this child and everything would be grand. But it isn't a perfect world, and the harsh reality is that there are too many sisters out there raising kids on their own; I don't want to be one of them.

ROMAN: *(Sitting beside her again)* You wouldn't be. I would be there every step of the way, through thick and thin.

FAY: You're the person who had to write me a letter to tell me our relationship was falling apart!

ROMAN: That's not even right, Fay.

FAY: One day you could up and leave. You could wipe your hands of the situation, like my father did, and I would be left to find a way to survive. I know what it's like growing up without a father in the house. I want better for my kids.

ROMAN: But I'll *be* a father. I *want* to be there for my child. This is a chance to start the next generation off right.

FAY: That's not fair to me—

ROMAN: Is it fair to me? Assuming I'm going to be the typical Brother who runs out on his family? Why can't I be the one who makes everything right, who gives you that perfect world? *(Taking her hands)* Together we can make this world what we want it to be.

FAY: *(Rising and pacing)* You can't promise that. *(Pause)* Don't you see that this isn't just about you? What about *my* life? Who says I'm ready to be there twenty-four/seven for someone else? I just got out here on my own. I finally found what I want to do in life, and it's starting to take off. Why should I be expected to put my career, and my social life, on hold for at least eighteen years?

ROMAN: That all depends on how you look at raising children. It's not the end of the world—

FAY: I didn't say that—

ROMAN: Well then, why don't you see it as the *beginning* of life? What better way to change the world, than to provide a little person with a whole new set of ideals and a new way of thinking? *(Silence, she turns away.)* So, what? Are you going to shut me out of this choice?

FAY: I don't think there really is a choice to be made.

ROMAN: I can't believe you're really going to be like this.

FAY: You're not ready to take on the responsibilities that come along with a child either. Shit, the way I do everything around here, it would be like having *two* kids. *(Pause)* I thought you felt the same way—we're not ready.

ROMAN: *(In a sudden burst, rising too)* Screw you! How can you decide for me whether or not I'm ready? The communication between us is definitely whack; how could you *not* know that there is nothing more important to me than raising a child—*my* child!

FAY: I'm sorry ... I didn't think you would get so mad. But that's just it; communication is necessary in order to raise kids. It's the key to making everything work, especially our relationship.

ROMAN: Then why did you shut me out? Everything I said in that letter boils down to the fact that I don't feel loved anymore. I mean, do you really still love me?

FAY: You *know* that—

ROMAN: No! I don't know *anything* anymore. I thought getting married and having kids would eventually be the path we'd choose to take—

FAY: The key word is *eventually.*

ROMAN: Well, what's wrong with *now*? If you love me, then why not now? *(Silence)* Because society dictates that we have to have a two-car garage and a million dollars in the bank in order to have a child? I thought we were supposed to be different. I thought we agreed not to follow those unspoken rules.

FAY: We still have to have a lot more than two dollars and a whole lot of promises!

ROMAN: *(Walks up to her, looks into her eyes)* Tell me something; do you love me? I'm talking about with all your heart ... the way I do you?

FAY: *(Pause)* Yes. I do.

ROMAN: Then what more do we need? *(They look at each other.)*

BLACKOUT

Carla Cabibi

Carla participated in one week-long intensive FYV workshop for teachers, during the summer of 2008. She had been teaching world history to high school students in Atlanta for two years. New to the profession, Carla took the workshop in the hopes of improving her own writing and communication skills. Although stating that she "rarely wrote," Carla had tried developing some plays for her students to perform, and she took to the form quite beautifully. She wrote this little jewel of a piece in three days. The play reflects her keen sense of humor, as well as her warm and sensitive nature. At the time of this writing, Carla was making "both valiant and desperate attempts to help world history seem relevant to tenth graders." She remembers the process of hearing actors speaking the lines of her play as "revelatory," because "the lines as they were spoken made clear the changes that were necessary. Also, my empathy and compassion for students under the stress of being 'in the spotlight' in class have increased a hundredfold." Although I knew Carla for a very short time, I include this play not only because it demonstrates how much craft can be cultivated in five days, but how much feeling can be evoked in little more than a single page.

This play is from the Not Listening *cluster and was written in response to Andrea Sperling's photograph on the cover of this book.*

Etude
Carla Cabibi

Characters:	NICK	Male, 11
	DAD	Male, 40s

AT RISE: NICK sits alone in a hallway. The muted sound of someone playing the piano can be heard. The boy looks at his watch, then he listens to the piano lesson underway. We hear the sound of a car horn outside. The boy moves as if to get up; then he sinks back into the chair and resumes listening. A few moments later, the car horn blows again. After some moments, NICK's DAD enters.

DAD: *(Exasperated)* Here you are. Didn't you hear me blowing the horn?

NICK: I heard.

DAD: Well, come on, let's go. *(He turns to leave, but NICK remains seated.)* Nick, I said let's go. What are you doing?

NICK: Listening. *(He tilts his head toward the music.)* I always listen to her lesson.

DAD: Not today you don't.

NICK: Shhh … This next part is tricky. I had trouble with it. *(Pause to listen)*

DAD: It's been a long day. I'm tired, and I don't have time for this. *(Starts to leave again)*

NICK: *(Pause to listen)* Hey, she did all right.

DAD: Good for her. Now let's go.

NICK: Do you recognize it?

DAD: Recognize what?

NICK: The music. *(No response)* Chopin?

DAD: Should I?

NICK: I've been practicing that same song for two weeks.

DAD: *(Sighing)* Your mother had the ear for music, Nick. Not me. *(Pauses, stares at NICK to get him going)* You used to complain about me being late picking you up from your piano lesson. Here I am, early—

NICK: You're not early. You're just not as late as you usually are. *(No response)* It used to piss me off that you were always so late. But then I started listening to this girl who comes in after me. *(Defiantly)* And now that's what I do.

DAD: Oh, so this is about a girl? I get it.

NICK: You *so* don't get it.

DAD: Is she cute?

NICK: It has nothing to do with cute.

DAD: Then what? What is this about? *(No response)* Jesus, tell me, so I can "get it" and we can go home.

NICK: I'm not leaving until I'm done listening.

DAD: This is ridiculous. The piano teacher is listening. It's her job.

NICK: *His* job.

DAD: Excuse me—*his* job. Why isn't it enough that *he's* listening?

NICK: *Because* it's his job. Don't you get it yet? *(No response)* Someone else has to listen.

DAD: *(He stares at NICK as something slowly dawns on him.)* When your mother used to … be the one who came and got you—

NICK: She never sat in the car and blew the horn. *(Pause)* She came inside and listened.

DAD: *(Pause. He looks around the room as if noticing the place for the first time.)* Where did she sit?

NICK: *(Motioning to a chair directly beside him)* Right here. She was always right here when I came out.

DAD: *(He eases into the chair, unbuttons his coat, and nods.)* Then what? What would she do?

NICK: *(Shrugs)* She'd smile. Even if I sucked. Then she'd ask, "Ready?" And we'd go home.

DAD: *(Pause)* So how did you do today?

NICK: I sucked.

DAD: What'd your teacher say?

NICK: He said I sucked.

DAD: Really?

NICK: Not exactly. He said I need to practice more.

DAD: *(Pause)* I guess we both need to practice more. *(Father and son listen to the piano lesson for a moment.)*

NICK: *(Taps DAD's leg)* We can go now, Dad. She's almost done.

DAD: *(Covers NICK's hands with his own)* No, it's okay. Let's listen. *(Their eyes meet briefly, and then they resume listening together.)*

BLACKOUT

Laura Clark

Laura took the FYV training along with the other seventh grade teachers on the faculty at the middle school where she was teaching. Her background was in the social sciences, and like many educators I have trained, she was more comfortable in the realm of facts than feelings; finding a warmer voice was crucial to her ability to connect with her students. However, she displayed a wonderful grasp of the rewriting process and worked on this play until it contained as much heart as it did facts. Laura then turn-keyed the FYV technique to the young bilingual students whom she taught; she did a remarkable job of leading them toward clear and authentic work. "I remember being shocked that the characters took on lives of their own. I worried that I wouldn't be able to come up with what they would say. Little did I know they would talk to each other in my head—day and night! The writing process highlighted for me that encouraging students to write was often much more about getting out of the way than about providing structure or lessons. The acting process was a valuable lesson about the importance of staying in the moment and expressing authentic emotions as a way of engaging people and affecting them." At the time of this writing, Laura was the full-time mother of twin girls and working on a number of freelance writing projects.

This, Laura's first play, was written as part of a cluster of plays entitled Revelations, *which were suggested by a photograph of sunlight on a stone wall (p. 38).*

Loca
Laura Clark

Characters: INES   Latina, 25
                      ALEX   Latino, 28

AT RISE: It is early morning. INES (wide awake and dressed in running clothes) has led ALEX (sleepy and dressed in sweats and shoes with no socks) to the top of the steps in front of the Harvard library. The plaza at the top of the steps is flooded in bright sunlight. Blinded by the light, ALEX desperately looks around for a place to sit down; he finds a bench.)

ALEX: Couldn't whatever this is have waited until a decent hour? *(Silence)* If you think you're going to get me into some kind of exercise program by getting me up before I can figure out what's going on; *estás loca.* I may not have had my coffee yet, but I'm not that confused. *(Looks down at his feet)* I don't even have my socks on. *(Gets up to leave)* Can I go back to my room now?

INES: Alex—

ALEX: You never go running this early; what's with you this morning?

INES: *(She sits)* I wanted to explain to you why I'm staying here.

ALEX: *(Confused, he sits)* You're going to start sleeping on the library steps again? *(Silence)* I thought the university agreed to let the maintenance staff send their children to the day care center. *(Silence)* Don't tell me they changed their minds?

INES: No, they haven't changed their minds, but—

ALEX: But what? Do you really think this is a good time to get involved in another protest? We have to be in New York in two weeks.

INES: That's what I'm trying to tell you. I'm not going to New York. *(Pause)* I'm staying in Boston.

ALEX: Very funny!

INES: I'm serious, Alex. I still don't quite understand it myself, but something amazing happened to me earlier this morning.

ALEX: What do you mean? Did you get a call postponing your clerkship?

INES: No. *(Pause)* I've decided not to take the clerkship ... I'm staying to head the Labor Rights office for Father Brannon.

ALEX: *(Stands up again)* Estás loca! When did he bully you into this?

INES: You know Father Brannon better than that—he didn't bully me into anything. He doesn't even know about it yet. I just found out myself.

ALEX: You just found out? What does that mean, Ines? How does someone "just find out" that she'll be turning down a clerkship with the chief judge of the Federal Court of Appeals in order to stay and run a two-bit office for the diocese? What the hell are you talking about?

INES: Could we be civil, Alex? I'm making a big decision here, and I really need you to try to understand.

ALEX: *(Starting to pace around)* Well, I don't understand. I don't understand at all.

INES: *(Holding him still)* Just listen for a minute, would you? *(He looks at her.)* Remember when Father Brannon told me how desperate he was for someone to take over in the labor-rights office, and how much he would love for me to stay and work with him?

ALEX: Do you remember how he *laughed* when he said it? He knew there was no way you would stay to do work any first-year law student could do.

INES: He wants the office to take on a new national role. That's not—

ALEX: You're more than that office, and he knows it.

INES: Please don't make him out to be the bad guy here; I'm the one who wants this.

ALEX: You're the one who wants this? You're the one? *(Pacing again)* No. What you want, Ines, is what's detailed in your thirty-year plan, in the green binder on your nightstand. Don't stand here and pretend you haven't planned your every move since you were fifteen years old around becoming the first Latina justice on the Supreme Court. Where on your spreadsheets and contingency plans does it say anything about turning down a federal clerkship to work with a priest?

INES: You don't need to treat me like a hostile witness! This is *my* dream we're talking about.

ALEX: I just don't get it, Ines. You've made so many sacrifices to get here—the college loans, the unpaid internships, and the constant—

INES: You think I haven't thought about all that? It's just that things changed for me this morning.

ALEX: How much could things have changed in one morning? You graduated at the top of our class at Harvard, Ines. Every law firm in the country—

INES: Will you please hold off on your "cross" for a minute, and let me explain?

ALEX: Ines, you were not meant to go work in a windowless office in the basement of a church. *(ALEX slumps back down onto the bench with his head in his hands.)*

INES: *(Pause)* Do you remember when we protested here, how beautiful the light was first thing in the morning? I would wake up as early as I could, just to watch it slowly creep across the sleeping bodies. *(Touches him to make him look up)* Look at the light.

ALEX: *(Looks up, squints)* It just seems bright to me, Ines.

INES: Now, yes; it's late. But don't you remember how beautiful it was then, first thing in the morning, and how happy I was?

ALEX: Sure, I remember.

INES: I thought I could always carry the memory of that light and how good it made me feel. For months afterwards, I used that memory to cheer myself up whenever I was feeling low. But over time, it stopped making me feel better; it just made me feel empty.

ALEX: Where are you going with this?

INES: *(She sits beside him on the bench.)* I jogged down here before dawn, because I wanted to get that feeling back. But the sun rose and nothing happened; I realized that the memory of the light was not enough … the light was only meant to illuminate what I needed.

ALEX: You're losing me here, Ines.

INES: I was so happy on those mornings because I woke up knowing that what I was doing mattered. *(Pause)* I can always clerk in New York next year, or the year after that. But if I walk away from Boston now, I will be giving up the opportunity to experience the sense of joy and purpose that I felt here.

ALEX: What about the sense of joy and purpose you would experience as a Supreme Court justice?

INES: I still want that. *(Pause)* The one thing I never accounted for in my green binder was that the spreadsheets were simply an abstraction—they keep my *life*. I can't wait thirty years for my life to matter.

ALEX: And what about *my* life, Ines?

INES: *(Pause)* We both know that you have to find your own path.

ALEX: Until fifteen minutes ago, my path *was* your path. I only interviewed with firms that had a New York office *and* a DC office, so that I could follow you wherever you went. Now I'm suddenly supposed to go find my own path?

INES: How long do you think we would have lasted, with you watching me work toward *your* dream?

ALEX: What's that supposed to mean? You had that dream long before we met.

INES: Don't you think I know why you can recite every detail of my thirty-year plan?

ALEX: Ninety percent of the students in our class dream about making it to the Supreme Court—that doesn't mean we all have what it takes.

INES: You're selling yourself short, Alex.

ALEX: I'm just being realistic.

INES: You're ignoring your own potential.

ALEX: And what about you, Ines? You can't ignore *your* potential without all of us paying a price.

INES: I understand the obligation that comes with what I've been given, but there's no reason to believe that my adolescent plans are the best way to fulfill that obligation.

ALEX: *(Looks at her sternly)* You need to give yourself some time to think this over. You can't change the whole course of your life based on one sunrise.

INES: In a funny way, the weeks I've spent pushing Father Brannon's offer out of my head have given me time. I didn't want this, but now I can't imagine things any other way.

ALEX: *(He rises.)* That's it then, Ines? You've made up your mind?

INES: Yes.

ALEX: I don't know what to say.

INES: *(Pause)* Now that's something, isn't it?

BLACKOUT

Patti Covich

Patti took the FYV training as part of her professional development, after a discouraging year of teaching drama at her high school. Patti was originally trained as an English teacher, but she was asked to double as the drama specialist at her school by dint of the fact that she had read Shakespeare! Although she had done some singing in college, she was neither an actor nor a director. Patti was so courageous in her participation with me that she returned to the classroom with a full toolkit to share with her young charges and began to work very successfully as a drama teacher. I love the humor in the piece, which never became situation comedy but remained poignant and true to the importance that the material held for her. It was this deepening comfort with authenticity that enabled her to develop true connections when she returned to the classroom. The following year Patti returned to take a master class; this play was written during that class. After several more years at her school, Patti adopted a child, went on to earn a degree in special education, and became a teacher consultant. "The thematic concerns of my piece voiced the thematic concerns of my life. It was quite a catharsis for me. I never considered myself a writer; I didn't know I had it in me! The training and coaching I received from the superlative staff and structure of FYV helped me to realize my potential. My self-esteem significantly increased; my technique in the classroom setting changed completely. Suddenly both my students and I loved my classes! Participating in FYV was the best thing I ever did for my personal and professional life."

This play was written for a cluster entitled Rain Dates, *in response to an image of a broken umbrella on the street.*

Third Generation
Patti Covich

Characters: MOM   40s
              ROBEY   Her daughter, mid-20s

AT RISE: CHARLOTTE TURNER is sitting by herself at a table for three in a restaurant in New York City. She has a small shopping bag and a purse

59

by her side. She looks in her makeup mirror and freshens her lipstick and then returns them to her purse. She is obviously waiting for someone special. She sips from her cocktail. The sounds of rain, thunder, and lightning are heard throughout the scene, but loudly now. Her daughter ROBEY (pronounced ROBE-EE) enters. She is wearing a garbage bag with holes poked out for her hands and head. Another garbage bag is tied around her hair as a rain bonnet. She is soaked and not happy.

ROBEY: *(Breathless)* Hey, Mom.

MOM: *(Mortified)* What are you wearing?!

ROBEY: It's all they had at the office.

MOM: Take that thing off right now!

ROBEY: *(Angry and hurt)* Ma, would you rather I got totally drenched—like I'm not drenched enough? *(Removes her bag and coat)*

MOM: Here we go again, Roberta. You can be such a misery. Are you always determined to rain on my parade? *(ROBERTA removes the plastic scarf from her head.)* Omigod! What happened to your hair?

ROBEY: Ma, it's been under a garbage bag!

MOM: Well, sit down. *(She pulls her down into the seat.)* Fluff it up, for heaven's sake. *(She does so with her hands.)* It's flat as a pancake. Here, let me tease it … *(She reaches for her purse.)*

ROBEY: Don't you dare pull a comb from that bag!

MOM: Roberta, you can really throw a wet blanket on any party, you know that? I'm not gonna let you get to me this time. *(Sips her drink deeply)* So … you have to wear a garbage bag on your head? What happened to your umbrella?

ROBEY: It's flown to Park Avenue by now. *(Slaps her MOM's hands away from her hair)* Leave my hair alone! Where's Daddy?

MOM: He's stuck on Vesey Street. No taxis.

ROBEY: Did we have to have dinner here? Doesn't he know I'm a vegetarian by now? I thought this was supposed to be *my* celebration. Why couldn't we go to La Metro?

MOM: Roberta, your father wanted to eat here. You can find a nice salad. *(Forcing the celebration)* So tell me already! How was it?

ROBEY: It was good. The people are friendly—the office is clean. I even have my own window; no view—but a window.

MOM: An executive office!

ROBEY: I'm an account executive, Mom. It's not that big a deal.

MOM: Your first day in a big company like Stuart's *is* a big deal, young lady, whether you realize it or not. You'll be able to buy that apartment of yours … *(The sound of a telephone ring is heard. MOM reaches into her purse and pulls out a small cell phone. In a high sing-song voice)* Hel-lo-o-o? *(Listens)* Oh yes, she's here. Where are you? *(Listens)* Oh my. Are you okay? *(Listens)* Well, we'll be here waiting for you. *(In a high sing-song voice)* Bye-bye!

ROBEY: Daddy?

MOM: Yeah. He's stuck on the IRT, somewhere around Delancey Street. He's all right. *(Reaches for something)* I have something for you.

ROBEY: *(Momentarily seduced)* Really, Mommy? *(MOM hands her a small package wrapped in silver from the shopping bag.)* What is it? *(ROBEY rips open the present. Inside the box, there is a white gold brooch with diamonds. ROBEY is shocked.)* Grandma Rose's brooch?

MOM: *(Kisses her—speaks sincerely)* Wear it in good health, my dear. You are a beautiful, successful woman now. It's time I pass it on.

ROBEY: Didn't you just call me a "wet blanket" and "a misery" two minutes ago? Now I'm a "beautiful, successful woman"?

MOM: Okay. A miserable wet blanket with—

ROBEY: *(Shoves the pin back to her mother)* Take the pin back, Mom.

MOM: I'm kidding!

ROBEY: Well, I'm not. I don't want that pin! Where am I going to wear it, Mom? To work? I don't go to country club parties every weekend. That's your lousy life!

MOM: Why are you so judgmental of my life? *(Softening)* Roberta, your life is just beginning. After you find someone and get married—

ROBEY: I already know who I'm marrying.

MOM: *(Takes another sip)* Listen, Roberta, how many times do I have to tell you, David is not the marrying kind. Someday you'll grow up and realize—

ROBEY: No, Mom. I'm not *you*! I can't live your life! Can you just accept me for who I am?

MOM: Of course, dear. I have never been prouder of you. You've just started this terrific job—

ROBEY: And don't mention my job again.

MOM: Why not? Aren't we here celebrating your job?

ROBEY: I don't feel like celebrating.

MOM: Well, excuse me for being happy! Is that such a crime?

ROBEY: No. I'm happy you're happy. After putting up with Daddy for twenty-seven years, you deserve it.

MOM: So what's the matter? *(Pause)* Okay, what happened? *(Silence)* Who hurt you?

ROBEY: Nobody hurt me, Mom. Everybody is perfectly nice; it's nothing like that.

MOM: Then what is it? *(Silence)* I want to know!

ROBEY: Mom, it's just that I … I … I gotta tell you—I hate that job!

MOM: What do you mean? Don't be ridiculous! It's only your first day—

ROBEY: It's horrible, Mom. The work is so boring. I don't care if Sach's wants "white gold spring clasps." I don't care if Charles Surrey fills his quota. It's all so ridiculous. What value am I creating?

MOM: *(Firmly now)* Roberta, you need to grow up. The most important thing is for you to make it in the world.

ROBEY: Am I supposed to just make money? At what price?

MOM: Would you rather live in a cardboard box?

ROBEY: I want to live where I can be happy—doing what I love to do.

MOM: Please don't start with that again. You can paint whenever you want, but Roberta—

ROBEY: Don't call me Roberta. My name is *Robey*.

MOM: No. Your name is Roberta Louise Turner. I should know; I gave you that name!

ROBEY: Mom, call me Robey. Everyone calls me Robey now. *(Studies MOM'S face)* Can't you understand? I'm not your old *Roberta* anymore. And I don't want to be stuck in an office all day. Mom, you may think it's glamorous, but, believe me, it's not. I don't want to end up like all those other women working nine-to-five jobs: gray hair, bleary dead eyes, taking care of other people's problems all day just so they can forget their own. Just work, and regret; a life they forgot to live.

MOM: And you don't want to live a life like mine, either.

ROBEY: No, I don't.

MOM: *(Sighs)* You'll get over it, dear. It's called growing up.

ROBEY: *(Glares at her)* Here I am, pouring my heart out, and you say, "It's called growing up, dear." You know what, Mom? This is a fiasco. I gotta go! *(Grabs for her garbage bag ensemble)*

MOM: *(Holds on to her garbage bags)* Roberta! Sit down.

ROBEY: Mom, let me go!

MOM: *(Holds onto the garbage bags, trying to stop her)* Don't you put that thing on in here!

ROBEY: Mom, you are so obnoxious! *(Runs out with the garbage bags. MOM is left in the restaurant, stunned but trying to look nonchalant. The telephone rings. We hear loud thunder, lightning, and pelting rain now.)*

MOM: Hel-lo-o-o? *(Drop in voice)* Yes, dear, where are you now? *(Listens)* Oh, well, why don't you call the car service? *(Listens)* Roberta just ran out. Excuse me, her name is *Robey* now. And she doesn't want my mother's pin—she wants a cardboard box and a garbage bag. *(ROBEY reenters and walks back to the table carrying her "Hefty" ensemble. She sits down at the table heavily. MOM gets off the phone as quickly as possible.)* All right, dear. See you soon. Bye-bye!

ROBEY: I can't leave now; it's a typhoon out there.

MOM: *(Hurt)* Oh, I see. You'll stay with your obnoxious mother just to stay out of the rain.

ROBEY: Ma, I swear, you don't even like me—all you do is try to change me.

MOM: I'm not trying to change you. Can't you see I'm just trying to protect you?

ROBEY: Protect me from what? Myself? I'm not that bad. It's not like I'm a heroin addict or anything.

MOM: I don't ever want to see you suffer. I don't want you to screw up your life.

ROBEY: Am I gonna melt? You'd rather see me drown than wear a raincoat you don't like. Can't you just let me live my own life and make my own mistakes?

MOM: Listen, Roberta; excuse me—*Robey*. Where did you get the idea that mistakes are fun? Believe me, they're not! I should know; I've made plenty. I was young once, too. I had dreams too.

ROBEY: But Ma, you've fulfilled your dreams.

MOM: No, Roberta, I had to give up many dreams along the way.

ROBEY: *(Interested)* What do you mean?

MOM: I could have married a kind man—like your David. *(Pause, takes a sip)* Even after you were born, I could have left your father and gone back to Robert—and back to acting. I wasn't so bad, you know—but I had children to raise. Robert waited for me for years, but if I had left your father—

ROBEY: *Robert?*

MOM: Yes, there was a young man named Robert once. He was a brilliant "starving actor." And he did everything he could to make me happy. He cooked me cheap spaghetti, bought me cheap flowers … and made me feel beautiful. He wasn't selfish like your father. Well, maybe selfish is the wrong word—

ROBEY: "Inconsiderate," "preoccupied"—

MOM: Right. But your father has some wonderful qualities too. He loves his family. He would do anything—

ROBEY: Except take his vegetarian daughter to a vegetarian restaurant.

MOM: I thought about leaving him; I could have left him—but how would we have lived?

ROBEY: Mom, I'm going to marry David; as you say, he makes me feel beautiful.

MOM: How long do you think that will last, Robey?

ROBEY: Forever! How can love die?

MOM: It can. Just like people.

ROBEY: I don't understand that. How is that possible? Where does it go?

MOM: I don't know. But I do know that if he doesn't let you do the things you want to do, you'll end up hating him.

ROBEY: But Mom, David *does* let me do the things I want to do!

MOM: No, not if he can't support you. How will he support you?

ROBEY: Well, he can't really—not as an artist. But that could change. And I can work.

MOM: Work where? Your job at Stuart's would support you—but you want to paint.

ROBEY: Yes, I want to paint, Ma. I *need* to paint. I'm just not happy if I don't. *And* I want to be with David. *(Pause)* Mom, please have faith in me. I might wear a garbage bag, but at least I know how to keep dry. *(Her mother looks at her for an extended beat. Telephone rings.)*

MOM: Hel-lo-o-o? *(Listens)* Yes, dear. Yes, she came back. Did you find the driver? *(Listens)* Good! Tell him to take you home. Or, you can meet me and Robey at La Metro. *(Listens)* Because she's a vegetarian. *(ROBEY is visibly delighted to hear this. She makes a strong gesture indicating her pleasure.)* Very good ... all right, dear. See you soon. Bye-bye! *(Hangs up the phone, looks at ROBEY)* Put on your Hefty bags and let's go.

ROBEY: Wait. *(Stopping MOM from rising)* I'd like to wear Grandma's brooch. Will you pin it on me? *(After a moment, MOM pins it on. ROBEY hugs her MOM.)*

MOM: Right now, I feel like my life ... has been good. *(Smiling at ROBEY, she gets her coat and umbrella quickly. She glances around the room.)* Let's go! *(They exit together to the sounds of rain, thunder, and lightning.)*

BLACKOUT

Franck Ramirez de Las Mercedes

I have known Franck for almost fifteen years; during that time, I have watched him evolve from a very angry young man who struggled to succeed in traditional schools to a mature and highly accomplished artist. Initially, Franck enrolled in a FYV Workshop in order to satisfy his English requirement at City as School—a "high school without walls" in New York City. His temper was so short that, although he had the natural fiery quality of a young Robert DeNiro, none of the other students in the acting class felt comfortable working with him. The chip on his shoulder was as large as his undiscovered talent. As he worked at developing craft, as well as improving his social skills, Franck began to write about his painful past and used his anger to fight for instead of with the characters whose stories he enacted in class. After two years, Franck, who was born in Nicaragua and often felt self-conscious about his accent, went on to give the commencement address at his high school graduation. Following that, he took several FYV Master Classes (the enclosed monologue from his short play Freedom *was written for one of those classes), and he continued to hone both his writing and acting crafts. Franck not only became comfortable with his beautifully accented voice, but he found a way to put his aggressive energy into a productive entrepreneurial venture, which also gave him an outlet for further self-expression: he created small painted boxes that could be sent as gifts and filled with whatever mood or sentiment the giver wanted to share. He was one of the first FYV alumni to be commissioned for our main stage; a scene from his play* Papa *follows. Franck has been a guest artist in several of our Teen Workshop presentations and performed in Khalil Hill's play* The Comeback Kid, *featured in this collection, at the launch of the* Find Your Voice *book. He is also a guest actor in our documentary film* Listening With Their Eyes. *After working as a researcher in television for many years, Franck is now a highly acclaimed visual artist, and he continues to use all of his voices to tell his stories and to benefit other young people. "I still remember the magic of seeing professionals acting in my play* Papa. *My whole experience with FYV equipped me with tools that I work with to this day." Frank's large-scale works and Public Art project have sparked great interest from the mainstream media and culture. He has shown his works with artists such as Romero Britto and Robert Rauschenberg and graced the cover of* Reader's Digest's *"Selecciones."*

> *This scene is from a play that was part of a cluster entitled* Four Views
> With a Room. *It was commissioned in response to the photograph on the
> cover of this book.*

Papa
Franck Ramirez de Las Mercedes

Characters: MARIO   Latino, late 50s
               MANUEL   Latino, early 30s, his son

*AT RISE: There is a knock at the door, and MANUEL, a young Latino
man who has been pacing, opens it to reveal an older Latino man—
MARIO, his estranged father.*

MARIO: Hijo! Como estas? *(MARIO makes an attempt to hug his son.
   MANUEL turns and walks inside and sits.)*
MANUEL: I'm fine, Mario.
MARIO: It's so good to see you!
MANUEL: Come in. *(MARIO walks inside and sits next to his son.)*
MARIO: I'm so happy to know that I'm a granddaddy. What did you
   name her?
MANUEL: Marlene.
MARIO: That's a beautiful name! *(Silence)* How is your wife doing? I'm
   sorry … I forget her name.
MANUEL: Laura! Her name is Laura. She's fine.
MARIO: Good, good. *(Looking around)* What a beautiful little chair!
MANUEL: You gave it to me for my fifth birthday, back in Nicaragua.
   I guess you wouldn't remember that.
MARIO: Are you kidding? Of course I—
MANUEL: It's going to be Marlene's now.
MARIO: And I'm sure she will love it.
MANUEL: *(Pause)* Can I get you anything?
MARIO: Oh, no thanks, I'm fine. *(Silence)* It's hard to believe you've
   kept it this long. *(Pause)* You always loved that little chair! *(Silence)*
   How's work? What's going on in the music industry these days?
MANUEL: Mario, I work in the traffic department for USA Networks.
   It's a TV station.

MARIO: Last I heard you were—

MANUEL: *(Gets up and paces)* How's *your* job?

MARIO: Well, it's a lot of pressure, and, as you know, I had to relocate ... but it's okay.

MANUEL: How's your son? Does he like Chicago?

MARIO: Little Mario is only in fourth grade. *(Pause, studies his son)* He reminds me so much of you, son.

MANUEL: You never saw me in fourth grade; how could he remind you of me!

MARIO: I meant, you are brothers ... there's a resemblance. I remember—

MANUEL: Remember? You didn't even remember what I do, or what my wife's name is.

MARIO: *(He quickly takes a present out of a bag.)* It's been a long time ... eh ... look, I bought this for Marlene. I hope she likes it.

MANUEL: *(MANUEL takes it and looks at it.)* Thanks a lot.

MARIO: It's a little music box! It plays the most wonderful melody. You used to love music boxes!

MANUEL: Did I?

MARIO: *(Laughs)* Yeah ... *(Awkward pause)* Manuel, there's no sense in—

MANUEL: What?

MARIO: Perhaps I can explain—

MANUEL: There's no need to—

MARIO: Look, I know I haven't been the best father—

MANUEL: No, you haven't!

MARIO: I want you to know that I want to be here for you, from now on—

MANUEL: What?

MARIO: If not for you, I want be there for little Marlene at least—

MANUEL: *(Rising)* Mario—

MARIO: Could we just sit and talk for another minute?

MANUEL: There's nothing to talk about. Why don't we just make this our usual once-every-five-year reunion and call it a day.

MARIO: *(Gets up and tries to reach for his son)* Manuel, I know how you feel—

MANUEL: *(Pulling away)* You have no fucking idea how I feel! For twenty years I kept silent; but I'm a man now. I'm a father.

MARIO: And I want to be there for you—

MANUEL: After all this time? Where were you when I *really* needed you?

MARIO: *(Pause)* I realize that I made a mistake by leaving, but we can start—

MANUEL: Over? We can just erase the past and start over? Like nothing happened? What about a childhood without a father?

MARIO: Son, I have to live knowing that I left you. I think about it every day—

MANUEL: Well, I *lived* it every day. I remember this chair too. You bought it so that I could sit and wait for you to come back from work. Every afternoon I would wait on the porch in my little chair. I would sit there quietly, patiently. Then, when I was six, you didn't come anymore. The only thing Mama said was, "Your dad loves you very much, and he'll be back for you." People think kids don't know what's going on.

MARIO: I *was* planning to—

MANUEL: You know what the worst part was? *(Pause)* That I turned seven, eight; I turned twelve … and I still waited. My life would have been so different with you around; if you had been there to guide me, to help me. How could we start over? And why do you think that you can make it up to me by coming to see my daughter with a stupid music box? *(He throws the music box to the floor; a couple of distorted notes play as he starts to walk away.)*

MARIO: Fine! I screwed up! That's why I'm here. *(Pause)* Manuel, I know that you must hate me—

MANUEL: I don't hate you. I *thought* I hated you, but the truth is that I feel nothing.

MARIO: Manuel, I came to America to build a better life for me, and for you, and for your—

MANUEL: Oh, you built a better life all right … just not with us.

BLACKOUT

This monologue is from a play that was part of the Liberty *cluster, in response to an image of the Statue of Liberty.*

Freedom
Franck Ramirez de Las Mercedes

(It is a pleasant summer afternoon. LOYA, a Latina woman in her late 40s, is walking through Battery Park with her son CHICO, who is in his late 20s. Although they live near each other, they haven't seen each other in a while; she is visiting with him for the Fourth of July. They stand gazing out at the Statue of Liberty; they have been arguing about patriotism, and there is tension. LOYA tries to get CHICO to forgive her for leaving him in Nicaragua as a child.)

LOYA

I'm going to tell you the truth son—for the first time. *(Trying to gather her courage)* You should know. *(Pause)* Maybe then you'll understand why I love this country so much. *(He snickers.)* Son, I didn't leave Nicaragua in search of anything—I was *forced* to leave. *(She has his attention now.)* After the fall of Somoza, the Sandinistas took it upon themselves to exterminate anyone who had been linked in any way with Somoza's government. Ironic, how *they* started doing things that the Somozas had been accused of doing! *(Shakes her head)* My father, your grandfather, had been a very respectable man, very well known. He had worked hard to become the minister of education; it didn't matter. He fled the country the minute it was official that the Sandinistas had won the civil war. *(Sighs)* Things were not that bad in the beginning for me. But when they wanted teachers to get involved in all kinds of political demonstrations, the education system changed. School plays had to be based on war and fighting—defending the Revolution! That was not my idea of education. One day, the principal of the school put me in charge of a political activity for the Sandinistas. He chose me as a mockery, because he knew my background. I refused to do it, and I knew things would get bad after that. They issued a warrant for my arrest *(in a sarcastic tone)* for "betraying my country." *(Looks into his eyes)* I either had to leave or rot in prison. *(Silence)* I was very good friends with the consulate general of Mexico, and I asked him for help. He got me a visa to Mexico. *(Takes his hands in hers)* Believe me, he tried to get all three of us visas, but on such short notice ... he could only get mine. *(Fighting tears)* Leaving you behind was the hardest thing I have ever had to do. In fact, I tried to change my mind once I had the visa in my hand, but I had no choice. *(Pause)* I will never forget that day; you were eight, and your sister was only six years old. *(A shaky smile)* You were being the tough little man you always were; you just stood there, quiet, motionless. I kissed you good-bye. You were so confused. *(Struggling to speak)* Right before I got into the car, Elena ran to me and wrapped her arms so tight around my waist; she was crying and begging, "Mommy, please don't leave, please don't leave me." *(Long painful pause)* My mother pulled her away from me. I felt as if she had pulled out my own heart, pulled away my whole life. *(She takes a moment to compose herself and then continues quietly.)* I got into the car, and I had to duck down all the way to the airport. *(Looks at him, begging forgiveness)* I left my own country like a criminal; that's not a story a mother wants to share with her kids. *(He stares)* It took so long for us to reunite. Chico, it wasn't easy getting you here, and it wasn't easy living here without you ... with the thought that I failed you as a mother, that I abandoned you. *(He looks at his hands.)* Maybe it's time you forgave me?

Gina Demetruis

Gina took the FYV training twice, once for her own professional development and then again as part of a faculty-wide development effort for the teaching staff of her small inner-city elementary school. Although originally trained as a drama teacher, she was blocked as a writer herself and feeling stale in her teaching. Gina had always harbored dreams of becoming a playwright; she simply needed to rediscover her love of writing, as well as her love of teaching. Participation in the training allowed this dream to flower in Gina and consequently in her classroom. "The workshop reawakened my desire to write, and that hasn't left me since. I also took the process and essentially duplicated it as an enrichment program for middle-school students with weak skills. Working dramaturgically really taught me how to listen with an ear for potential ... and the group effort reminded me about the importance of bonding with my students." Gina wrote this play during her second training, and I subsequently selected it for inclusion in the Find Your Voice *book, as an exemplar of the kind of professional-level work to which teachers can be connected and reconnected. More importantly, she exemplified the way in which teachers can be led to reconnect to their love of teaching. Notice the subtle humor in the piece, which moved the character's sheer cynicism to tragic hopefulness as she honed the "wants." Gina's middle-school students created and enacted dozens of powerful plays of their own, and she created original musicals with fifth and sixth graders in an afterschool program at a New York City public school.*

Gina wrote this play for a cluster entitled Something Old and ... *in response to a photograph of things hidden beneath a bed.*

CIRCLES
Gina Demetruis

Characters: ZANE   Male, mid-30s
             ANDREA   His wife, mid-30s

AT RISE: ZANE is lying on the couch with a crumpled New York Times *spread over his face and body. Only his feet, protruding at one end, let us*

One Vision, Many Voices

know that a human is present. There is a large bookcase and a door upstage of the couch. ANDREA quietly enters from that door and walks down to the couch. She looks at the figure under the papers and then sits on the man.

ZANE: Ughh!

ANDREA: I'm sorry. I didn't know there was a life form under all this.

ZANE: Uhhh. *(He shifts under the paper.)*

ANDREA: You are a life form, aren't you? I wouldn't want to pressure you with any high expectations. *(She picks up a piece of the newspaper.)* This newspaper's from last week. Look, I know "easy does it" is your new motto, but are you supposed to take it so literally? I mean, shouldn't you at least change your paper? *(There is no response.)* Hey! *(She slaps the newspaper.)*

ZANE: I'm trying to sleep.

ANDREA: Well, I admire your tenacity, 'cause you've been trying for the past forty-eight hours. Not everyone could stick with it like that. *(There is no response. She gets up.)*

ZANE: Ooof!

ANDREA: Sorry, I don't want to wrinkle my new dress. *(Silence)* I went shopping earlier, to celebrate. It's your thirty-first day without a drink, so I bought a new dress. Look. *(She does a slow turn, but ZANE remains completely motionless under the paper.)* The man at the store said it showed off my best assets. I was just happy to hear I still have assets. I mean, I'm only thirty-five, but sometimes I feel a lot older. Now that you're getting sober, that'll help. It's gonna rejuvenate both of us. *(She pauses and stares at the couch.)* Do you think it's too short? The dress? *(ZANE raises the newspaper slightly and peers out at her.)* Well, it shows off my legs. They're still pretty shapely, don't you think?

ZANE: *(He lets the paper drop back on his face.)* Do we have aspirin?

ANDREA: You should have seen the guys down the street. I wore the dress home from the store, and when I passed those old guys on the corner, the ones who play dominoes, their eyes got so big I thought they'd pop right out of their heads. Their whole board flipped over. *(Pause. She deflates.)* Store clerks, old men, and a husband who's buried under last week's newspaper. *(She sits down with her back against the couch.)* Who am I? *(Without looking behind her, she holds out her hand.)* Could you hold my hand? Honey? Honey! Honey, could you just hold my goddamn hand for a minute!

ZANE: I'm trying to sleep.

ANDREA: I'm trying to stay alive! For the past seven years, I've been caught up by this tornado that pulls everything up into a frenzy. For seven years I followed your tornado, and I've tried to clean up the mess left behind. And now you're getting sober, and you come and go from those AA meetings like a phantom and then close yourself up in this room. You made me a full partner to your drinking, and now you're getting sober and you shut me out! Where's my payoff? What's in it for me? Say something. Say something! *(There is no response. She goes to the door and slams it shut but remains in the room, leaning against the wall behind. ZANE slowly sits up. He stands and walks a step, unsteadily, toward the bookcase.)* I'm sorry.

ZANE: *(Shocked)* Shit!

ANDREA: I'm sorry, again. *(ZANE sits back on the couch, visibly shaken.)*

ZANE: Shit. *(ANDREA sits by his side.)*

ANDREA: I don't know what got into me. I'm so proud of you. Really, I'm just anxious. *(Pause)* Say something.

ZANE: Nice dress.

ANDREA: *(Playfully through her tears)* Please hold me. *(They embrace on the couch.)*

ZANE: Anything to eat?

ANDREA: Of course. *(She doesn't let go of him.)*

ZANE: I'm really starving.

ANDREA: *(Letting go)* I'll go fix something. But Zane, come eat in the dining room. Okay? Not in here. Let's eat together.

ZANE: Okay. Call me when it's ready. *(ANDREA gets up with a noticeably lighter physical presence and almost floats past the bookcase toward the door. He watches her go, and then she suddenly stops. ZANE tenses as he waits in the silence. ANDREA turns slowly and moves back toward the bookcase. He looks away.)*

ANDREA: Zane, where were you going?

ZANE: *(Without turning to look at her)* What?

ANDREA: Where were you going?

ZANE: When?

ANDREA: When you thought I'd left the room.

ZANE: I wasn't going anywhere, I was just standing.

ANDREA: You were heading over here. *(ZANE now turns and looks directly at her standing in front of the bookcase.)*

ZANE: Was I?

ANDREA: You bastard! *(She starts throwing books on the floor.)* Where is it? Where is it?

ZANE: *(Soothingly)* Andrea. Come on, what are you doing?

ANDREA: *(Still looking)* Where is it?

ZANE: *(Firmer)* Andrea! *(ANDREA turns around, holding a bottle of vodka.)*

ANDREA: I knew it! You lying bastard! *(He tries to pull it from her, and a tug of war follows.)*

ANDREA: You goddamn lying bastard.

ZANE: Give it to me. Let it go!

(The bottle drops and breaks. They both stare at it. Pause)

ANDREA: Well, you could quit now, you know.

ZANE: *(With humor)* It's all right. I've got another one under the couch.

ANDREA: This is not a damn joke—this is our life.

ZANE: I really don't want to have this conversation right now. *(He walks back to the couch.)* I'll clean this mess up later. You don't have to worry.

ANDREA: I'm not worried about the mess. *(He lays down and puts a paper over his face.)* That's what I do, I clean up the mess.

BLACKOUT

This monologue is drawn from the previous play.

Circles

Gina Demetruis

(ANDREA, a woman in her mid-30s, is desperately trying to get a response from her alcoholic husband ZANE, who has been trying to quit drinking.

He is lying on the couch with a crumpled New York Times *spread over his face and body. Only his feet, protruding at one end, let us know that a human is present. ANDREA looks at the figure under the papers then sits on the man. He groans loudly.)*

ANDREA

I'm sorry. I didn't know there was a life form under all this. *(Pause)* You are a life form, aren't you? I wouldn't want to pressure you with any high expectations. *(She picks up a piece of the newspaper.)* This newspaper's from last week. Look, I know "easy does it" is your new motto, but are you supposed to take it so literally? I mean, shouldn't you at least change your paper? *(There is no response.)* Hey! *(She slaps the newspaper.)* I know you're trying to sleep, and I admire your tenacity, 'cause you've been trying for the past forty-eight hours. Not everyone could stick with it like that. *(There is no response. She gets up.)* I don't want to wrinkle my new dress. *(Silence)* I went shopping earlier, to celebrate. It's your thirty-first day without a drink, so I bought a new dress. Look. *(She does a slow turn, but ZANE remains completely motionless under the paper.)* The man at the store said it showed off my best assets. I was just happy to hear I still have assets. I mean, I'm only thirty-five but sometimes I feel a lot older. Now that you're getting sober, that'll help. It's gonna rejuvenate both of us. *(She pauses and stares at the couch.)* Do you think it's too short? The dress? *(ZANE raises the newspaper slightly and peers out at her.)* Well, it shows off my legs. They're still pretty shapely, don't you think? *(Pause)* You should have seen the guys down the street. I wore the dress home from the store, and when I passed those old guys on the corner, the ones who play dominoes, their eyes got so big I thought they'd pop right out of their heads. Their whole board flipped over. *(Pause. She deflates.)* Store clerks, old men, and a husband who's buried under last week's newspaper. *(She sits down with her back against the couch.)* Who am I? *(Without looking behind her, she holds out her hand.)* Could you hold my hand? Honey? Honey! Honey, could you just hold my goddamn hand for a minute. *(Pause)* I'm trying to stay alive! For the past seven years, I've been caught up by this tornado that pulls everything up into a frenzy. For seven years I followed your tornado, and I've tried to clean up the mess left behind. And now you're getting sober and you come and go from those AA meetings like a phantom, and then you close yourself up in this room. You made me a full partner to your drinking, and now you're getting sober and you shut me out! Where's my payoff? What's in it for me? Say something. *(Silence)* Say something!

Linda Faigao-Hall

It is difficult to summarize my connection to Linda; I began to commission and produce her work over a decade ago. We were both members of the Women's Project, where I found her voice both moving and informative. I shared her frustration that her work was not getting attention beyond the Asian-American theatre community, which was one of the missions of my company. Linda created works for me several times, went on to study the FYV approach in a master class; participated as an actor in several of our rehearsed readings in the educational program; and then served as assistant director of the company from 2005 to 2009. Although we are from very different cultures, we share a passion for authentic, well-built plays, hold master's degrees in English literature, and have a history of early father loss. With Linda I have learned, again, the universality of human suffering and human aspirations. Over the past decade, I have served as midwife to many of her stories, and she, in turn, has been one of the greatest proponents of disseminating the dramaturgical process that has been my signature approach. What follows are excerpts from several of the colorful and touching plays that we premiered together. The developmental process was never easy—finding a common language rarely is—but the results were always fruitful. Linda remembers that, "The cluster entitled Four Views With a Room, *was my first encounter with this method. I felt as if I had been asked to complete a wish list and everything was granted—it was playwright heaven! I wanted: time to write the play, a dramaturg with highly developed coaching skills and a specific method, actors to read the play at different stages of its development, and a* full production. *Who does this? It was the most generous, the most supportive, environment I had ever found myself in. This was a workshop set up to produce plays, not just write them, and it was driven by a specific process that helped a playwright find not just her voice but also her character's voices. The use of the triggering photograph focused one's creative juices; it narrowed down one's options, but it was open enough that all four playwrights ended up with four very different views. I was hooked. I was invited to participate in two more workshops. I need to point out that all of the plays I developed in the FYV workshops have found themselves in other subsequent equity productions in New York, in venues like the Harold Clurman and the Samuel*

Beckett in *Theater Row* and at the *Ensemble Studio Theater*, among others. *The FYV method drives my playwriting, my teaching, and the way I live my life. It's total. In my teaching, it helps me empathize with my student's fears of speaking up in class; in my writing, it helps me discover what my characters want and how they fight for what they want, and in my life, I attempt to be heard without being belligerent. The most difficult is applying it to my life and my relationships—which means everyday is a 'process'. I can never thank Gail enough."* Linda assisted me in the editing of this anthology, as well as in all of the other recent work of the company. She also teaches writing at Mercy College, and she continues writing plays.

This scene is from a play that was commissioned for the cluster of plays entitled Nothing You Can Say, *all of which explored breakdowns in communication (p. 32).*

Duet
Linda Faigao-Hall

Characters: PETER   Male, Asian, 30s
              JEN LI   Female, Asian, 30s

AT RISE: PETER and JEN LI have both returned to their childhood home, where their father is gravely ill. When they were young, although they were both prodigies, their father chose to train only PETER. They have been estranged for a long time, and there is tension in the air. PETER enters and clears his throat. JEN LI turns around with a start.

PETER: I'm sorry. I didn't wish to startle you. *(Awkward pause)* Where's Dad?
JEN LI: He's asleep.
PETER: How is he?
JEN LI: Dr. Sam said he'll make it.
PETER: *(Silence)* And how are you, Jen Li?
JEN LI: Fine.
PETER: *(A long silence)* Other than Dad's stroke, I guess you could say I'm fine, too! *(Another long pause)* And Tommy?

JEN LI: He's coming tomorrow. With his dad.

PETER: Great! I brought him a lot of souvenirs that I picked up on my tour. *(Silence)* And his music? The last time he was here, he did a wonderful Chopin mazurka for me.

JEN LI: He's discovered jazz; he's playing the sax.

PETER: The sax! Then I'll take him to meet Wynton.

JEN LI: I'm sure he'd be thrilled. *(Another long pause)* Your European tour went well?

PETER: They told me the critics would be tough, but it didn't feel like it to me. There was a lot of good press.

JEN LI: Except for Vienna.

PETER: *(Pause)* How did you know that?

JEN LI: I read it in *People.*

PETER: Funny thing is, I felt I'd never played better. I decided to do Scriabin there. The etudes; C-sharp minor and D. Both of them! It was reckless. *(Clearly enjoying himself)* Luciano—I mean Pavarotti—was there. He came backstage to congratulate me and took me to dinner with his family. *(He catches himself.)* It was tiring, though. I mean—I don't want to be tedious. Traveling. It's not as much fun as it looks. *(Silence)* Ma tells me you're setting up a children's orchestra at St. Ides.

JEN LI: I didn't know I'd love teaching so much. And how talented some of these kids are, considering hip-hop and rap, Smashing Pumpkins.

PETER: I'm sorry?

JEN LI: It's a rock group.

PETER: Oh.

JEN LI: It always surprises me that there are still children who want to play Bach.

PETER: Why would anyone not want to play Bach?

JEN LI: I forgot. You've got your own world, as I have mine. I hope you don't mind, Peter; I'm really very tired. It's been a long day. *(JEN LI turns to go.)*

PETER: Do you know how long I've imagined this conversation?

JEN LI: And this is how you planned to start it?

PETER: Please. I'm sorry. I'm messing it up. *(Pause)* When you went to live with Ma's relatives, I thought all you needed was time. I didn't know you'd never speak to me again. You never gave me a chance.

JEN LI: To say what? How sorry you were?

PETER: I was.

JEN LI: How you would feel sorry for me for the rest of our lives?

PETER: In the beginning I did, yes; but that didn't last, Jen Li.

JEN LI: Well, I hated you for a long time. I couldn't touch my violin for a year. Couldn't hear a single phrase of music without bursting into tears. Couldn't pass by Carnegie Hall, or read the *New York Times,* without praying I wouldn't see your picture … or any of your concerts being reviewed. I lived with envy. It sat in my heart, taking up space.

PETER: I'm sorry, Jen—

JEN LI: Let me finish. I didn't start to play again; I just came crawling back to Dad. I asked for his forgiveness. I went back to school. To my music. It was the only thing I knew how to do. It was in my blood. In my bones. It's who I am. I had no choice.

PETER: When I heard you'd married William, I was so happy for you.

JEN LI: And after that, Thomas. Tommy came. That's when I decided I was going to teach. I realized that I would never be the artist I'd dreamed of becoming, but I accepted it without feeling I failed; I'd always done my best.

PETER: I hoped that you would put it all behind you. *(Steps toward her)* But you continued to shut me out of your life. Why?

JEN LI: You betrayed me, Peter. You betrayed my trust! So what if I forgave you; I could never trust you again.

PETER: Tell me how I can make it up to you!

JEN LI: How can you make up for something that happened fifteen years ago?

PETER: I can't. I can only deal with what's here now. You're a wonderful wife. A devoted mother. Someone with the gift of music, who's made it a passion to find others who have it. That's not a job, Jen Li—that's a vocation. Was this really the future you were dreading?

JEN LI: What I've made of my life is to my credit; it's got nothing to do with you.

PETER: So what does that mean, that we'll always have this between us?

JEN LI: All these years, why do you care?

PETER: Tommy. He's eight and getting older. How do you explain us to him?

JEN LI: I don't.

PETER: When Ma called me about Dad's stroke, I didn't know what to think. It scared me. We're all we have, Jen Li. *(Pause)* You're all I have.

JEN LI: You haven't married, Peter.

PETER: And I'm beginning to think I shouldn't! No woman would have me. I mean I've tried, but it doesn't work. I travel so much, I have no time. I'm too obsessed with what I do.

JEN LI: Are you saying you're not happy?

PETER: It's lonely. *(Silence)* Sure, I have friends, but I don't really know if it's me they love or my music. *(Pause)* But when I play, I don't know where I end and the music begins, so maybe it doesn't matter.

JEN LI: You haven't answered my question. Are you happy, Peter?

PETER: *(Pause)* Yes, I'm happy. In spite of it all, I can't think of my life being any other way.

JEN LI: Why couldn't you just lie a little! *(She turns around and walks away.)*

PETER: Do you know why Dad chose me?

JEN LI: *(She stops, her back to him.)* You were more talented? You had greater potential? You were the eldest? You're a man? *(Smirks)* The way your career has soared these past few years, you've surpassed all our expectations. Ma was right; we share in your glory. But that's all we share. *(Starts to leave again)*

PETER: Because I was weak.

JEN LI: *(She turns around to look at him.)* What?

PETER: Dad said I could never survive the disappointment, but you were strong enough to go on with your life and make the best of it.

JEN LI: He said this?

PETER: When he told me I was the one he'd chosen, I was delirious with joy. I knew right away I would break our promise to insist that he support both of us or neither. That's how I knew how right he was. You would've stood by it.

JEN LI: *(Long pause)* Why didn't he tell me that?

PETER: Would you have understood it then?

JEN LI: I don't know if I understand it now.

PETER: Take a good look at what you've got. Realize that all of it, even my betrayal, is a part of you. Change one tiny thing, and you wouldn't be who you are right now. *(JEN LI is lost in her thoughts.)* Let it be, Jen Li. Embrace it. *You* have it all.

BLACKOUT

This next scene is from a play that was commissioned for the cluster entitled, Four Views With a Room, *and written in response to the image on the cover of this book.*

The Interview
Linda Faigao-Hall

Characters:	PERLA	Filipina, 20s
	DI	Female, Caucasian American, 40s

AT RISE: PERLA enters DI's open apartment, in response to an advertisement for a roommate. DI is upside down in a yogic pose in a corner of the room, with her eyes closed; she is not moving.

PERLA: *(Softly)* Hello …? *(No response, louder)* Hello …?

DI: *(With a start)* I didn't hear the bell.

PERLA: The door was open.

DI: Oh. I guess I forgot to close it. I had open house today until three; you're my four o'clock, aren't you? *(DI does not uncoil herself, she remains in yogic position. PERLA peers at her, trying to find her face.)*

PERLA: No. *(Glancing at her watch)* It's six-eighteen.

DI: I meant that you're late.

PERLA: I'm sorry. My uncle and I were in the Bronx; we got lost. *(Silence)* Is the share still available?

DI: Yes.

PERLA: Oh, good. How much is it?

DI: Name's Diane Anderson.

PERLA: *(Puts out her hand but she can't find DI's, so she drops it.)* Perla Amihan-Tudela.

DI: That's exquisite. *(Pause)* Does it mean anything?

PERLA: Pearl Harvest.

DI: Wow. And what's that from—South America?

PERLA: Philippines.

(Overlapping)

PERLA: We speak English! DI: You speak Spanish!

PERLA: The Philippines is one of the largest English-speaking nations in the world.

DI: *(She straightens herself out.)* Far out. I love Asian culture.

PERLA: Which one?

DI: *(Pause)* All of them, I guess. My daughter's been to India, Nepal, and Tibet. *(Laughs)* Her friends went to Europe; she went to Asia. The road less traveled. *(Pause)* So how's the government? You know, life after Marcos? And the shoe lady ... there was a special on her the other day, where they are now ... that kind of thing.

PERLA: I missed it. *(DI leads the way into the next space.)*

DI: We'd be sharing the living room and the kitchen ... *(She points offstage.)*

PERLA: How lovely!

DI: I have a small catering business, very specialized. Gourmet health food. Most of my clients are vegetarians.

PERLA: That's what I like about America! Half the world is starving to death, but here you choose not to eat meat.

DI: Half of the world is eating tofu. *(PERLA makes a face. DI catches it.)* It's nature's perfect food.

PERLA: That's good to know. *(Awkward pause)* So how much for the share?

DI: Four-fifty.

PERLA: Four-fifty?!

DI: I don't believe in taking advantage. It's bad karma.

PERLA: Four-fifty! I'll take it! So when can I move in?

DI: *(Throwing her a quizzical look)* Don't you want to see the bedroom?

PERLA: I'm a bit pressed for time. My uncle and I have an agreement: if I can find a safe, affordable apartment before he leaves, I can stay. If not, then I must go back home with him to the Philippines.

DI: Doesn't he know that finding a place to live is serious business? Sharing one is even more so. *(She leads the way into the next room.)* This used to be my daughter Jeanie's room. Please excuse the mess. I've been sorting since last week. It's the first time I'm throwing some of her things out. *(Pause)* So why don't you sit down and relax, Pearl. Take your time. I like to take things very slowly, myself.

PERLA: *(Picking up a batch of postcards)* Oh! May I?

DI: Jeanie sends them to me.

PERLA: *(Pouring over the cards, studying them intently)* I have a collection of American postcards; my uncle used to send them to me when I was a little girl. For a long time I thought he traveled around the world because all the pictures were so different from each other. It was only when I grew up, I realized all these places were in the same big country.

DI: That's what we've got: space. A lot of it. *(Pause)* Too much of a good thing, I think.

PERLA: How is that?

DI: Think of the country as a whole—its physical landscape—the sheer size of it. You have a problem, you don't have to deal with it; you can just get up and go. I hate it!

PERLA: I love it!

DI: *(Awkward pause)* So what are you into, Pearl Harvest? May I just call you Pearl? You can call me Di.

PERLA: Pearl is fine. I'm into … my second semester at NYU.

DI: Okay! *(Pause)* Any other interests?

PERLA: No.

DI: I find that very hard to believe!

PERLA: *(Defensively)* I used to be political.

DI: Okay. That's good. Political is good. What kind of politics are you into?

PERLA: Used to be. Not anymore. It's not even worth discussing. *(Picking up a book)* You have a catalogue on the *whole earth*?

DI: It does sound pretentious, doesn't it. *(She picks it up and puts it on one of the piles.)* It's old, I'm throwing it out.

PERLA: *(Picking up another book)* The Tao Teh Ching. *(She pronounces the Ts.)*

DI: The *D*ao *D*eh Ching. *(Pronouncing it correctly)* I love this book. Do you know it well? *(Taking the book from PERLA and putting it in a different pile. DI will sporadically sort things out during the next few minutes.)* This stays.

PERLA: I know *of* it. Never really read it.

DI: That's ... *(thinks 'bad' but says:)* surprising.

PERLA: The Philippines is ninety-eight percent Catholic. We read the Bible. We're not very exotic. *(Examining a collage on the wall)* Now this I find intriguing. Did you do it?

DI: Yes. Whoever moves in will have to live with it.

PERLA: I can live with it. *(Something in the collage catches her eye.)* Look at that ... Molotov cocktails! Are those Molotov cocktails?

DI: *(Taken aback)* What? Where? *(Looking at the same spot)* Oh. No. They're sketches of *buttons*. *(No response)* Peyote? *(PERLA shakes her head.)* I guess you could say they're just as lethal.

PERLA: How?

DI: It sets one off the beaten track. One day your daughter is worrying about prom night, the next she's reading *Doors of Perception. (Pause)* Molotov cocktails ... exactly what kind of politics were you involved in, Pearl?

PERLA: Does it have a title?

DI: I call it "Work in Progress." What kind of politics was it, Pearl?

PERLA: It's a collage, isn't it.

DI: A friend of mine once sublet her apartment to somebody who was secretly buying ammunition for the IRA.

PERLA: *(Interested)* Did he accomplish his mission?

DI: *(Peering at PERLA)* Fortunately, my friend found out in time. Why, do you support the IRA?

PERLA: Where's Jeanie now?

DI: This space is very, very special to me; that's why I need to be extremely cautious. It can't handle negative energy.

PERLA: *(Looking around)* So this is Jeanie's room—

DI: She moved out; it's mine to do with as I wish. *(Determined)* How political were you, exactly?

PERLA: She hardly took anything with her. *(Tries to exit)*

DI: *(Blocking PERLA's way)* I've never seen a Molotov cocktail, have you?

PERLA: They're crude, but effective. *(DI doesn't budge.)* I used to cover anti-Marcos groups. My family published a local newspaper back home, and when my parents gave it up, I decided to run it myself. Two months ago, I closed it down. I had no choice, it could no longer support itself. But there was a time when it was the best newspaper in my province. And during the Marcos regime, it was the most influential underground newspaper in the country. People were thrown into prison just for reading it.

DI: You ran a paper? You look so young—hardly a day over eighteen!

PERLA: I'm way older than that, but thank you. It was my family's calling.

DI: And you said you had no interests!

PERLA: I thought you meant basket-weaving, stamp collecting ... you know, hobbies.

DI: So your family was involved with what was going on there?

PERLA: We were right in the center of it. The Tudelas were always in the center of things. One of our ancestors successfully led a rebellion against a Spanish friar in 1860! A grand-uncle was imprisoned by the Japanese during World War II for treason!

DI: Please don't get me wrong, I'm not necessarily against all political movements—

PERLA: So can I move in tomorrow?

DI: Did I mention in the ad that I need a character reference?

PERLA: No, you didn't.

DI: Well, I do.

BLACKOUT

> The following monologue is from the previous play, which was commissioned for the cluster of plays entitled Four Views With a Room.

The Interview
Linda Faigao-Hall

(A young Filipino woman tries to explain her shady past in order to convince a prospective American landlord that it is all behind her now. She is unaware of the radical effect of her story.)

PERLA

A little over ten years ago, some pro-Marcos people had my parents thrown in jail. They were tortured until they were dead. My two older sisters disappeared a few weeks later, but they never touched me; I was only thirteen. I guess they thought I was too young to cause them any trouble. They were wrong. *(Pause)* The only relative I had left was my uncle; he was in the States, unable to help. It was a long time before I could weep over any of this. I didn't weep when they dragged my parents from their bed in the middle of the night, or when my sisters were abducted. *(Pause)* I just fled to the mountains. I found my place there; I became a Sparrow, the armed guard of the underground. We were trained to appear suddenly—without warning—and to leave as quickly as we came. Just like sparrows. The Marcos dictatorship called us *terrorists;* but to many people, we were heroes. *(Pause)* When I shot one of the men who threw my parents in jail, I thought I would feel guilty, remorseful. I thought that finally—finally—I could weep ... but not even then. *(Beseechingly)* I killed only him. I asked to do it; I trained for a year. I thought of nothing else. *(Laughs bitterly)* Love of country is an illusion; it's revenge that's real! Maybe that's why after I shot him, I quit. I went back home. By that time, Marcos was gone, and Aquino had taken over. My uncle sent me money, and with it, I resumed publishing my parent's paper. For ten years, I ran it. Then, a few month's ago, my sisters' graves were discovered. They asked me to identify what was left; only then did I weep. The time to move on had come at last. *(Silence)* What more can I say? I shot him. It's over and done with; and the past, it's all behind me. The paper, my parents, my sisters, the cause; it's history. And whatever else I did it for—I gave it all up.

This scene (p. 33) is from a play that was commissioned for a cluster entitled The St. Nicola Cycle and was suggested by the photograph on p. 38, which Linda saw as a beam of light on an apartment building.

Pusong Babae
(The Female Heart)
Linda Faigao-Hall

Characters: ROGER   Male, Caucasian American, 40s
               ADELFA   Filipina, 20s

AT RISE: A Filipina mail-order bride tries to convince her abusive American husband to return to Alcoholics Anonymous.

ROGER: I don't deserve you. There's no hope for me.

ADELFA: You only do it when you've had a few drinks.

ROGER: I know. I know.

ADELFA: So don't drink. *(Pause)* I'll make sure everything's picked up in the house.

ROGER: That's no way to live, making sure nothing sets me off. *(Shakes his head)* Everything sets me off these days, a speck of dust on the dining room table.

ADELFA: A grain of rice.

ROGER: Please.

ADELFA: I just need to get my details right: don't look through other people's garbage, buy fresh orange juice instead of concentrate, lots of pulp, not just some pulp—but if it's pink grapefruit, *no* pulp—and no meat. No animal products!

ROGER: Meat isn't good for you.

ADELFA: I still don't understand what that means.

ROGER: It's also one way of saving the planet. Don't you want to save the planet?

ADELFA: Who? Me? *(Silence)* What happened to the AA, Roger?

ROGER: It's been so hectic; I can't find listings as fast as I can sell. I may need another broker; the one I've got can't keep up!

ADELFA: If you didn't drink, we wouldn't have any problems ... we'd have a good life. *(Silence)* Don't you want a good life?

ROGER: There's always something.

ADELFA: No, there isn't always something.

ROGER: That's because you expect so little.

ADELFA: This is little to you? You have a beautiful house. Your business is booming. I send money home every month. My own family is able to move to a bigger apartment. My brother is recuperating. Life is good. Why do you need to drink at all?

ROGER: I've had a hard life, Adelfa.

ADELFA: But you don't have a hard life now.

ROGER: You don't understand. To you, life is simple. Food, clothing, and shelter. That's it.

ADELFA: No. You need health, too. Food, clothing, and shelter don't mean anything if you're sick. And family. Family is essential.

ROGER: I told you I'm not ready to have a family.

ADELFA: I'm talking about mine.

ROGER: Thank God, they're doing well. *(Pause)* They should be, with all the money I send them.

ADELFA: I said I could work for it. I'm not afraid of real work. Make me your secretary. I'll go to computer class, learn word processing.

ROGER: No way. My friend Tony got himself a foreign wife from Romania. Tony sent her to Microsoft Excel, and, next thing you know, she ran off with a classmate from the Ukraine. He says next time he has a new wife, he's gonna keep her home with her passport under lock and key.

ADELFA: You can trust me.

ROGER: It's not about you, Adelfa. It's the nature of money. And women. Money and women. Once a woman gets hold of money, that's it. Next thing you know, they're out the door. That's what happened with all my other wives.

ADELFA: Other wives? *(A long pause)* How many, Roger?

ROGER: Two.

ADELFA: Two? Two. Like me?

ROGER: No way. Nothing like you. You're one in a million.

ADELFA: Why didn't you tell me?

ROGER: I was afraid you'd lose interest. American women, they're very high-maintenance. They want everything. They want it all. And when they do get it all, it's still not enough. Babbs, my second ex-wife, when she asked for money it was always for something—a car—the latest model Miata. When you ask, it's so your brother can live another day. That's why I looked for someone like you. Someone who'd been poor. Who'd be grateful. Who'd never take anything for granted. I knew damn well there wasn't a woman in this country who'd fit the bill. That's when the mail-order bride thing came to me. There's something to be said for poverty.

ADELFA: There's *nothing* to be said for poverty.

ROGER: All right. Maybe you know better. *(He kisses her.)* Now that you know about the others, can you still love me? That's all I want to know.

ADELFA: I will never leave you, Roger. What you've done for Anghel, I could never pay you back.

ROGER: That's what I told my therapist, I said: "I think she's really grateful. It's happening. This one good thing," which is you, "is happening to me. I'm making progress."

ADELFA: Is that what he said?

ROGER: No. That's what I said. *(Silence)* You know what they're like. They just sit there and listen. And if you ask them a question, they turn around and ask you the same thing.

ADELFA: Maybe he's not very good. Maybe you should find someone else.

ROGER: I pay him a hundred bucks an hour, he'd better be good.

ADELFA: *(Pause)* One hundred dollars an hour? Four hundred dollars a month!

ROGER: *(Laughing)* That's what I love about you. Everything amazes you. Scented toilet paper. Ricki Lake! *(Nods)* That's right. I'm paying someone four hundred dollars a month just to listen to me yap.

ADELFA: That could feed a barrio for a month. *(ROGER laughs, ADELFA doesn't.)* So besides American women, what else are you angry about, Roger?

ROGER: *(Pause)* My parents. Splitting up when I was ten. This moment, as we're talking, they're still arguing over the barbeque grill. My custody was the only thing that got resolved, and that was because I turned eighteen. *(Silence)* What about *your* father, Adelfa? There's just the three of you?

ADELFA: He left.

ROGER: How old were you?

ADELFA: Four.

ROGER: So we both know what it means to be abandoned. A child's worst nightmare.

ADELFA: I don't remember anything about him. He's a faded photograph my mother pins inside her dress next to her heart.

ROGER: Make no bones about it, your soul remembers.

ADELFA: But *I* don't, so leave it alone then.

ROGER: You can't. That's not how it works.

ADELFA: Go back to AA. I'll go with you. Or to Alanon. I know all about it; I went to the library.

ROGER: *(Stiffening)* You did? When?

ADELFA: *(Quickly)* The other day. *(Awkward)* I was thinking about you.

ROGER: *(Pause)* You're the best thing that's ever happened to me.

ADELFA: We deserve each other.

ROGER: Do you mean that? Tell me what I can do for you, to make it up.

ADELFA: I don't want anything—don't buy me anything.

ROGER: I never in my life heard a woman say "don't buy me anything."

ADELFA: You know what I want? When you're like this, when you listen, when I can talk to you—that's what I want. Then I feel hopeful. Hope is a wonderful thing, Inay says. You can see the stars.

BLACKOUT

This monologue is drawn from the previous play.

Pusong Babae
(The Female Heart)
Linda Faigao-Hall

(ROGER, 35, struggles with an anger problem and tries to explain himself to ADELFA, the Filipino mail order bride he's been abusing.)

ROGER

Do you know the sound of despair? *(Silence)* The sound of breaking glass. *(Pause)* I grew up wearing shoes in the house. Otherwise I'd step on shards of glass and china my father threw in his rages. No matter how hard Mom tried to clean up, she could never find them all. Haven't you noticed the kitchen? *(No response)* There's nothing in there you can break. Thank God for acrylic! *(ADELFA takes his hand.)* You and I are more alike than you think. That's why I need you to be patient with me. What I do to you, this is not who I am. *(Silence)* I wish I'd met you sooner. Or I had different parents. Or I was someone else. I'm so fucking aware of what's wrong with me. I can take responsibility for all the choices I've made and do all those enlightened things, but it doesn't stop me from hurting you. I can keep going to therapy and talk until I am blue in the face, but it's still like turning over mud; the same garbage over and over again. *(She doesn't follow.)* I have so much love in my heart for you. I can feel it—this sweet solid thing that sits in my heart, waiting to be let out.

Tova Friedman

Tova took only one FYV Workshop, in her last year of high school, a time when she was going through a good deal of personal flux. She wasn't able to complete her training, but she did complete this powerful play before departing. The two courageous teenage actors who performed it on stage in the spring of 2000 were greeted by rapt silence and then thunderous applause from their appreciative high school-aged audience (p. 31). I decided to include it in this collection because, although initially buried under layers of sarcasm and jargon, Tova ultimately painted an incredibly short but affecting portrait of adolescent vulnerability. "This was a very private piece, but I encourage myself to try everything. Working with a live audience was amazing, and an experience everyone should get. Everyone who feels shy should open up to their fears and perform." At the time of this writing, Tova was a psychology major at the City College of New York, with a minor in arts in education, and engaged to be married.

This, Tova's first play, was written for the cluster of plays entitled Into the Light, *all of which were set in a white room.*

Basement
Tova Friedman

Characters: ZIP   Female, 16
                  ROSE   Female, 16, her friend

AT RISE: ZIP files her nails while ROSE looks through a book. They are in the basement of ZIP's home, spending the weekend together.

ZIP: So, what are you thinking?
ROSE: I'm thinking: how did you ever find this book?
ZIP: *(Smiles)* Oh, it was easy.
ROSE: Who wrote it anyway? *(Pause)* You?
ZIP: Come on, we both know my work could never be that good!
    (Laughs)

ROSE: No joke; how do they come up with these books? Like, *hello!* If I owned a bookstore, and I was ordering my inventory, and I saw *Fun Things to Do When You're Bored*, I wouldn't even pick it up. Then again, that's just me.

ZIP: I was just trying to be nice by finding something to do during our weekend. *(Pause)* Aren't you sick of just hanging out every weekend?

ROSE: Yeah! But I love your basement.

ZIP: You love my basement—or the fact that my mom filled the refrigerator with food for the whole weekend?

ROSE: You don't wanna know!

ZIP: Hey—

ROSE: Ah, shut up, you know I love ya!

ZIP: Of course you do; how could anyone *not* love me!

ROSE: Conceited much?

ZIP: I'm not conceited.

ROSE: Okay, you're right; you're just a freak.

ZIP: *(Pause)* You think I'm a freak?

ROSE: What are you talking about; you're the biggest freak I know!

ZIP: Hey ... shut-up ... or I'll tell!

ROSE: *(Pause)* You'll tell what?

ZIP: I'll tell your parents ... about that party!

ROSE: Okay, that's enough; we don't need to be talking about that.

ZIP: Oh, yes we do! Think back. Don't you remember ...?

ROSE: Shut up. *(Laughs nervously)* Freak-a-zoid!

ZIP: You made me write on your ass, in permanent marker, that you loved Danny? Then we went and played strip poker.

ROSE: Oh, yeah. That *was* a bit freaky! But while we're on the topic, let's talk just pure, plain, old-fashioned embarrassment—

ZIP: What are you ...?

ROSE: Don't you remember when we went to Jim's party and you, my sweet pea, did five naked jumping-jacks with Chuck watching?

ZIP: I felt really stupid after that.

ROSE: *(Softening)* I know. I'm just having a bit of fun. *(Pause)* Hey, I'm in the mood for a cigarette; how about you?

ZIP: Jerk, you know I don't smoke.

ROSE: I was being polite. *(Laughs)* Come with me over to the window.

ZIP: I wish you would stop smoking.

ROSE: I know, you remind me every time I look at you.

ZIP: I don't want to see you get sick, that's all.

ROSE: I thank you for that. It's just a bit aggravating sometimes. *(Pause)* But it is good to hear that you care. *(Long pause)* You trust me, right?

ZIP: What are you talking about?

ROSE: I've had something I've wanted to tell you for a while now, that's all.

ZIP: What is it?

ROSE: Well, I kind of ... umm ... it's a secret.

ZIP: What is?

ROSE: I'm sorry, I just can't tell you. Yet.

ZIP: Yet?

ROSE: Yeah, yet. I'm *gonna* tell you.

ZIP: When?

ROSE: When the time's right. *(Smiles)*

ZIP: And when's that?

ROSE: I don't know.

ZIP: What about ... now?

ROSE: *(Pause)* Okay, but it's going to be hard; so please be patient.

ZIP: Okay.

ROSE: Well ... I like someone.

ZIP: You do?

ROSE: Yeah.

ZIP: Who? *(Silence)* Do you still like Chuck? Because, you know, its okay; I would understand.

ROSE: No; it's someone who means a lot more to me than him.

ZIP: So who?

ROSE: It's ... umm ... well—kind of a girl.

ZIP: "Kind of a girl"?

ROSE: I really like this girl.

ZIP: A girl. *(Pause)* I didn't know you liked girls.

ROSE: I never have before, but I guess I do now.

ZIP: *(Sitting back)* Wow, that's—

ROSE: Please don't feel weird around me now.

ZIP: No, I don't. I just don't know what to think.

ROSE: I don't either. I—

ZIP: You what?

ROSE: I feel this connection to her that's different. *(Studies ZIP for her reaction)* I haven't known her for too long but, she's really pretty, sweet, fun, easy to talk to. I just feel this chemistry between us, you know?

ZIP: Yeah. That's nice. *(Pause)* So who is this great person?

ROSE: First you have to answer something; when I tell her my feelings, do you think she will like me back?

ZIP: Of course she will. She'll be pleased to know that a great person likes her! *(Pats her hand)* You have the kindest heart I know; you always want to make people feel better. And you always put others before yourself; you're the best person to have around in *any* situation.

ROSE: Thanks!

ZIP: Now, will you *please* tell me who it is?

ROSE: *(Said with pride)* You!

ZIP: *(Awkward pause)* What?

ROSE: You, Zip Johnson.

ZIP: What are you talking about?

ROSE: I'm talking about me. For a while now I've been dreaming about the time when I got the courage to tell you that I care for you. *(Pause)* And not like those *guys* you date, but for *real* reasons. I know there's more to you than what other people see. I see you, and I want to have the pleasure of waking up in the morning next to you. Just knowing you and having your karma around, makes me feel good inside.

ZIP: You don't know what you're talking about; you *can't* feel for me like that. *(Tries to rise, ROSE stops her.)*

ROSE: Yes, I can. *(Pause)* It took a lot of courage to say what I had to say, and now to hear *this?* That what I said was *wrong?* I don't know … it's just so messed up. *(Looks into her eyes)* I told you my inner feelings; I trusted you.

ZIP: I don't believe you. How can I believe you?

ROSE: How can you *not* believe me? *(Takes her hand)* It's so damn simple.

ZIP: *(Pulling away)* What are you trying to get at? Are you trying to get me to admit something that's not true?

ROSE: No. I don't want *anything* from you.

ZIP: *(Jumps up)* You're lying. *(ROSE looks away.)* Why are you doing this? What's wrong with you? How could you fuck with my head like that, for kicks?

ROSE: *What*? Who said I'm "fucking with you"? *(Rises, faces her)* Why don't you believe that what I say is the truth?

ZIP: Look me in the eyes and tell me—

ROSE: What?

ZIP: No, I changed my mind. I don't want you to; I don't want to hear it even if it *is* the truth. *(Starts to walk away, then ROSE's voice stops her.)*

ROSE: The only reason you don't want me to tell you face to face is because you're afraid. *(Goes to ZIP)* What happens if, when I look at you, you start to realize that I'm telling the truth, and that the truth is not only about me?

ZIP: What are you implying?

ROSE: *(Softly)* Are you scared because you feel the same way?

ZIP: Are you saying I'm a *lesbian*?

ROSE: Liking a girl does not mean you're a *lesbian*.

ZIP: *(Takes a step back)* Listen, Rose, just because you're a lesbian doesn't mean the whole world is. I'm not gonna say that I *am* one, even if it makes you feel better about yourself. *(ROSE suddenly grabs her and kisses ZIP passionately on the lips. ZIP pulls away in disgust—wiping her mouth on her sleeve.)* What did you do that for?

ROSE: I don't know. *(Pause)* Can we forget about this?

ZIP: I was hoping you'd say that.

ROSE: Yeah, and I just did.

BLACKOUT

Patrick Gerrity

Patrick studied with me for several years while I was in residence at the high school where he was in attendance. During that time he grew from a charming boy to a young man who could take his own comic gifts seriously. Like many adolescent boys I have trained, Patrick hid his insightful, sensitive nature behind a wall of jokes. His acting study helped to safely lift that mask, and Inventions *reflects the vulnerability he came to reveal. This was his first fully realized play, the last one he wrote before graduating. The play reflects both his keen sense of humor and the poignant awareness of human frailty that was beginning to emerge. "It was a great experience. I remember trying to figure out why two people would be in an all-white room [which was the trigger for this particular cluster of plays]. All I could think of was death, or a painting accident. I figured painting would be funnier. This was my first entrée into the theatre world, and it was performing in FYV that made me want to break into radio/television; it helped bring me to where I am today." At the time of the writing, Patrick was director of technical support for City Lights Media, a television/film production company. In his spare time, he was doing sound design for movies and television.*

This, Patrick's first fully realized play, was written as part of a cluster of plays entitled Into the Light; *each was set in an all-white room.*

Inventions
Patrick Gerrity

Characters: ROBERT Male, 24
             NANCY   Female, 25

AT RISE: ROBERT and NANCY have been living with each other for three years. They are standing in an all-white room following a freak painting accident. Next to ROBERT is a white bag. Next to NANCY there is a white chair with a white coat on top of it.

ROBERT: I'm so sorry; I didn't know *that* was going to happen.
NANCY: The hell you didn't.

ROBERT: I'm sorry. I thought if I used the Paint Hose, it would save time.

NANCY: You know; that's just like you, Rob. You're always trying to find a way out of things. You're so lazy.

ROBERT: I'm not lazy. You're always finding reasons to criticize me; why don't you just do it yourself! *(Starts to leave the room)*

NANCY: If that's what it takes to get some work done around here, then fine. *(NANCY takes a paint brush and starts completing the paint job. ROBERT turns back to watch her.)*

ROBERT: *(Long pause)* Look, Nancy, I'm sorry—

NANCY: Don't say you're sorry. You've been doing stupid things since I met you. *(Paints angrily)* Remember that time you made the Human Turn-Signal? It would tell the people behind you where you were going?

ROBERT: That was a great invention.

NANCY: Remember what happened? It short-circuited and almost burned my ass!

ROBERT: That was only once.

NANCY: It was *only once?* *(Silence)* That was just one of the stupid things you invented. And now the Paint Hose!

ROBERT: The Paint Hose was a wonderful idea.

NANCY: Real wonderful; now I feel like I'm living in a Gap commercial.

ROBERT: *(Starts imitating a GAP commercial)* "I just can't get enough, I just can't get enough. Every time ..."

NANCY: Stop that! This is *not* a time for joking!

ROBERT: Oh, come on; it's not *that* bad, Nancy. You always said I would be put in a white room someday!

NANCY: *(Agitated, throws down paint brush)* Can't you be serious for one moment? I am so tired of you always making fun of every situation.

ROBERT: I thought that's what attracted you to me in the first place.

NANCY: Well, Robert, maybe I made a mistake.

ROBERT: *(Pause)* What are you trying to say?

NANCY: I don't know.

ROBERT: This isn't just about the white room anymore, is it?

NANCY: Yes and no. I mean, it's about the white room and everything else.

ROBERT: You can't say that *all* of my inventions were bad.

NANCY: Yes, I can.

ROBERT: Okay, what about the Talking Phone Book for the Blind?

NANCY: There was no stop button on it; I had to hear it from A to Z every time I opened it.

ROBERT: All right; how about the VHS Tape Drive for the Computer?

NANCY: It made the computer twice its normal size; we couldn't put it anywhere.

ROBERT: The Y3K Compliant Computer?

NANCY: I rest my case.

ROBERT: Okay. I get it; I'm a *failure*. Is that what you want me to say?

NANCY: No, Robert, I didn't say you were a failure. *(Pause)* I just don't think this relationship is going the way I wanted it to.

ROBERT: The way *you* wanted it to! How about *me*, Nancy? I've had to put up with some crazy things that you've done too.

NANCY: Like what?

ROBERT: Remember the time you said you were going to pay for dinner? *(Short pause as NANCY shakes her head.)* After we finished eating, you realized that you had forgotten your wallet. I had to wait there, with all the waiters looking at me like I was tomorrow's special, while you ran home to get money!

NANCY: Now you're trying to blame everything on me? All right; if that's the way you want to act. *(Starts to walk to the door)* Excuse me.

ROBERT: Well then, go ahead and leave. *(NANCY hunts for the door, finds it, but the door won't open; she is trapped in the room.)*

NANCY: I can't believe this; you painted the door shut!

ROBERT: I could open it with the Open-Says-A-Me but, as you said, "it's stupid."

NANCY: *(Glares at him)* Just give me the goddamn door opener.

ROBERT: What's your hurry? *(Moves toward her)* We've been together for three years—all of a sudden you want to avoid me like the plague?

NANCY: *(Tries to open the door some more before giving up)* I just don't think we're compatible.

ROBERT: *(A pause while something dawns on him)* You've been having talks with your mother on the phone, haven't you? *(No response)* That's why you're always on the phone for so long.

NANCY: Well, I *have* been talking to my mother a lot. And she *has* been telling me that I should move on; that I'm not getting anywhere in this relationship.

ROBERT: And you believe her?

NANCY: Look around, Rob. We live in a one-room apartment on the Lower East Side. You can't hold down a job that pays more than minimum wage, and I'm getting stressed trying to make ends meet for both of us; trying to pay for your *inventions*. It's just not working.

ROBERT: So you're giving up, just like that?

NANCY: I've been trying to make this work for the last two years—

ROBERT: Two years! You've been feeling this way for two years, and *now* you tell me?

NANCY: You were always so busy with your inventions; I never had a *chance* to tell you.

ROBERT: I always had time for *you*.

NANCY: No, you didn't. *(Pause)* That's why I had to find someone who did.

ROBERT: What?

NANCY: Those long phone calls ... they weren't to my mother.

ROBERT: Then who?

NANCY: I've been seeing this guy—

ROBERT: I can't believe this! This is incredible! You've been seeing another guy?

NANCY: He gives me something you just can't provide.

ROBERT: What? What does this guy have that I don't? *(Short pause)* You know what? Don't even tell me! I don't want to know! You want to go with this guy, than *go!!!* (Grabs the tool from the bag next to him, walks over to door, puts the tool into the doorknob, and opens the door wildly) There ... go! *(NANCY exits quickly, and he yells after her)* WHEN THAT GUY *(imitating Nancy)* "DOESN'T HAVE ANY TIME FOR YOU" EITHER, YOU'LL REALIZE THAT I

WAS THE MAN FOR YOU; AND THEN YOU'LL BE BACK! *(ROBERT slams the door. About two seconds later a knock on the door is heard. ROBERT smiles, then goes and opens it. NANCY is standing there.)* Back already?

NANCY: I forgot my jacket.

BLACKOUT

Sarah Goldstein

Sarah studied with me throughout her years at a high school where we were in residence. She saw herself primarily as an aspiring actor when she began, and she was indeed much less self-conscious about taking on the life of another character than were most of her peers. In fact, she often got so caught up in the feelings she was portraying that she forgot anyone else was there! As she worked to develop the craft of "inter-acting," Sarah's work became rich beyond her years, and this carried over to her writing as well. Her first few attempts at a play were highly dramatic but too unfocused to produce. Looking back, it is hard to imagine that those nascent attempts came from the same young woman who authored this perfect little jewel of a play, whose brevity, focus, attention to character detail, and hyperawareness of psychological nuance brings to mind such writers as Harold Pinter, Raymond Carver, and JD Salinger. Note how little happens and yet how much is conveyed by the way the characters relate. Sarah wrote this in a summer master class at the end of her junior year in high school. "I remember feeling very encouraged and respected even though I was younger than almost all of the other participants. I also remember the strange sense of revenge in writing about a broken relationship, while being in one myself!" At the time of this writing Sarah was working as a reporter at Business Magazine, Inc., *and hoped someday to be an editor. Although no longer acting, she still likes being in the spotlight!*

The trigger for Sarah's play was a photograph of a wrapped box, and Sarah chose to explore hidden feelings rather than a hidden object.

Swimming at Coney
Sarah Goldstein

Characters: NATHAN   Male, 18 *(he looks older)*
HANNAH   Female, 18

AT RISE: NATHAN and HANNAH sit on a crowded city beach; they are no more than three feet from the water. NATHAN is shirtless and a little too pale for the sun; he is in excellent shape and sits relaxed, holding

104

a cigarette in his hand, from which he drags no more than twice. His focus is on the pier in the distance, behind HANNAH. HANNAH is thin and healthy-looking; she appears to have had more exposure to the sun. She is wearing an opened button-down shirt, exposing a light-colored bikini; she is fidgety and throughout the scene will dig and re-dig her feet into the sand.

NATHAN: *(HANNAH slaps NATHAN hard on his back.)* What the fuck was that?!

HANNAH: You're like those water buffalo.

NATHAN: Like what?

HANNAH: Those water buffalo. You know—they let flies rest on them. *(Silence)* I had to flick a fly off you.

NATHAN: Huh? A fly?

HANNAH: Uh huh. You just let it sit on you.

NATHAN: Nah.

HANNAH: There was a fuckin' fly on you. I had to flick it off. You just let it sit there.

NATHAN: No I didn't.

HANNAH: Yes you did.

NATHAN: I didn't just let it sit there if I let you flick it off. *(Pause. HANNAH looks at NATHAN and smiles. NATHAN flicks his cigarette.)*

HANNAH: Do you want to swim?

NATHAN: Huh?

HANNAH: Do you want to go swimming? *(HANNAH rises.)*

NATHAN: Where you goin'?

HANNAH: *(She tests the water.)* For a swim. Come on.

NATHAN: Hold on a minute. Sit down.

HANNAH: *(She obliges.)* Come on … all you're doing is sitting here. Let's go.

NATHAN: Will you wait a second? Wait till we finish the conversation.

HANNAH: What conversation.

NATHAN: The one we're having.

HANNAH: We're done with the conversation.

NATHAN: Well, I'm not done with my cigarette. *(Pause. NATHAN flicks cigarette. HANNAH rises again.)* Will you sit down? *(NATHAN pulls at her wrist gently and HANNAH sits. NATHAN thumbs HANNAH'S stomach absently.)* Brown as a bean.

HANNAH: Stop.

NATHAN: What?

HANNAH: Stop touching me.

NATHAN: Huh? I can't touch you now?

HANNAH: I'm going for a swim.

NATHAN: Why?

HANNAH: Why? *(Silence)* The water is beautiful. I want to swim. You're just sitting. And I wish you wouldn't smoke at the beach. It's … I don't know; it's unclean. *(NATHAN takes a drag of his cigarette.)* It looks dirty.

NATHAN: What?

HANNAH: The smoking. But you do look so … oh, I don't know. I guess you look so goddamn cool when you smoke. You're beautiful. *(Pause)* Remember the last time we came here, you told those fishermen that we had just gotten married and we were on our honeymoon? Then they gave us all the fish they had caught that day as a wedding gift. Fuckin' A! As if we would eat fish off Coney Island. *(Laughs)* Do you remember that?

NATHAN: Sure.

HANNAH: *(She takes off her shirt and throws it on top of a pile of belongings above where they are sitting. She stares at the pile of clothes.)* Why don't we have fun anymore?

NATHAN: I have fun.

HANNAH: We don't have fun.

NATHAN: Speak for yourself. I have fun.

HANNAH: Then I wish you would share some of your joy. *(Long pause)* It's hot. I'm going swimming. *(Rises)*

NATHAN: *(Stops her)* Will you wait a second?

HANNAH: No. I want to swim.

NATHAN: Think you'll have enough fun if you go swimming?

HANNAH: I don't think—I didn't say … *(flustered)* No! Why am I still here talking to you? I'm going swimming.

NATHAN: The water looks pretty gross. It's polluted.

HANNAH: It looks all right to me.

NATHAN: If you won't eat the fish out of it, how are you going to

106

submerge your body in it? *(Pause)* Will you stop doing that with your feet, shit's making me nervous. *(Pause)* You have pudgy feet, you know that?

HANNAH: I do? *(Studies them)* I like my feet.

NATHAN: Yeah, they're okay feet, but they're pudgy. Kind of like little-kid feet. *(Pause)* Damn it's hot.

HANNAH: I think my feet are fine.

NATHAN: You're still on that? Shit, it is hot.

HANNAH: What do you mean I'm still on that? You want me to point out all your imperfections? Like you're some real gift.

NATHAN: What are you talking about? Relax. Jeez.

HANNAH: *(HANNAH studies her feet.)* I'm fucking relaxed, all right? I just don't see how you come off criticizing me when you're certainly not perfect.

NATHAN: I thought I was "beautiful."

HANNAH: Wow, you were listening.

NATHAN: I'm sweating like crazy. *(Pause)* Go get us some ice cream, woman.

HANNAH: Did you just …?

NATHAN: Kidding! You know I'm kidding. *(Pause)* But really though—it's hot, huh?

HANNAH: You want ice cream?

NATHAN: Sure. I mean, if *you* do.

HANNAH: Yeah, that would be nice. It would be nice. What do you want?

NATHAN: Chocolate-vanilla swirl, chocolate sprinkles. Hmmm … *(He fishes in back pocket.)* I only have a ten.

HANNAH: I have singles in my wallet. I got it.

NATHAN: It's a long trip to the boardwalk; put on your shoes so your feet don't burn.

HANNAH: Right. Always concerned for my well-being. *(She rises and exits. NATHAN watches her as she walks off. NATHAN takes a long drag, throws his cigarette up the beach. Slowly he stands and walks into the water up to his waist; he begins to swim.)*

BLACKOUT

Sharifa Hayle

Sharifa began her FYV training while on a scholarship at a private high school in the Bronx. Unlike many of the other students, Sharifa was already highly outgoing and possessed a beautiful God-given singing voice. During the terms that we worked together, I began to see that—like many extraverts—Sharifa could also be very private about her feelings and was more comfortable "posing" than truly revealing. Always a sweet and giggly presence, as she explored the darker emotions exemplified in this monologue (sadness, anger, aggression)—and began to be more comfortable just listening when someone else was in the spotlight— Sharifa's raw talent grew into an impressive craft. And these abilities carried over into her writing as well. As with many other girls, especially pretty and talented girls, I constantly battled Sharifa's resistance to taking herself seriously, but when she did, she had some powerful things to say. "Fourteen years ago, I was struggling with marginalization and sadness. My family had hard times, our house burned down, and no one had yet asked this 'Black girl' to the prom (someone eventually did). I had no outlet until I got to FYV." I was delighted to learn that, after college, Sharifa decided to undertake theological training in order to become a minister. I could imagine no greater nexus at which her various voices might meet, and no greater outlet for her intelligence and humanity. "There's no way I could write or teach/preach effectively without this background. Not only for the confidence and grounding it gave me, but also because I was encouraged to explore motivations and felt needs beyond the spoken word, in order to connect and communicate honestly." Sharifa married and continues to teach and preach.

This monologue is from a play in the If I Knew *cluster, which featured the fantasies of a group of students at their commencement from high school.*

Shakira
Sharifa Hayle

(SHAKIRA, an African-American teenager, and her friend ROXANNE—a serious student—have gotten together after school. ROXANNE has finished

her homework and is trying to read a book. SHAKIRA is restless and hasn't done any work yet. After ROXANNE chastises her, she explains why it simply isn't worth the effort.)

SHAKIRA

I don't have to do every single assignment! It's not like the teachers are checking my work anyway; they're too busy checking us for guns. *(ROXANNE stares at her.)* I'm passing—okay? *(ROXANNE is unconvinced.)* I'll be graduating with you. *(No response)* It's *my* problem, so mind your business, Roxanne. *(A long uncomfortable silence; ROXANNE goes back to her book.)* I didn't mean that the way it sounded. *(Pause)* I came home from school the other day and saw my father flipping through the classified ads again. Did you know that he graduated with honors from Georgetown? *(Silence)* When he was young he once had an interview with this fancy law firm. They said, "I'm sorry, you're not what we're looking for; but there *is* a custodial job opening up that you might be interested in." I bet they got a good laugh out of that one. *(Pause)* My father has gone on a hundred interviews since he got laid off last year, and they all seem to say "you're not what we're looking for." This is 1993, and my father is still nothing but a nigger with a degree.

Khalil Hill

I met Khalil over a decade ago, when he was just beginning his years as a student at one of Manhattan's prestigious private middle schools. Although he was clearly very bright, he was disaffected and had a collection of rough-and-tumble street kids who followed him wherever he went. I quickly came to see his disaffection as extreme shyness and his friends as a loyal group of followers who knew a visionary when they saw one! He studied acting with me for several terms, and as he came out of his shell, he came to be known for his painfully authentic portrayals of vulnerable teens. The first play he ever wrote follows. In that particular training, I took the members of the workshop to Phoenix House, the rehabilitation center for substance abusers, where they each interviewed a teenager in recovery who was almost their same age. Khalil met with a young man who was about to be graduating and was taken by his ambivalence about getting out. His subsequent portrayal of this tender friendship between the young man and his roommate won him an ovation when it was performed to general audiences, as well as a grateful embrace from the real "Jason," on the evening when Phoenix House bought all the seats. It is such a vivid example of how completely a story and relationship can be rendered in only a few pages that I have used it as the sample play in our Teen Training Manual *for the past ten years. It was also performed live at the launch of my* Find Your Voice *book, and it never ceases to touch people, no matter how close or far they may seem to be from the realities of these two characters' lives. "While the memory of the creative writing has mostly passed away, the thrill of viewing my piece onstage has endured these fifteen years. There is a power and an arrogance in telling stories which are not our own. I hope my interpretation benefited the characters whom I based the play on, and catalyzed some closure to their experience." Khalil is a physical therapist and at the time of this writing was at work on a novel.*

This, Khalil's first play, was written as part of a cluster entitled Ashes, Ashes We All Fall Down.

The Comeback Kids
Khalil Hill

Characters: DARRYL   Male, African-American, mid-20s
               JASON   Male, African-American, mid-20s

AT RISE: The room of two Phoenix House residents. It is midnight. There are two beds parallel to each other. The person that checks the bed walks in with a flashlight and then exits.

DARRYL: Jason ... Jason ... Yo J, wake up man! *(No response. DARRYL throws a pillow at him.)* Jason, wake up!

JASON: What, man?!

DARRYL: *(Pause)* I don't know ... I wanna ... I wanna talk, man, it's your last night.

JASON: Well, I wanna sleep.

DARRYL: All right, fine. *(Pause)* Have a nice life. *(DARRYL puts head down on pillow)*

JASON: *(Stares at him)* C'mon, Darryl. C'mon, D. *(Silence)* What, you're not gonna talk to me anymore? *(Mocking him)* C'mon, baby. *(He gets up and goes to DARRYL's bed.)* What, you don't love me any more? All right, give me a little kiss. No tongue, I promise.

DARRYL: *(Half laughing, half angry, he throws Jason back to his bed)* Get off, man!

JASON: I'm sorry ... *(Gets serious)* I'm just ... I don't know ... I'm really scared.

DARRYL: Why? You're going back to the city, man. You're getting your life back. Damn, I'm in this place for five more months.

JASON: I know, I know. *(Pause)* But what am I going back to?

DARRYL: Aren't you going to see your family?

JASON: Why? So I can watch my mom smoke crack with my brothers? Forget that, man.

DARRYL: You don't even wanna see what they're doing?

JASON: What they're doing? They'll always be doing the same shit! Smoking crack, getting drunk, having kids. Damn, man, I don't have a family.

111

DARRYL: *(Not in a corny way)* You got me.

JASON: Yeah, two former crackheads. Talk about a dysfunctional family! *(They both laugh.)*

DARRYL: But, seriously, why are you so upset?

JASON: This is gonna sound really stupid. *(Pause)* I've been having this dream every night since my parole officer said I could get outta here ... and ... forget it, this is really stupid.

DARRYL: Come on, man. What happens in the dream?

JASON: *(Sighs)* All right. I'm walkin' down this street in Brooklyn, and I see John and Arlo and Eric and all these other guys I used to smoke crack with. And as I approach them, my heart just keeps pounding faster and faster and faster. Every step. Boom ... Boom ...*(Showing with his hand)* When I get up to them, their faces are so dark and their eyes so evil, no pupils ... scariest shit I've ever seen! And then John stares right at me. *(Acting it out)* "Hey, Jason! Hey, everyone, look at Jason. What, Jay, you don't smoke crack with the rest of us niggers? What! You think you're better than us? You'll always be a crackhead. *(Mimics pulling out a gun)* Yo, Arlo! Gimme the pipe! Take a hit, Jay! Take a smoke, kid! You know you love it." I say no. He puts a gun to my head and clicks the trigger back. BOOM! *(Looks at DARRYL)* I hear a loud shot and then it's over ... *(Pause)* I know it sounds really stupid ...

DARRYL: *(Cutting him off)* Naw, man. It's not stupid. Don't sweat it, man, you said it yourself. Half those guys are dead or in prison.

JASON: I know. But still, man, it scared the shit out of me.

DARRYL: Forget it. At least you're doing something. You're going to be a cook. In five years from now, we'll be dining at your cafe.

JASON: Yeah, right. Whose gonna invest in a former crackhead? *(Pause)* No matter what I do, I'll always be another screw-up from the ghetto. No matter what I try to make of my life, it'll always be there. *(Pause)* I wish I could just change my name, change my face, be a normal person. Wake up, go to work, pay rent. *(Laughs sarcastically)* Can you believe that shit? I wish I could pay rent. *(More serious)* I know this sounds dumb, but I just want a clean slate.

DARRYL: Why do you do this?

JASON: What?

DARRYL: Why do you sit there feeling sorry for yourself? You're so lucky. Where would you be if you hadn't come here? You'd be dead. You're getting a second chance. You're getting to start all over, so stop whining. You're getting a chance to live, man.

JASON: You're right, but I don't know. It's like I've always been the strong one in this program. Everyone looks at me and says, "That one! He's gonna make it!" But I never believed it myself.

DARRYL: Forget it, man. Forget it. It's your last night. Yo, I, um, got you something. Even though you're the jerk that you are. *(They both laugh.)* It's, um, I don't know ... a going-away present. *(DARRYL reaches under his bed and gets out a box.)* Here, take it. *(He gives it to him.)* It's a piece of shit, man. I made it in jewelry class with Ms. Bess. *(JASON opens it.)* It's nothin, man ... it's a stupid ring with our initials on it. It's probably not worth five bucks. *(JASON puts it on.)*

JASON: You know man, when I first came here, all I cared about was getting high, having gold, and getting all of these material items ... but this, man, this means more to me than all of that shit put together. *(Looks up at DARRYL)* Brothers?

DARRYL: *(Slaps his hand)* Brothers! *(Hands held still, he stands up and hugs him. After a beat, DARRYL laughs.)* This is getting too corny.

JASON: You're right. This is like *90210.* *(Both laugh.)* But seriously, thanks, man! Whenever I'm feeling alone, I'll look at this and know I got someone who gives a shit about me. *(Pause)* I'm getting kind of tired, I think I'm going to bed.

DARRYL: Yeah, me too. *(Both get into their beds.)*

JASON: Goodnight, dick! *(DARRYL laughs.)*

DARRYL: Goodnight, jerk! *(Both laugh.)*

BLACKOUT

This monologue is drawn from the previous play.

The Comeback Kids
Khalil Hill

(JASON, an African-American man in his mid-20s, reluctantly tells his roommate at a residential drug treatment facility about a recurring nightmare that has plagued him, and why he's afraid to graduate.)

JASON

I'm walkin' down this street in Brooklyn, and I see John and Arlo and Eric and all these other guys I used to smoke crack with. And as I approach them, my heart just keeps pounding faster and faster and faster. Every step. Boom ... Boom ... *(Showing with his hand)* When I get up to them, their faces are so dark and their eyes so evil, no pupils ... scariest shit I've ever seen! And then John stares right at me. *(Acting it out)* "Hey, Jason! Hey, everyone, look at Jason. What, Jay, you don't smoke crack with the rest of us niggers? What! You think you're better than us? You'll always be a crackhead. *(Mimics pulling out a gun)* Yo, Arlo! Gimme the pipe! Take a hit, Jay! Take a smoke, kid! You know you love it." I say no. He puts a gun to my head and clicks the trigger back. BOOM! *(Looks at DARRYL)* I hear a loud shot and then it's over ... *(Pause)* I know it sounds really stupid, but still, man, it scared the shit out of me. No matter what I do, I'll always be another screw-up from the ghetto. No matter what I try to make of my life, it'll always be there. *(Pause)* I wish I could just change my name, change my face, be a normal person. Wake up, go to work, pay rent. *(Laughs sarcastically)* Can you believe that shit? I wish I could pay rent. *(More serious)* I know this sounds dumb, but I just want a clean slate.

Shawn Hirabayashi

I met Shawn when we were both members of the Circle Rep Lab in NYC. I found his voice to be both highly intelligent and very funny. Our first collaboration was on a cluster of plays entitled Holding Patterns, *which used the image of a single airplane in the sky as the trigger. I was completely delighted by his notion of a plane stopping in midair and the ways in which he used that surreal event to authentically reveal the very real-life issues that the characters were grappling with. Shawn returned the following year, to participate in a cluster entitled* Steam, *featuring four plays that were each set in a steam room. Once again, Shawn created a highly surreal construct in which to play out the very real racial tensions he explores in the play. During the next few years, Shawn went on to teach and inspire high school students in our educational programs, and he assisted in our professional development efforts to turnkey this method into the curriculum of a local middle school. Shawn remembers that the "process affirmed the idea that within any action lies a gem that can be found with patience and nurturing."*

The following scene and monologue are from a play that was commissioned for the Steam *cluster of plays, which had to be set in an all-white room.*

20th Century Sauna
Shawn B. Hirabayashi

Characters: MAX Male, African-American, 30s
             KIM Female, Asian-American, 20s

AT RISE: A surreal sauna in which there are no bursts of steam. MAX and KIM—two strangers—have been inexplicably trapped inside together for several hours, where they both had the same vision of themselves dying violent racially motivated deaths. They are unsure as to whether they are still "in this world," and have been sharing their philosophies about life and death.

MAX: I don't appreciate your making fun of my beliefs.

KIM: Sorry. *(MAX smiles.)* What's so funny?

MAX: The flowing white robe. When I was ten, maybe, it came to me that the angels and God wouldn't be wearing any clothing. Why would they, if they were spirits? I asked my mom about it. She tried to convince me otherwise, but I was pretty adamant. So she brought out the Ivory soap.

KIM: She washed your mouth out? I didn't know people really did that.

MAX: She didn't literally wash it out. She'd make me hold the bar of soap in my mouth. I'd say something she didn't like, and she'd say, "Open up." I was sitting there breathing through my nose and going, "Ahn ah a eh ow?" And she said, "Not yet." When she saw me really squirming, she said, "I don't want to hear anymore about God being naked." "Yeh ahm." She took the bar of soap, and I spent the next half hour rinsing and spitting.

KIM: Dylan, my brother, was the one who always got punished. I was the good one.

MAX: I don't know if I was worse than my sister Francine. She was just better at not getting caught.

KIM: *(Pause)* Is that what's happened? Were we the ones caught?

MAX: You think we're being punished?

KIM: You think this is a good thing?

MAX: I don't think there's a cause and effect here.

KIM: A random act of violence? A crazy skinhead goes a-shooting and we're the unlucky ones?

MAX: Yes.

KIM: Where's your God in that?

MAX: I don't know.

KIM: I don't deserve to be killed.

MAX: Who ever does?

KIM: I can't believe in a God who would have me killed for no reason.

MAX: Then go home! There is no God, you're not dead. Just open the door and walk out of here. Go on. It's been real. See you later. Don't let the door hit you on the way out.

KIM: Don't be mean.

MAX: I don't understand either, Kim. But I have to *believe*.

KIM: *(Pause)* So what do we do here?

MAX: Wait.

KIM: For how long?

MAX: Until … until we've forgotten.

KIM: I don't want to forget.

MAX: How else will the pain go away?

KIM: I wish I had my clothes. I'm not comfortable being in stages of undress even when I'm alone.

MAX: Then why were you coming to a sauna?

KIM: I'm on a diet, a diet that involves a cleansing of the system, part of which is accomplished by sweating in a sauna.

MAX: You don't look like you need to diet.

KIM: I've got about a few pounds on me that I don't want. *(Pause)* That I *didn't* want.

MAX: Maybe here, you won't have to eat at all! How about that? No eating, no dieting. No clothing. Just us.

KIM: *(Indicates robe)* If we're not supposed to have clothes, what are we doing dressed in these things?

MAX: Maybe its part of a transition. Showing up naked would be too much of a shock.

KIM: I agree with you there.

MAX: *(He rises to undress.)* When we're ready, we strip and move on.

KIM: Well, I'm not ready.

MAX: *(Starts to pull down shorts)* Shed our past lives, so to speak.

KIM: I'd prefer if you didn't.

MAX: I think it makes a lot of sense.

KIM: Max, wait! Please. Maybe you're right, but I'm very uncomfortable here. Could you just wait a little bit? *(MAX leaves his shorts on.)* Thank you.

MAX: I guess we've got all the time in the world. *(He sits.)*

KIM: This is crazy. I don't know about you, but I wasn't supposed to die this way.

MAX: How were you supposed to die?

KIM: I don't know. It wasn't worth thinking about because it wasn't going to happen for a long time.

MAX: It's not such a horrible surprise to me. There were too many statistics to ignore them.

KIM: Statistics on being shot in the back?

MAX: The average life expectancy of the African-American male is less than any other group. And that's not because of health or diet.

KIM: Where did you get that?

MAX: I work in insurance. I *worked*, I should say.

KIM: So you went around thinking you could be attacked?

MAX: Not so much consciously, but it was there.

KIM: You think its *okay* that some pea-brain skinhead shot us?

MAX: I didn't say it was okay. I said it didn't surprise me as much as it did you.

KIM: *(Pause)* Why did he call me *mud*? You think he meant dirt, or garbage?

MAX: *(Looks at her, surprised)* You don't know?

KIM: No, Max. I don't.

MAX: You were aware that skinheads existed, right?

KIM: Yes. I just didn't pay any more attention to them than I felt they merited.

MAX: And look where it got you.

KIM: Do *you* know what *mud* means?

MAX: Yes.

KIM: Well, look where it got you.

MAX: I'm the walking statistic, remember?

KIM: *(Turns away)* Don't tell me, all right. I don't want to know.

MAX: Is ignorance really bliss?

KIM: If you're going to tell me, tell me. If not, then shut up.

MAX: *Mud people.* The white supremacists' term for *you*. In their world there are niggers and Aryans; everybody in between is a mud person. After they're done with race, they've also got their kikes and papists and ad nauseam.

KIM: *(Stares at him)* What do you get from knowing shit like that?

MAX: What do you get from *not* knowing it?

KIM: A world that's a little less ugly.

MAX: A world built on illusion.

KIM: You read about something, and you come to believe it, and then you make it so. You empower it.

MAX: You're saying that our getting shot was *my* fault?

KIM: I'm saying that dwelling on the ugly *makes* the world ugly.

MAX: You're saying that you're willfully ignorant.

KIM: I'm saying I have choices.

MAX: Good for you.

KIM: You've got choices too.

MAX: Not like you think.

KIM: What do I think?

MAX: You think a world that's *nice.* Somehow you've been able to maintain that illusion. *(Pause)* At least until now.

BLACKOUT

The following monologue is from the longer play that was commissioned for the Steam *cluster.*

20th Century Sauna
Shawn B. Hirabayashi

(MAX, an African-American man in his 30s, finds himself mysteriously imprisoned in a surreal sauna along with an Asian-American woman named KIM. They experience a shared vision of their own racially motivated violent deaths. After many hours together, in this monologue, he tells KIM how he thinks their deaths will be remembered, and why he disagrees with her belief that their deaths will have an impact on the racist world they have lived in.)

MAX

The first time Dionne held my hand, like this *(squeezes KIM's hand)*, not while walking or something, was the first time I met her father. We had been seeing each other for maybe a month, and she invited me to her family's for the Fourth of July. They had this cottage on Lake Michigan; there was going to be a *weenie roast* on the beach! *(He snickers.)* The day was pretty much perfect; if any of her family had a problem with me, they hadn't shown it. Just a fun time by all. *(Pause)* It worked out that Dionne's father and I were the ones left on the beach to put out the fire. We were tossing sand on the embers when he said he'd like to be "completely honest with me." He said he liked me—that I was "a great guy." He was concerned, though; about our children. Mind you, Dionne and I hadn't even thought about marriage yet! When I asked him what his concern was, he said, "Mixed race. It'll be really hard on them." I asked him if he was telling me to break up with his daughter. He said, "I'm asking you to think about your future. It's not an easy world." I held my tongue, but I was aggravated; my head was spinning. I wasn't going to tell Dionne, because I figured what could she do? When she did get it out of me, she held my hand to her face. Just that. *(Silence, he places KIM's hand against his cheek.)* If our story is in the papers, it'll be tucked away somewhere where nobody will see it. And if somebody does find it, there will be more in it about the asshole who did the killing than about us. Stuff about how horrible his life was. The reporters will dig until they find that *detail,* that *thing,* that makes him different. And that thing will make everybody comfortable with what happened. Then they will forget. *(She starts to argue, but he continues.)* But I'll tell you what *will* happen: Stephen and Jenny will come to understand that their father was killed before their eyes for no reason other than the color of his skin, and they'll become infected with hate. As much as Dionne, their community, and their church try to balm the wound, it won't heal. Somewhere, deep inside, they will hate. Every white person they meet will feel uncomfortable, because they will sense that hate. If the children try to hide it behind a smile, it will only make it worse. People will wonder what they're hiding. And if these same people ever do find out about what happened to me, their reaction will be, "*I* didn't do it. It's not *my* fault."

This scene (p. 36) is from a play that was commissioned for the cluster entitled Holding Patterns, *which was suggested by a photograph of an airplane in the sky.*

On a Plane
Shawn B. Hirabayashi

Characters: SIMONE   Female, French, 50s
              CARL   Male, Japanese-American, 60s, her husband

AT RISE: When an airplane freezes above their apartment, SIMONE tries to get her ailing husband to take action.

SIMONE: *(Hanging up the phone)* They have no idea why it's frozen.

CARL: Of course not.

SIMONE: They suggest we go elsewhere. In case the plane falls.

CARL: Why don't they make sure their damn plane falls somewhere else?

SIMONE: I'm just telling you what the woman said.

CARL: It's a conspiracy to get us to move. They want to expand their airport.

SIMONE: Don't be ridiculous.

CARL: You can't trust them. Any of them.

SIMONE: Carl, the government is not after you.

CARL: You don't know. You weren't there. They threw us in camps. Took away all our possessions.

SIMONE: Yes, yes, I know. It was horrible.

CARL: Don't make fun of me.

SIMONE: But you say it all the time. Frankly, it's boring.

CARL: I'm sorry my heritage bores you.

SIMONE: Carl, the camps are not your heritage; not an important part of it. *(Pause)* Do you remember what Pierre called you when he could finally speak?

CARL: Old fart.

SIMONE: He held your finger and called you *Oji.*

CARL: Why shouldn't he?

SIMONE: Our American grandson with a French name calls you Oji, because it's Japanese for *grandpa.* That's your heritage. A wonderful, beautiful heritage. *(Pause)* What do you think his children will call you?

CARL: Dead old fart.

SIMONE: Watching Pierre hold you by the pinky, it struck me that we've been together almost forty years. Forty years, in a way, led to that moment of joy. It made me laugh. Then you looked at me, and you laughed, too.

CARL: I never knew my grandfather.

SIMONE: You laughed, too, Carl.

CARL: He's a funny-looking kid.

SIMONE: He's beautiful. Like our daughter. Like you.

CARL: Not me.

SIMONE: You're still a very handsome man.

CARL: Maybe once, not anymore.

SIMONE: To me, you are.

CARL: This is not me.

SIMONE: Who is it?

CARL: Some crap piece of shit shell.

SIMONE: Isn't that redundant?

CARL: Yes, goddamn it, it is. All of it. One huge fucking redundancy.

SIMONE: Please don't curse.

CARL: I'll do anything I want.

SIMONE: *(She tries to lift him out of his chair.)* I've had enough. The plane may fall at any time; we are going.

CARL: *(He pulls away.)* No.

SIMONE: I don't want to die.

CARL: Do what you feel you have to.

SIMONE: Do you want to die?

CARL: I've already got one foot in the grave.

SIMONE: So you've been saying for five years now. Isn't the foot moldy? Or do you change feet?

CARL: Go ahead, make fun. We all do what we can to cope.

SIMONE: Some of us sit on our ass, while others clean and cook and chauffer them to doctor appointments.

CARL: You're free to leave at any time. No one's keeping you.

SIMONE: Why do you think I do these things for you?

CARL: I've never asked you to stay; I told you, you should find a whole man.

SIMONE: *Tu es emmerdant.*

CARL: Don't like it? Leave.

SIMONE: What would you do if I left?

CARL: Have a party.

SIMONE: *(Pause)* It's not so much what you say that's bothersome; it's the attempt at cruelty.

CARL: It's not cruelty. It's just the facts.

SIMONE: You've been crazy about me ever since we first met.

CARL: I felt sorry for you. Away from your home. Alone. I took pity.

SIMONE: *(Beginning to collect her things)* Perhaps a visit to the children. Then Bergerac. Clothes, photographs of the children, documents. Toothbrush. Is there anything in particular that you want to take?

CARL: I am not going anywhere.

SIMONE: You would abandon me?

CARL: Abandon means to leave. Movement. You're the one moving, not me.

SIMONE: This situation calls for movement.

CARL: Not in my mind.

SIMONE: Then we are of different minds.

CARL: Oh, are we?

SIMONE: Yes. At least since the stroke.

CARL: Finally. Finally it's out in the open. You hate me for being a cripple.

SIMONE: You are not a cripple.

CARL: Then why do you hate me?

SIMONE: I don't hate you. You hate yourself.

CARL: You hate me because I'm not the man you married.

SIMONE: You were never the man I married. Or you were, but only for that moment. Then you grew and changed, and I did as well. It was stimulating.

CARL: Until now.

SIMONE: Until now.

BLACKOUT

Haru Ikeda

Haru trained with me for several years while he attended high school. Although initially very shy and nervous, he distinguished himself as a courageous actor in roles as diverse as a werewolf in a sit-com parody and a young man accused of date rape. He also distinguished himself as a writer of biting wit when he wrote a parody of a talk show whose host unwittingly promotes racism and distorts the news. After that performance and during that post-show discussion with the audience, Haru began to speak very candidly about the kinds of prejudice he had encountered as a Japanese-American male, and the anger that surfaced began to serve him well. He wrote this particular monologue for the Ashes, Ashes *cluster of plays, which were based on interviews with real teenagers who were in recovery from substance abuse at Phoenix House. As always, these were fictionalized accounts, so the student playwrights had the freedom to embellish the biographies with details from their own experiences. He remembers, "The 'torn earlobes' advertisement was a real ad that I saw on the subway one day!" and that FYV "provided me with the confidence one needs for self-expression and internal harmony." At the time of this writing, Haru was an operations supervisor for commercial and residential properties in California.*

Geometry Lesson Number Five
(Circles: they begin at one point and end at the same point)
Haru Ikeda

(A twenty-four-year-old African-American drug addict explains her past behavior during a group therapy session at a rehab program.)

JEN

Guilt can eat you up sometimes. I know. *(Pause; the counselor encourages her to continue.)* I went to work once while I was high. *(Looking around at group defensively) Once.* The patient's name was Mrs. Frunknip! *(Snickers)* She was this cranky bitch who wanted her old teeth to shine like her new car. *(Swallows hard)* I was cleaning her molars; you use this special drill. I can handle it without any problem, but that day ...
I mean ... it goes really fast. If it gets out of hand, it automatically

124

shuts off because it has this switch. But I *had* to get that molar. *(Getting agitated)* I just *had* to. There was this one spot I just couldn't reach. So I kept pushing it in. And pushing it in. And pushing it in. The drill was shutting itself off but I kept switching it back on. Next thing I know my boss is grabbing me, and then I hear the sounds; the sounds of her screaming and choking on her own blood. And I look down at my nice white dress and it's stained in red. I mean there's blood all over my hands, my name-tag, my everything. *(Long pause, she stares at the floor)* There was an investigation and trials and interrogations and more trials. I lost my job. I can't ever work in dentistry again. *(Long pause, the counselor encourages her to continue.)* That's why I decided to come here. *(Pause)* I was hunting for a job, and I was on the subway one day. I started reading those completely random advertisements like: "Torn earlobes? We can help." And "Want beautiful feet?" *(Snickers at the memory, then sobers)* Then I saw this ad with all these homeless people on drugs; it said, "When you're back from the living dead … give us a call." *(Hard to say)* I thought to myself; I don't want to ever be like that. And then I realized that I *am* like that! *(Laughs bitterly at herself)* I have no control. That's why I'm here. *(Looking around at group)* I go off without control; without an automatic switch when things get rough.

Lesley-Diann *(LD)* Jones

LD participated in a FYV training that was offered to the entire faculty at the New York City elementary school where she was teaching. She had taken some drama in high school but had never written a play before. At first, the piece was a natty argument between a stereotypical desperate female and a haughty gay man. As she focused on what each character really wanted in life, they evolved into real people. After many drafts, this piece came to reflect the combination of self-deprecating humor and buoyant spunk that distinguished her warm personality. At the time of this writing LD was the principal of the Warner Girls' Leadership Academy in Cleveland, Ohio, and newly married. "How very true it was to my life—having been the bridesmaid so many times and not the bride. In July 2006, 'I' was the bride! After going through the FYV process twice—and enjoying it so much—I implemented it into the writing workshop model at school with my elementary school students. It worked."

This, LD's first play, was written for the cluster, Something Old and…, *in response to a photograph of a vase on a table.*

The Back Room
Lesley-Diann Jones

Characters: AMALIA   Female, African-American, 35, never married

           STANLEY   Male, Caucasian American, 33, lives with his partner

AT RISE: Small pottery/arts and crafts/jewelry store divided into two parts. It's mid-day on a Sunday during spring. The store is crowded with people shopping for gifts; some are wedding gifts, since there is a very popular wedding registry in the front room. Couples shopping for rings are in the back room. AMALIA, dressed up from church, enters and looks at pottery rather quickly. A salesclerk approaches her.

STAN: Hi! I see you're back!

AMALIA: *(Embarrassed)* Yeah, it's me again.

STAN: Looking for another wedding gift?

AMALIA: Got one in two weeks.

STAN: How did the last couple like the vase?

AMALIA: Which couple are you talking about? I feel like I spend every Sunday afternoon in this place shopping for wedding gifts! *(Picks up a martini glass and studies it)* I'm sure they liked the vase. I hope they liked it! *(Puts martini glass down)* You liked the vase, didn't you?

STAN: Oh, absolutely! It was wonderful—and very well priced!

AMALIA: *(Picks up a platter and studies it along with the price)* What do you think of this platter? *(Reassuring herself and not waiting for a response)* I like the colors. Very soothing, wouldn't you say so?

STAN: It's handcrafted by a local artist who's new to the store. *(Pause)* And who would this one be for?

AMALIA: *(Sighing and placing platter back on shelf)* This wedding present will be for Sheila and Robert. *(Pause)* It will be my tenth wedding as a bridesmaid, and my seventh wedding as a guest.

STAN: You actually count them?

AMALIA: *(Laughs)* Trust me; the numbers are true. The good news is that the majority of the couples are still together.

STAN: *(Smiling)* Well, that is good news. *(Silence)* Do you want to see another vase? Or something else in that color?

AMALIA: *(Notices the back room)* I see you're busy as usual today in the back room; couples shopping for wedding rings! The front room, the back room. *(Indicates with hands)* The front room. The back room. The front room for gifts and me, the back room for rings and couples.

STAN: You'll get there, honey.

AMALIA: God, if one more person tells me something like that: "Good things come to those who wait"; "Rome wasn't built in a day"; "The best is yet to come"—

STAN: Are you seeing anyone? That's half your battle, if you are.

AMALIA: Well … it depends on what day you ask me. Or should I say, month? February certainly was a busy month for me. Nine blind dates. *(Silence)* Did you hear me? I said nine blinds dates! There was Josh, and then Eric, and then Isaac, and then … what

on earth was that guy's name from Long Island? *(Silence)* See that's
what happens … you forget the guy's names! Well, tomorrow's guy
is older; maybe he'll be more mature.

STAN: Maybe this is the one!

AMALIA: I hope so! Who's got time to waste? My eggs are dropping as
we speak! And Lord only knows when he'll start shooting blanks!
(Looking on STAN's finger for a ring) What about you? I don't see a
ring on your finger.

STAN: *(Whispering)* Girl, you think you have problems? My boyfriend
is "Mr. Commitment Phobic." He doesn't believe in the "church
vow" thing. He says that living with him and knowing he loves me
is all I should be concerned about.

AMALIA: I see.

STAN: Sometimes I don't even think it's worth putting up a fight.

AMALIA: Not worth it? *(Silence)* You love him, don't you?

STAN: Of course I do. But we have enough strikes against us already;
with society's hang-ups about our status, why push the envelope?

AMALIA: *(Silence)* I think he's not the one for you.

STAN: What?

AMALIA: You obviously don't share the same goals. I say, leave him.
There are too many fish out there and you need to start fishing.
Trust me, I know!

STAN: Really. So I should spend countless nights going out on blind
dates with guys whose names I forget? So I can shop on Sundays
for everybody else's wedding gifts? I don't think so. I may never get
a gift, but at least I got the guy!

AMALIA: And I may not have "Mr. Right" yet, but at least I'm hopeful.
I'm not gonna settle for just anyone because he meets *half* my
needs.

STAN: Just because he doesn't want to get married doesn't mean we
should be separating. It's life, sweetie, with its mixed-up games and
all. And if there's one thing I've learned, it's that if you get lemons,
you better start making lemonade! And my lemonade couldn't be …
(Takes finger, puts it into mouth and tastes it) sweeter!

AMALIA: Well, I don't want lemonade. I want champagne in two
crystal intertwining glasses, while I'm dressed in my sweetheart-cut,
silk organza Vera Wang gown. And we'll dance to "Save the Best

for Last" and then cut into our five-layer chocolate-raspberry cake, with my twelve bridesmaids cheering me on. And the photographers will be shooting away. And it won't just be in color. No. We'll have black-and-whites too, because it took us an ancient time to get to the damn altar! So ... Mr. "I'll Settle for Sweet Lemonade" ... while I'm waiting for Mr. Right, I, Miss Amalia Jackson, will keep on looking for my name on the place-card table at weddings, and I'll keep pushing other ladies-in-waiting out of my way so I can catch *my* bouquet. And I'll keep praying to the mighty good Lord to send me my man. *(Pushing vase in his chest)* Here! I'll take this vase for Sheila and Robert. It'll be a charge; gift wrap and delivery as usual. And I want you to know one more thing ... it's only a matter of time before my ass gets to the back room.

STAN: *(Pause)* What color wrapping paper would you like?

BLACKOUT

This monologue is drawn from the previous play.

The Back Room
Lesley-Diann *(LD)* Jones

(AMALIA, an African-American woman in her late 30s, has never married. She is shopping for a wedding gift in the front room of a local gift shop—yet again, while couples shop for rings in the back room. She blows up at a salesman who suggests that she might be setting her standards too high.)

AMALIA

I don't want *lemonade.* I want champagne, in two crystal intertwining glasses, while I'm dressed in my sweetheart-cut, silk organza Vera Wang gown. And we'll dance to "Save the Best for Last" and then cut into our five-layer, chocolate-raspberry cake, with my twelve bridesmaids cheering me on! And the photographers will be shooting away! And it won't just be in color! No. We'll have black-and-whites too, because it took us an ancient time to get to the damn altar! So—Mr. "I'll Settle for Sweet Lemonade"—while I'm waiting for Mr. Right, I, Miss Amalia Jackson, will keep on looking for my name on the place-card table at other people's weddings, and I'll keep pushing other ladies-in-waiting out of my way so I can catch *my* bouquet, and I'll keep praying to the mighty good Lord to send me *my* man! *(Pushing vase in his chest)* Here! I'll take this vase for Sheila and Robert. It'll be a charge; gift wrap and delivery as usual. And I want you to know one more thing … it's only a matter of time before my ass gets to the back room!

Susan Kim

I became aware of Susan's work when her agent submitted her for participation in one of our main stage clusters. I was immediately drawn to her authentic yet offbeat voice, and I invited her to participate in the upcoming Steam *cluster, for which we asked the participating writers to create short plays in which two people found themselves in an all-white steam room together. Although developed in separate workshops, her decision to set a play that deals with the very real issues of misogyny and racism, in a surreal setting, was eerily reminiscent of Shawn Hirabayashi's solution to the same creative problem. (See* 20th Century Sauna, *featured earlier in this collection.) I have found these "echoes" from play to play—all of which are conceived in isolation—to be one of the most exciting aspects of the FYV method of play development. Susan Kim coauthored two graphic novels, and at the time of this writing was developing a series for the Disney Channel, as well as coauthoring a nonfiction book,* Flow.

The following two scenes are from a play that was commissioned for the Steam *cluster of plays.*

The Door
Susan Kim

Characters: HELEN Female, Asian-American, 50s
MIRI Female, Asian-American, 20s

AT RISE: A surrealistic, white steam room that MIRI has been mysteriously transported to and locked in. A door opens and HELEN enters; she is dressed in a robe and flip-flops. She also wears a walkman and carries a plastic basket full of toiletries and a bottle of water. Her upper face is heavily bandaged, so she feels her way to a bench with arms outstretched; MIRI cowers in a corner, still in her jacket and clutching her backpack.

HELEN: Hello? *(Pause)* Is someone there? *(Pulls off headphones)* Who's there? *(Silence)* Who are you? What do you want?

MIRI: Do you work here?

HELEN: God, no. *(Pause)* Do you?

MIRI: No.

HELEN: Really? *(Whispering)* In that case, do you have anything to eat?

MIRI: No. Where am I?

HELEN: Where does it look like you are; it's a steam room, isn't it?

MIRI: I meant, what *is* it? Who *are* you?

HELEN: *(Holding out her hand)* I'm Helen Choo; nice to meet you. *(MIRI doesn't shake it.)*

MIRI: But what's going on? Where *are* we?

HELEN: I don't really know.

MIRI: What do you mean? How did I get here?

HELEN: Sorry.

MIRI: Shit … *(Goes to the door and tries it again, and finding it locked, turns back to her)* Well, what city is this? Are we still in New York? *(No answer, pounds on door again)* Hello? Is anyone out there?

HELEN: I'm not trying to be difficult; it's just that I'm as much in the dark as you are. So to speak.

MIRI: Are you blind?

HELEN: Are you young?

MIRI: I'm twenty-two. Why?

HELEN: I just can't imagine anyone older than thirty asking such a rude question. *(Gingerly touches her bandages, wincing)* But to answer you, *yes*—it would appear I am blind. For the time being, I hope. It seems I've had some kind of a *procedure*.

MIRI: A what?

HELEN: It's a euphemism. Don't worry; I'm sure you'll find out eventually.

MIRI: *(A sudden realization)* Shit, I am such a retard ... *(She scrabbles through her backpack. Fishing through it, she pulls out a cell phone and starts dialing feverishly. HELEN listens attentively.)*

HELEN: They don't work.

MIRI: What?

HELEN: Is that a telephone? If it is, congratulations on finding one, but I don't think any of them work. *(MIRI slams it back into her bag.)* I'm surprised they left one lying around.

MIRI: They didn't. It's mine.

HELEN: What do you mean? You carry one around?

MIRI: Well, yeah.

HELEN: You're kidding.

MIRI: Did you say your last name was Choo? What are you, Chinese or Korean?

HELEN: Korean. Hey, are you Asian, too?

MIRI: Why do you want to know?

HELEN: I don't know. Because ... most non-Asians would assume it was Chinese, I guess. Don't you agree?

MIRI: Is this a hospital?

HELEN: No. It's definitely a building, though—or at least a complex of rooms. This is just *one* of them; there are dozens more—

MIRI: But who runs it? *Why* am I here?

HELEN: To lose weight?

MIRI: That's bullshit. Why am I here?

HELEN: How the hell should I know why you're here; why *are* you here?

MIRI: I have no fucking clue. I never saw this place in my life; I just woke up a second ago and ... Jesus. Do you think I was kidnapped?

HELEN: Possibly.

MIRI: But who would wanna kidnap me? My family doesn't have any money. *(Pause)* Do you think I was drugged?

HELEN: Do you feel drugged?

MIRI: I can't tell. I don't think so. Please, you've got to help me. I'm not supposed to be here; I think they wanted someone else. There's obviously been some kind of mistake … *(HELEN laughs.)* What's so funny?

HELEN: You'll have to bear with me … my memory's shot. It's like that cheese—Swedish or Swiss—full of holes? But as I recall, the same thing pretty much happened to me too.

MIRI: You mean you were kidnapped too?

HELEN: Of course, that was a long time ago—

MIRI: But how did they do it? *(Feels her own head, rolls it around on her neck to test for injury)* If someone knocked me out, I'd still feel it—wouldn't I?

HELEN: What was the last thing you remember?

MIRI: Last thing? *(Pause)* Shit, I can't remember anything! It's all so fucked up—

HELEN: Yes. It's already started.

MIRI: What has? What are you talking about?

HELEN: I don't mean to be rude, but are you *sure* you don't have anything to eat? Like in your pockets, maybe? *(Silence)* A cookie? Half a sandwich? Gum?

MIRI: Sorry.

HELEN: *(Picks up a bottle of lotion)* Believe it or not, I actually tried eating some of this the other day; the coconut was driving me insane! *(Starts applying lotion to her legs)* Talk about mistakes—

MIRI: It was food!

HELEN: What was?

MIRI: We were at dinner someplace; me and my boyfriend—someplace fancy. It was our first real date, and I felt stupid cause of the way I was dressed. *(Pause)* Shit. Why can't I remember? *(Paces nervously, tries the door again)* Hey, where'd you come from?

HELEN: Beats me. Somewhere in New Jersey?

MIRI: I meant just now. How'd you get in?

HELEN: I came in through the door, what do you think?

MIRI: But it's locked.

HELEN: Not from the outside, it isn't. *(MIRI bangs on the door repeatedly and then starts kicking it.)* Will you stop that? *(No response)* I said, will you stop? You're going to hurt yourself.

MIRI: *(Still kicking)* Maybe someone will hear.

HELEN: There's no one out there.

MIRI: Isn't there another way out of here?

HELEN: No. And I seem to remember, once upon a time, doing a very thorough search of this room. And I mean *very.* *(MIRI kicks the door one last time.)* Look, if you really want to leave, I'm sure someone will let you out. Eventually.

MIRI: Well, they better show up, and it better be soon.

HELEN: Yes, yes. Just sit down and relax, all right? You're making me nervous. *(MIRI sits down.)*

MIRI: They better answer some of my questions, too.

HELEN: Oh. You mean like: *"Who's in charge?" "What's really going on around here, anyway?"* and *"How the hell did we get here in the first place?"* Good luck.

MIRI: You really don't know anything about this place? *(HELEN shrugs.)* Shit.

HELEN: The bottom line is: I avail myself of their services; they seem perfectly adequate. I haven't had any complaints, other than that I honestly don't know what the hell is going on around here.

MIRI: What kind of *services?*

HELEN: What do you think? There's the steam, the sauna, the mud room, the eucalyptus room—

MIRI: But I can't stay. I've got stuff to do.

HELEN: Yes, well … didn't we all?

MIRI: I'm serious. My boyfriend's gonna be wondering where I am. He's gonna be worried … *(Glances at a watch that isn't there)* Shit … they took my watch!

HELEN: Yes—they do that.

MIRI: So how do you know what time it is?

HELEN: Are you kidding? I haven't known what time it was since I got here. But the strange thing is, I've found that time doesn't really work the same way in here as it does out there. As a matter of fact, I've come to the conclusion that in here what time does, essentially, is *stand still.*

MIRI: What? *(A buzzer goes off. The sound of hissing immediately follows. It is quite loud, making any conversation impossible. Steam fills the space. After a few seconds, it stops.)* Jesus.

HELEN: Trust me—you get used to it. It can even be vaguely pleasant, if you let it.

MIRI: But how do you breathe?

HELEN: Carefully; through your teeth. *(MIRI wipes her brow and tries to breathe. HELEN stretches out on the bench.)* Aren't you hot?

MIRI: What?

HELEN: I said, aren't you hot?

MIRI: No.

HELEN: You'd feel a lot better if you took off some of your clothes.

MIRI: How do you know I have them on?

HELEN: By the smell. *(Sniffs with some distaste)* You're wearing jeans … and something leather. Am I right? *(MIRI is self-conscious.)* It doesn't matter … *(Sits up and gropes her way along the bench)* I think they have some bathing suits and things around here somewhere. *(Lifts up a bench section that hinges open, takes out a bathing suit)* They're not exactly what I call "le dernier cri." As a matter of fact, I wouldn't even wear the robe at first; it makes you look incredibly fat! But I guess that doesn't really matter here, right? *(Holds it out, MIRI doesn't take it.)* Well? Aren't you going to put it on?

MIRI: No.

HELEN: Not that it's any of my business, but why not? Don't think it'll fit? *(Tosses it to her, MIRI catches it, looks at the tag.)*

MIRI: It's not that. I just don't trust it.

HELEN: Trust what; how clean it is?

MIRI: I just don't like being told what to do.

HELEN: I'm not telling you to do anything. Roast alive. See if I give a shit.

MIRI: I didn't mean *you*. I meant … whoever's out there.

HELEN: Out where?

MIRI: We're in here, and we can't get out … and there's like this bathing suit in here, and it just happens to be my size? That's not, like, a coincidence; you know what I'm saying?

HELEN: No; what are you saying?

MIRI: *(Pause)* You think they want us to take our clothes off?

HELEN: And why would they want us to do that?

MIRI: I dunno. To … see us naked?

HELEN: Try again.

MIRI: What else could they be trying to do? Maybe they're watching us somehow; maybe they've got cameras. Maybe they're filming … everything we do?

HELEN: No, no. You're way off base.

MIRI: How do you know?

HELEN: I may have lost my ability to think, but I can still recognize a stupid hypothesis when I hear one. *(Lying down, she puts on her Walkman, starts to turn it on.)*

MIRI: No, but listen; why is it so goddamn hot? Why do they keep pumping steam in here? *(HELEN takes off the headset.)* Are they trying to torture us? Why? What did we do, anyway? But why else would we be here? You see what I'm getting at? *(HELEN laughs.)*

HELEN: You're feisty; that's cute!

MIRI: *(Jumping up)* Stop patronizing me, okay? I'm trying to figure out what's going on.

HELEN: And you think you're entitled to some kind of answers and solutions.

MIRI: Well, yeah. I mean, shit—don't you?

HELEN: I don't think anything anymore, quite frankly.

MIRI: That's pathetic.

HELEN: Is it? I mean, if the door's locked, it's locked. And you know what? Sometimes it's not. Why? I don't know. Who's in charge? Who cares! Does it really matter? Sit down and stop making so much noise; my head's about to explode. It's hot enough as it is.

MIRI: How am I supposed to relax? I'm fucking roasting to death.

HELEN: Yes. But that's the one thing you actually have some control over, now, isn't it?

BLACKOUT

The Door
Susan Kim

| Characters: | HELEN | Female, Asian-American, 50s |
| | MIRI | Female, Asian-American, 20s |

AT RISE: HELEN and MIRI are prisoners in the same surrealistic steam room—neither able to remember how or why they got there. HELEN has been there for a long time, and her face and eyes are heavily bandaged, making it impossible for her to see. MIRI goes to the door, takes out a pen, tries to pry it open.

HELEN: *(Hearing sounds)* What's that? *(Pause)* What are you doing?

MIRI: I don't suppose there's like a screwdriver or something around here?

HELEN: Sorry. *(MIRI keeps working.)* God, I'm glad you're here. I'd forgotten how much I missed it.

MIRI: What?

HELEN: People. You can get as starved for company as you can for food, did you know that? *(Silence)* What's your name?

MIRI: Miri.

HELEN: Miri. That's pretty.

MIRI: So tell me what you know about this place. What's outside this door?

HELEN: Some of the hallway, I guess; I'm not really sure of the layout. There's a swimming pool. Then there's a weight room, a cardiovascular circuit, the operating room, a tanning parlor … everything's really well-maintained; you could practically eat off the floors. If there *were* anything to eat, that is.

MIRI: What are the other people like?

HELEN: *(Pause)* What other people?

MIRI: The other … whatever they are. Prisoners.

HELEN: No, that's good! "Prisoners." I like that. *(Snickers)* There aren't any.

MIRI: So who uses all this stuff?

HELEN: Nobody. You're the only person I've ever seen in here.

MIRI: No way. Really?

HELEN: Weird, isn't it? We're kind of like *No Exit,* as written by Jack LaLane.

MIRI: Christ. *(Gives up on door, paces)*

HELEN: Look on the bright side; at least you don't have to wait in line for the Stairmaster.

MIRI: Are you kidding? I hate that kind of shit.

137

HELEN: You mean health clubs? Staying in shape?

MIRI: I'm just not into aerobics and tanning salons and all that crap.

HELEN: Why not? *(Pause)* Are you fat?

MIRI: No.

HELEN: Is that why you don't want to put on the bathing suit?

MIRI: *I said I'm not fat, okay?*

HELEN: *(Pause)* I used to think it was all pretty stupid myself, you know. But one cruel comment, one unflattering photograph—it can change your life; did you know that? *(Silence)* What do you look like?

MIRI: Why do you want to know?

HELEN: Habit. It's weird not being able to see someone you're talking to, someone in the same room. Looks are so important when you're just getting to know someone, don't you think?

MIRI: No.

HELEN: Sure they are. I mean, God; it's Darwinian.

MIRI: How do you mean?

HELEN: Animals prefer symmetry: the size of wings, the ratio of the head to the body. They *hate* differences. They're trained to at best ignore, at worst destroy, any differences they detect.

MIRI: But we're not animals.

HELEN: Are you kidding? Why do we love beauty? Why are we repulsed by ugliness and deformity? *(Pause)* Who's your favorite actress, by the way?

MIRI: I don't have one.

HELEN: Mine is Julie Christie. God, is she stunning. At least she was until she got so old. *(Pause)* So what do you look like?

MIRI: This is weird.

HELEN: You can see what I look like—roughly, at any rate. I'm a dumpy, middle-aged Asian woman in search of a waist. So now, it's your turn.

MIRI: *(Pause)* Well ... I guess I look kinda normal.

HELEN: I see. Hair color?

MIRI: It's ... whatever. Normal. You know.

HELEN: No, I don't know. That's why I'm asking.

MIRI: Brown. I mean, it used to be brown; but I dyed it. Now it's kinda ... orange.

HELEN: And your eyes?

MIRI: They're brown too.

HELEN: Height? Weight? Build?

MIRI: You know; nothing special. I'm kind of normal.

HELEN: You're not much of a wordsmith, are you?

MIRI: What do you want me to say? I'm *normal.* I'm average. I look like anybody.

HELEN: And what does *anybody* look like?

MIRI: You know; typical. I look like your typical twenty-two year old Asian woman ... with orange hair.

HELEN: Ah-ha! The details emerge. So you are Asian as well.

MIRI: Well, yeah. I'm Korean-American.

HELEN: Well, why didn't you mention that earlier? We could have bonded. And here I was, feeling like some kind of freak.

MIRI: I dunno; it didn't seem relevant.

HELEN: Since when is race not relevant?

MIRI: You know. It's not that big of a deal.

HELEN: To you, maybe. *(Pause)* Or were you just embarrassed?

MIRI: You mean about being Asian? That's ridiculous.

HELEN: Is it?

MIRI: Of course it is.

HELEN: So why are you being so defensive?

MIRI: I'm not.

HELEN: It's all right. I can't stand the assumptions people have about Asian women either. It doesn't even matter if the stereotypes are positive; because they're all so fucking presumptuous. As if anyone could know who you are by the shape of your nose, the fold of your eyelid. Aren't you sick of it all?

MIRI: Well—

HELEN: Of course you are; we all are.

MIRI: I mean ... once in a while you get an asshole giving you a hard time. Not that often, though.

HELEN: But often enough.

MIRI: Well—

HELEN: Do you mind if I touch you?

MIRI: What? *(HELEN crosses to her, groping her way.)*

HELEN: On the face. I just want to make sure.

MIRI: That I'm Asian? Just take my word for it, okay?

HELEN: Calm down; I'm not a dyke. *(Sits beside MIRI)* I can't even remember the last time I was in the same room as another human being. I just want to make sure that you're actually here and not an audio tape being piped in as some kind of cruel joke.

MIRI: Believe me, I'm here. *(Moving over)* I wish I weren't, but I am.

HELEN: But I don't know what you look like. Not really. I just know what you told me.

MIRI: Why would I lie?

HELEN: Why would anyone lie about their appearance—because they can't stand the way they look? Please. May I? *(She reaches out. MIRI hesitates, then takes HELEN'S hand and guides it.)*

MIRI: Hold on. You're about to poke my eye out. *(She places HELEN's hand on her face. HELEN lightly runs her fingers over MIRI's face.)* I wouldn't care if you were a lesbian, by the way. Lesbians are cool.

HELEN: Well, I'm not. *(Still feeling her face)*

MIRI: My college roommate was gay.

HELEN: How nice for you.

MIRI: Why do you call them *dykes*, anyway? Are you like a homophobe?

HELEN: No.

MIRI: How old are you? Do you even know any gay people?

HELEN: Let's keep this civil, okay? *(She finishes.)* How did you break your nose?

MIRI: *(Pause)* How could you tell?

HELEN: It's not hard; you've got a whopper of a bump there, and it's very crooked.

MIRI: No it isn't. *(Feels it)* Is it?

HELEN: You never noticed?

MIRI: Well, no. Not really—

HELEN: *(HELEN touches MIRI's nose.)* Right over here—before your nose flattens out. Is it very disfiguring?

MIRI: No! I mean, I don't think so—

HELEN: I don't know. A flat Asian nose with a huge bump on the bridge does not sound very attractive to me.

MIRI: Hey! Fuck you. *(Gets up and paces)*

HELEN: Does your boyfriend mind?

MIRI: No. Of course not—

HELEN: Did he actually *say* he doesn't mind? Or are you just assuming he doesn't?

MIRI: I—

HELEN: Because all men are obsessed with appearance. They can be downright fascistic about it, too: "Are you sure you need that extra helping?" "Your hair looks better long," "Can't you wear a belt with that? You look like a fire plug." *(Pause)* Sometimes I wonder what the world would be like if men didn't care what we looked like. Or maybe it's just us. Maybe it would be different if *we* didn't care that they did—

MIRI: Tomas isn't like that. He *likes* the way I look.

HELEN: Really? *(Pause)* Have you been together long?

MIRI: No.

HELEN: Uh huh.

MIRI: I mean … he *says* he likes the way I look. *(Pause)* Although it's kinda funny … I don't look anything like the kind of girls he normally likes.

HELEN: And what's that?

MIRI: Well, like his girlfriend in college; she was really beautiful. I mean, like tall, with big boobs. And she had this long red hair—

HELEN: And let me guess; that's why you dyed yours?

MIRI: No! I mean … shit. I don't know; I never thought of it that way. I mean … maybe. Yeah; maybe I did. Pretty fucking stupid, huh?

HELEN: Of course not. You're in love, right?

MIRI: I don't know. Yeah, I guess. He's cool.

HELEN: So. How did you do it, anyway?

MIRI: Do what?

HELEN: Break your nose.

MIRI: Oh. It was a game of football. I was like thirteen.

HELEN: What happened?

MIRI: Okay. You know how when you play touch, some asshole always wants to tackle?

HELEN: Sure.

MIRI: My cousin Leo landed on my face, bam, like that. *(She demonstrates.)* Everyone said you could hear the crack all the way indoors. Man, there was blood shooting out of my face like it was a fire hydrant.

HELEN: God, don't remind me. The coppery taste in your mouth—

MIRI: My dad didn't even take me to the hospital. "Nose not broken," he said, "you just take beating."

HELEN: Just what my father would have said—

MIRI: Not that there's anything they can do for a broken nose. Anyway, I didn't cry or anything. My dad said I was tougher than a boy.

HELEN: Well, it's noticeable ... but I wouldn't worry about it if I were you. That's an easy one.

MIRI: An easy what?

HELEN: Fix. Obviously.

MIRI: Who said I want to fix it?

HELEN: Why wouldn't you?

MIRI: I dunno. Why would I?

HELEN: Because. It's what they do here.

MIRI: It is?

HELEN: And get this—it's free.

BLACKOUT

The following is a monologue drawn from the longer work that was commissioned for the Steam *cluster.*

The Door
Susan Kim

(HELEN has been trapped in an otherworldly health spa for many years, where she's receiving unlimited plastic surgery. She tries to justify her contentment there when a newcomer asks HELEN to break out with her.)

HELEN

I told you they give you magazines here? Beauty magazines mostly. Some fashion, with the articles ripped out; I guess the ones they don't want you to read. Well, I was flipping through a magazine once, and I came across this—I can't imagine why they let this one through. *(She pulls a tattered magazine article out of the pocket of her bath robe.)* Here. *(She unfolds it.)* It's about this old couple who lived in Minnesota. When she was younger, this woman was in trouble somehow; a political prisoner maybe? She'd spent years in some kind of camp, and at night they used to shackle her to her bed. Anyway, the woman was eventually set free and made her way to America. She met a man, and they got married. But this woman started having nightmares. They got so bad that she started sleepwalking. Her husband would wake to find her gone, and he'd go out looking for her. At first she'd just wander around the house, and he'd find her asleep in the living room. But later, she started heading outdoors; out onto the street and down the road. If he locked the doors at night, she'd unlock them in her sleep. It got so bad that he had to install a chain link fence around their property, and these big search lights. Even so, he was afraid she'd hurt herself in the house; falling down the stairs or tripping over the furniture. So he started locking and then bolting the bedroom doors. And finally, you know what he ended up doing? *(Silence)* He bought a long chain and some leather dog collars—and shackled her to the bed!

Jan Kodadek

Jan began her FYV training right before entering high school. She was an incredibly bright and precocious girl, who was having some difficulty fitting into traditional academic classrooms. She eventually ended up at a "high school without walls," and she attended biweekly FYV workshops for four years—traveling up to two hours back and forth, to and from her home on Staten Island. As Jan gained an outward maturity and confidence that was on par with her innate journalistic curiosity, she was able to focus her thoughts and responses to the point where she became one of the more interesting writers in any given workshop. For this particular cluster, a commission from the Jewish Museum that would accompany their exhibit on Remembering the Holocaust, Jan discovered that a relative in her own family had been a "hidden child." She came to class equipped with old photographs and loads of details, and she wrote a moving play that contained this monologue. In the actual performance, two Latino teenagers performed the roles of mother and son! The actor who portrayed the son, Jayson Torres—whose work is also featured in this text—was asked to memorize and passionately deliver a Hebrew prayer while lighting a candle of remembrance. Jan recalls, "I never had the opportunity to meet a lot of my family members, as many were killed in the Holocaust. It's a subject that my family rarely speaks of. However, it is present as an undercurrent—from the number tattooed on my uncle's arm, to the stories told by my cousin, to the box of photos of family members who look vaguely like me but whom I will never have the chance to meet and get to know. Writing this piece was an opportunity to give voice to something unspoken and to show how the effects of such a massive tragedy resonates through generations and, at the same time, transcends race, social class, nationality, etc." At the time of this writing, Jan was a marketing and events director in the fashion, sports, and entertainment industries. She was also the co-owner of a lifestyle company and online snowboard shop for women.

This monologue is taken from a play written as part of a cluster entitled The Art of Memory, *in response to a commission from the Jewish Museum of New York City, where it was ultimately performed (p. 36).*

Hidden Child
Jan Kodadek

(CHANA, a Jewish woman in her 50s, and her teenaged son DAVID, are in the attic of their house, with a box of old photos that DAVID has never seen before. He caught her looking through them and finds one of a boy—her brother—who looks like himself. She tries to tell him why she has kept her past a secret.)

CHANA

I had a pretty happy childhood in Antwerp; until one day Gestapo officers hung posters up saying that every Jew had to go to the synagogue and register. Once we got to the synagogue, we were loaded into cattle cars. My mother, father, brother, and grandmother were in the car with me. *(It's hard for her to continue.)* The train stopped after three days, and we were greeted by German shepherd dogs and SS guards yelling: "*Mach schnell, mach schnell*." *(Pause)* I never wanted to tell you all this. *(She covers her mouth with a tissue; he takes her hand to encourage her.)* The SS guards separated the men to one side. My dad and my brother were on that line. They were made to take their clothes off. Again the Nazis separated us. My mother and I were on the right line; my grandma was on the left line. *(Pause)* They shaved my hair off and took my jewelry; then they gave me a striped uniform which didn't fit me. *(Pause)* They tattooed a number onto my arm. *(DAVID reaches for her arm, but she yanks it away.)* I had it removed. *(Silence)* I was lucky because they put me in a bunker with my mother. We both had jobs in the laundry, and somehow she got word to my brother about where we worked. *(Pause)* He was your age. *(Swallows hard)* He would sneak to the laundry and bring us an extra blanket, or a few slices of bread. *(She tries to hold back a flood of emotion.)* I don't want to go on. *(DAVID puts his arm around her—urges her.)* My mother got sick with typhus. She had a fever, but she kept going to work because if she didn't they would have killed her anyway. *(Long pause)* I woke up one day, and she was dead. *(She looks right at DAVID.)* I took her blanket and shoes before someone else could.

Robert (Bobby) Lopez

I have known Bobby since he was about ten years old. He was one of the first young people I coached when I left New York University and began to develop this method for younger learners, under the aegis of the Children's Aid Society in Greenwich Village. Although we initially used existing musicals to work on the development of "voicing" and social skills, once the agency agreed to my creating original work and bringing a more culturally diverse group of learners from their other neighborhood centers into the mix, the nature of the experience changed completely. Bobby was already a gifted pianist when I first met him, a loner who was chronologically younger than his unusually adult intellect and artistic ability would indicate. Though he could comfortably speak and sing in front of others, he was less comfortable expressing his emotions. As a way to get him writing within his comfort zone, I offered Bobby the opportunity to write underscoring and lyrics for the clusters of original plays that were being written by the other members of the teen workshop. Having heard him play, it was no surprise that the music he composed for us was extraordinary, but the lyrics that emerged were also prodigious—witty, poetic, provocative, and profound. Bobby went on to write scores for many clusters of plays in which he also performed with greater and greater depth of feeling. After graduating from Yale, Bobby took several FYV master classes, wrote music for our Main Stage productions, and was eventually selected to participate in the prestigious BMI Musical Theatre workshop. The piece that he developed there, Avenue Q, *went on to win him a Tony Award!* "The acting training I received from Gail continues to be a part of the way I try to get into a character's head as I'm writing. I'd done a lot of creative writing [as a child], but never really put music and words together. And the practical experience of writing so much theater music, and getting to see it performed at such an early age, was invaluable. My writing has changed a great deal over the years, as have I, but the groundwork was laid back then, very soundly. The piece in this collection was the first time I ever tackled the subject of growing up—a theme I kept exploring in college in another musical, and then in Avenue Q. The lesson is always that you're never done growing up, never done learning—and it is nice to discover in rereading this piece now, *almost twenty years later, that the lesson still holds true. I was amazed that the image of the 'thousands of tiny little patterns that the branches and leaves of a tree make' was something I had been planning on trying to sneak into my next show, in the final number! Uncanny!" This monologue is from the one play that Bobby wrote, early on in his tenure in the FYV workshops; it deals with a very young couple who have become old before their time.*

This monologue was written as part of a cluster of ten plays that dealt with growing up.

I Want My Mommy
Robert (Bobby) Lopez

(PATTY is a 16-year-old who has recently married and moved in with her 16-year-old boyfriend, against their parents' wishes. Here she tells a friend who has come to see them in their tiny, half-empty apartment, why she did it.)

PATTY

I didn't really *want* to leave them. I loved my parents … and they loved me. *(Pause)* They actually always pampered me. I got whatever I wanted—toys when I was little, clothes and lessons when I got older, and always love and affection. *(Bittersweet smile)* I was really happy … until I began to notice things. Not ugly things—beautiful things. Things like the thousands of tiny little patterns that the branches and leaves of a tree make when you look up at the sky. *(Her friend looks perplexed.)* I noticed those kinds of things while I walked home from school, and then I would get home. *(No response)* I realized that I was always happier outside of my home than inside; because nothing there really belonged to me. *(No response)* That's the way my parents acted. When they said things like: "Did you practice your violin?" it sounded like: "Did you practice *my* violin?" And whenever I cut loose, or got in trouble, or let my hair down, they were always reminding me that *they* were in charge. Everything I had was purchased with *their* money. *(Silence)* There's no beauty in things that don't belong to you. When you owe what you have to someone else, it loses its value. Do you understand? *(Her friend shrugs.)* The only time that I ever really felt free was with Charles. *(Smiles)* With Charles, I could walk for miles and not say a thing and still know what he was thinking. With Charles, there was no obligation ... except to love him. *(Smile fades)* When I told my parents we were getting married, they got really upset; they thought they'd failed in bringing me up, somehow. But I told them that as much as I loved them and appreciated all that they'd given me, I needed to live with Charles for awhile. *(Hears herself)* I mean, *forever.*

Lucy Matos

Lucy took her first FYV workshop on the recommendation of the arts coordinator for the district in which her elementary school was based. Lucy was both founder and principal of her school and was seeking a way to give everyone on her small fractious faculty a shared experience and a shared language. Her hope was to unify their vision and their energy. She decided to take the training with another group first, so that she would know exactly what they would be getting into! Although Lucy was game for this new challenge, she found herself bravely confronting several obstacles. One was a long-standing anxiety about expressing herself on paper. Lucy had grown up in a Spanish-speaking household and, even after attending college and graduate school, she still mistrusted her own abilities with the language. This is a syndrome that I've encountered with many people from bilingual homes, and the FYV methodology has been unfailingly successful at helping to provide "ownership" of a language that still feels like it's only being borrowed. Lucy's first attempt at a play yielded a creative but rather impenetrable monologue. She also anguished about her ability to memorize material, and working on her monologue each week proved to be more stressful for her than running a school! However, she finally got through the entire piece, and by the time the final performance of the plays rolled around, she turned in one of the most authentic and riveting performances of the evening. When she took the training again with her staff, the acting work came quite naturally to her, and she was now able to write a complete two-character play. And when she took it again for a third time with the faculty of Bank Street College, where she had attended graduate school, she produced this little jewel of a play. After many rewrites, which were designed to help her say exactly what she meant in English, the play earned her a rousing ovation in final performance. For Lucy, "The characters became a part of my psyche. When I revised and revised, it was their voices I heard in my head. Find Your Voice is a process that I've internalized. It is alive, and the learned skills have become a habit. Revision is a necessary and important part of my current work; FYV was my boot camp." Lucy went on to join the board of FYV, Inc., and is one of the educators whose profile is featured in the Find Your Voice book. At the time of this writing she was serving as coach/facilitator for the New School Intensive, under the umbrella of the Leadership Academy, in New York City.

Lucy wrote this play (p. 37) during her third FYV Training. It was in response to a photograph of a used tea bag, for a cluster entitled Offerings.

Safety Net
Lucy Matos

Characters: ROSARIO   Latina, 40s
               CARMELA   Latina, Puerto Rican-born, 70s

AT RISE: ROSARIO enters her mother's bedroom carrying a cup of hot tea.

ROSARIO: Mama, here's your tea. *(CARMELA does not respond.)* Hot, three sugars, just the way you like it.
CARMELA: *(Pause)* Why are you bringing me tea?
ROSARIO: Because I know you like tea first thing in the morning! *(No response)* And I wanted to do something nice for you; after last night. *(Puts tea down)* Mom, you did a great job organizing Poppy's memorial. It was beautiful ... he would have loved it.
CARMELA: *(She nods.)* Your father loved his family and friends. I'm glad you liked what I planned. *(Pause)* I could have used more of your help. *(No response)* In the past couple of weeks, you've been unavailable.
ROSARIO: Unavailable?
CARMELA: What's going on with you?
ROSARIO: Nothing is going on.
CARMELA: I know you, and I know when something is going on.
ROSARIO: *(She sits.)* I was waiting until Poppy's memorial was over to tell you.
CARMELA: Tell me what?
ROSARIO: *(Pause)* That I'm leaving New York in a couple of days; I've accepted a job.

CARMELA: How long have you been planning this?

ROSARIO: For a while.

CARMELA: All along, I thought you were grieving your father; instead, you were planning your escape.

ROSARIO: Just because I've decided to move doesn't mean I'm not grieving. It doesn't mean I no longer care about him.

CARMELA: And what about *me*? How much do you care about what happens to *me*?

ROSARIO: I care enough to spend time shopping for your favorite books, and lotto tickets. I care enough to spend sleepless nights thinking about how I will support your interests long distance. *(Pause)* Just the other day you said you still had a lot of living to do; I have a lot of living to do too.

CARMELA: Well, it appears you have been preparing. *(Folds her hands in her lap)* Tell me more about this job; I don't even know where you're going.

ROSARIO: I'm going to Stanford.

CARMELA: Connecticut?

ROSARIO: *Stan*ford in California.

CARMELA: How many miles away from New York is that?

ROSARIO: *(Pause)* About three thousand.

CARMELA: Why can't you get a position at NYU, or Columbia, or somewhere in New Jersey?

ROSARIO: I don't want to work in New York or New Jersey; I want to return to Stanford.

CARMELA: I don't understand what "return to Stanford" means. You were there once; why do you have to move so far away again?

ROSARIO: *(Pause)* I can't explain it; it's just something I have to do. *(Pause)* It's time for me to move on, Mama.

CARMELA: "Move on"! You sound like you're quitting a job. How about a letter of resignation: "Dear Mom, I am leaving New York. I am no longer your child. Your loving daughter, Rosario."

ROSARIO: What do you want from me? I've told you my plans.

CARMELA: No ... you've told me you're leaving. You haven't told me your plans—what do you expect from this move?

ROSARIO: I'm going to Stanford to write my book, a book that I started ten years ago. I never got past the first chapter. My dream is to finish this time.

CARMELA: So, my biggest fear has come true.

ROSARIO: What's that?

CARMELA: That I will die alone.

ROSARIO: My leaving doesn't mean that you'll die alone.

CARMELA: How will I continue to live without you? *(Hard to say)* You've always been my safety net. The minute you were born, I knew I would be safe as long as I had you to take care of me.

ROSARIO: You've been my safety net too. *(Pause)* Now, I have to find out if I can balance life *without* the net.

CARMELA: Why can't you find that out without leaving?

ROSARIO: The temptation to depend on you is too great.

CARMELA: That's what mothers and daughters do; they depend on each other. *(Growing angrier)* Why are you abandoning the natural order of things?

ROSARIO: *(Meeting her rising frustration)* I could never abandon you or what you've taught me, but I have to go and try out all of the theories I have about the world ... and I have to do it without you.

CARMELA: I feel left out.

ROSARIO: *(Reaching for her hand)* "It's time for you to get out from behind the curtain"; those were your words. *(No response)* Remember when you told me to stop letting others take credit for my work, my ideas? You taught me to have strong convictions, to work hard, and to love when it's not easy to love; and that is why I have to go.

CARMELA: *(Pulling away)* Let's not argue. We'll think about it some more; tomorrow, when I'm less tired and you're calmer, we'll make a decision.

ROSARIO: *(Rising)* There is no *we* ... *I've* made my decision. I am very calm and very sure this is what I want. *(Squats beside her)* Mama, you're part of me the way I'm part of you. Every time I speak, or make a choice, *you* are a part of that.

CARMELA: *(Turns away)* It was bound to happen.

ROSARIO: What?

CARMELA: That some day you would need something more than what I had to offer.

ROSARIO: But I do need something more from you; I need your blessing to go forward. I want to discover and conquer the unknown parts of *me.*

CARMELA: *(Closes her eyes)* Rosario, you are exhausting me. It's very simple; I am your mother. I want you by my side until the day I take my last breath. *(Looks into her eyes)* Can you promise me that you'll be there at the end?

ROSARIO: *(Returning her gaze)* Of course I'll be there at the end.

CARMELA: Even if you are a million miles away?

ROSARIO: Even if I am a million miles away.

CARMELA: *(Pause)* Maybe I should go with you.

ROSARIO: *(Jumps up)* You can't go with me; this is *my* journey! Now, do I have your blessing?

CARMELA: This is very hard for me. *(She takes the cup of tea and sips.)* Agh. This tea is cold—

ROSARIO: Mom, I need an answer. *(Silence)* I need to know that you'll be okay with my going.

CARMELA: *(Pushes the tea towards ROSARIO)* Make some more tea, the way Poppy used to, and then I'll listen. Okay? *(ROSARIO reaches for the cup, and CARMELA takes her hand.)* Did I tell you your cousin is coming over on Saturday? *(No answer)* She would love to see you. I hope you're not leaving this Saturday.

BLACKOUT

Daniel Missale

Dan Missale took the FYV training once, during his senior year at the high school where we were in residence. The development of this piece is thoroughly outlined in the Find Your Voice *book and represents a journey toward self-awareness, as well as a journey toward craft. The free-write, treatment, and first draft can be read on p. 20. Dan went on to attend Antioch College, and at the time of this writing was teaching in Poland.*

This, Dan's first play, was written for part of a cluster entitled Timepieces, *in response to a photograph of a timepiece reflecting clouds.*

The Only Drug
Daniel Missale

Characters: PUCK Male, Caucasian American, 17
WILL Male, Caucasian American, 29

(PUCK and WILL are sitting in the living room. They are getting ready to go out to their neighborhood pub. WILL opens up a bag of coke. PUCK is watching him.)

PUCK: I need to talk to you.
WILL: Hang on. I want to fuel up before we go to the pub.
PUCK: That's what I need to talk to you about.
WILL: What?
PUCK: You've been hitting it pretty hard lately. I think you should take it easy.
WILL: Okay, "Dad."
PUCK: I'm serious. You need to chill with that stuff tonight. I don't want to have to carry you home, like last night.
WILL: Worry about your own life, and stop worrying about mine.
PUCK: I'm your brother ... your life is my life.
WILL: That's so adorable.
PUCK: I'm being serious.
WILL: Don't take me so seriously.

PUCK: Stop avoiding the issue.

WILL: What issue?

PUCK: That I'm younger than you, but I have to be your parent.

WILL: You're a parent to me? Who finished raising you, and never complained about it?

PUCK: I know ... and I'm thankful for—

WILL: Then stop giving me grief.

PUCK: I just don't want you to be like Dad; turning to some drug when things are tough.

WILL: That's what you think I do?

PUCK: Yes!

WILL: You don't know what you're talking—

PUCK: *(Snaps)* Ever since you got that new boss, you've been drinking all the time ... *(He points to the coke.)* And now you're doing that shit.

WILL: I'm not Dad.

PUCK: I don't want us to be like him.

WILL: It's your choice what to make of yourself. Don't worry about what other people's affect on you will be. The sooner you understand that, the sooner you'll be at ease. *(WILL snorts another line. PUCK stops him.)*

PUCK: How can I be at ease? I need you to be there for me. I need a brother to look up to.

WILL: I'm not going anywhere. I'm always here for you; you can look up to me.

PUCK: Look at what I'm looking up to ... a coke addict and an alcoholic. And I see myself becoming the same.

WILL: Meaning?

PUCK: I notice myself drinking a lot for no reason at all.

WILL: And you blame me for that?

PUCK: My friends joke around about me becoming an eighteen-year-old alcoholic, and it was funny at first. But it's not a joke anymore, it's weighing me down. And I don't want to be weighed down. I want to do stuff with my life. Time is moving on. I want to go to college; I don't want to flunk out of life. *(Silence)* I tried some of your coke last week.

WILL: You did what?

PUCK: Coke, blow, nose candy —

WILL: *(Snaps)* I know what you mean.

PUCK: All of the shit I'm talking to you about now, it just went away. It felt amazing. I finally felt good about me.

WILL: There isn't anything wrong with you.

PUCK: I'm getting sucked into your lifestyle.

WILL: I never said, "Hey, this stuff is great. Try it."

PUCK: That's bullshit.

WILL: What?

PUCK: I said that's bullshit! I see you do things, and then I want to do them too. You don't have to say anything. *(PUCK picks up the bag of coke.)* This shit is gonna kill us.

WILL: *(Tries to get bag of coke)* What the hell do you want from me?

PUCK: I want you to be an older brother who cares about me.

WILL: I care about you.

PUCK: If you cared about me, you'd stop me. *(PUCK spreads the coke on the table and tries to snort some.)*

WILL: Stop it! *(WILL pulls PUCK'S head up.)* I said stop it! This stuff is expensive.

PUCK: *(PUCK throws the rest of it at WILL. WILL drops to the floor and struggles with the bag, trying to scoop up the remaining coke.)* That shit is all you care about.

WILL: I don't know what to tell you.

PUCK: Tell me that you're going to stop. I haven't had a parent for five years. I need you to really be a father to me now.

WILL: I can't do that.

PUCK: Why? *(Silence)* Why can't you?

WILL: Cause I'm not your fuckin' father. Your father left you, and your mother gave up on you. And they left me, only an eighteen-year-old kid myself, to raise my little brother. I handled it the best I could.

PUCK: Your best wasn't good enough. *(PUCK rises, starts to leave.)*

WILL: You're gonna leave me now too? *(He grabs him.)* Where you gonna go? *(Silence)* We need each other, brother. *(WILL grabs a couple of beers and holds one out to PUCK.)* Here, have a beer. *(Pause, puts his arm around PUCK.)* C'mon, we won't go to the pub tonight. *(He pushes the beer into PUCK'S hand)* Alcohol … it's the number-one drug prevention in the world! *(WILL smiles at PUCK. PUCK does not smile back. PUCK takes the beer, hesitates, then drinks it.)*

BLACKOUT

Gail Noppe-Brandon

It is probably apparent from the volume of my output that one of the through lines over the past twenty years of workshops has been me! I have had a love affair with words since I was old enough to write poetry by flashlight under my covers at night. But it's not the words I love as much as the stories that they tell and what these stories reveal about the storyteller. Both my grandfather and mother were great "tellers," and I follow in their tradition. I also love to listen to stories, and it has been my joy and honor to have been blessed with the privilege of midwifing so many stories into being. What follows are pieces I wrote in response to diverse triggers, which knocked on various doors of my imagination. I continue to write daily.

The following monologue is from the first musical commissioned by FYV. It was itself a cluster, featuring the sung and spoken stories based on the accounts of five formerly homeless people and five volunteer participants of a Habitat for Humanity building project (p. 32).

Building
Gail Noppe-Brandon

(LARRY, a formerly homeless African-American man in his 30s, vies to be selected for a Habitat Housing project, in which he'd have to do two years of sweat equity to earn a home. He explains how he ended up on the streets, how he got rehabilitated, and why he deserves to be selected for this program.)

157

LARRY

I've actually worked all my life ... I just had the wrong attitude about it. I thought people who worked for a living were *suckers*. See, my father was a Princeton graduate; but back then he could only get work as a janitor ... a janitor, for god's sake. *(He studies the faces of the interviewers.) He* turned to the church, but *my* role models were the dealers and pimps; they were big earners so they got everyone's respect. *(With some bitterness)* The local *gangsta* liked using us teens because we were in and out of juvie so fast, it kept his training costs low. I dealt all the way through high school ... and then college ... and then in the service too. It was the American way! *(Silence)* When I got out of the service, I became a corrections officer. I dealt to other cops, even to the lawyers. Business was booming until they started that random drug testing program, then I quit and trained to do EMS work. I did the job high for five years—because it was very stressful. *(Shakes his head)* I was saving people's lives and putting them in danger at the same time. *(Looking at the floor)* I got so dissipated from the drugs. I had two kids, and no relationships to go with them, because all of my women eventually left me. My own sister threw me out on Christmas Eve ... Christmas Eve, for god's sake. *(Pauses to collect himself)* I started sleeping in empty cars and abandoned buildings. At that point, my habit was fifteen hundred dollars a day. The more I did, the more I needed to do. I couldn't even stay in detox; I just went there to eat or sleep. *(Looks at interviewers)* My parents didn't want to see me. So, cold as it was, I slept in the parks. *(Hard to say)* One night a guy came over to me and said: "Hey, man, I've been watching you. You don't have to live this way." He gave me the address of a shelter. A shelter. *(Sitting up straighter)* I was an educated man ... I had no business with a shelter. That's when I really saw myself—how low I'd fallen. *(Tries to continue)* I started going to Narcotics Anonymous. At first I only went for the free donuts! When I saw how much those people wanted to help themselves, I agreed to go to a rehab program upstate. Eventually, I joined the staff there. *(Looking right into their eyes)* I had been drugging for *ten* years by then—my whole young life. I became a counselor because I was tired of the hurting side ... I wanted to be on the helping side. *(Lifting his chin up)* I did my time. I got my life back. I got my kids back. *(Pause)* I even started going to church.

> *This scene is from a longer work that was commissioned for the* St. Nicola
> Cycle: *a pair of plays suggested by a photograph of a beam of light across
> an old church (p. 38), and based on a story in the newspaper.*

Double-Cross
Gail Noppe-Brandon

Characters: PACO   Latino, late 20s
              MAG   Female, Caucasian, 40s, a nun

*AT RISE: A convent in the Cuban section of Washington Heights. PACO,
who raped SISTER MARGARET (MAG) several days ago, reappears
seemingly from out of nowhere—MAG jumps.*

PACO: *(Trying to keep her quiet)* Mi Hermana ... shh.

MAG: I'll scream ... *(He crosses to MAG, kneels and takes her hand gently.
At first she tries to pull away, but he quiets her, assures her. It is clear
that he means her no harm whatsoever.)*

PACO: No, no, no ... don't run away. I won't hurt you ever again. *(The
tug-of-war continues; she breaks free.)*

MAG: How do you dare to come back here?

PACO: *(She stands apart from him, like a scared animal. He assumes a
supplicant position.)* I risked everything to come and beg you to
forgive me.

MAG: How do you even look at me now?

PACO: *(Immediately drops his gaze to the floor)* Your face is my
salvation.

MAG: Is that why you ravaged me from behind ... so you wouldn't .
see my face?

PACO: No. *(Pause)* That wasn't me.

MAG: Even with your hands pressed over my eyes, I knew it was you.

PACO: It wasn't really me.

MAG: It was you! You had the key; you knew the schedule ... you knew
I'd be alone—

PACO: Listen—

MAG: You haven't been showing up to clean here; you've been hiding
in your shame.

PACO: I've been sick—

MAG: Because it was you.

PACO: It was the devil, Sister.

MAG: Paco, it was you.

PACO: It was my father's devil.

MAG: Get out!

PACO: You see? My mother was right.

MAG: Now you drag in her good name? Have you no shame at all?

PACO: Sister, I have nothing but shame.

MAG: Then have some respect for the dead.

PACO: She's not dead. *(MAG is silent.)* She's somewhere in Arizona, hiding from my dad.

MAG: Why are you lying again? She died in childbirth; everyone knows that.

PACO: That's only what he told them. They had a fight … he beat her. She lost the baby … then she left. *(Silence)* You are the only mother that I've ever really known.

MAG: Which makes what you did to me all the more vile.

PACO: Yes. That's why she didn't take me; I had his devil inside.

MAG: Don't be absurd; you were just a child.

PACO: My mother could see things. She saw his devil in me.

MAG: *(Pause)* You've hurt someone before?

PACO: Yes. *(Pause)* I hurt her. *(Silence)* She pushed for three days to birth me; I almost ripped her in two.

MAG: Childbirth is painful; all mothers experience pain.

PACO: *(A painful admission)* But she has never forgiven … all these years and not one card.

MAG: *(Pause)* Maybe she left you behind so he wouldn't come after her; so he would still have something.

PACO: He looks at me and sees her. *(Feeling his face)* I used to resemble my mother … before he broke my jaw.

MAG: *(Pause)* You said you got into a fight at school. How come you didn't tell me the truth?

PACO: Cause he would have shot me dead. Now it's only his to tell—in confession, on his knees.

MAG: I could have helped you.

PACO: You did help me. You gave me a job so I could buy my way out of his life. *(Pause)* You were my angel on earth.

MAG: *(Long pause)* Until last month. *(He looks at her, waits.)* When I told you Sam was coming back.

PACO: Sister, that was wrong.

MAG: You knew this job wasn't permanent.

PACO: Two years is a very long time; people get attached.

MAG: That's why we gave you notice so far in advance.

PACO: *(Vehemently)* Notice to leave my home? This is like home to me here!

MAG: Your temper is always flaring—even now when you try to repent—

PACO: *(He reels himself back in; contrite, apologetic, points to her chair.)* Sister, you taught me to read in that chair. This church is like my house.

MAG: This is God's house, Paco. *(PACO hangs his head.)* This is a sacred place.

PACO: *(Pause, he's afraid of the answer.)* Am I going to burn in hell?

MAG: I don't determine your fate.

PACO: But you can forgive me. Can't you? *(Silence)* You always taught me to forgive.

MAG: *(Pause, a new and disturbing idea)* Maybe there are some things that can't be forgiven.

PACO: *(Dropping to his knees, in true agony) Madre mia*, please don't say that! *(Trying to straightjacket his own terror, rocking back and forth)* I feel so sick all the time. I'm drowning in my own sweat. *(Crawling to her)* You have to help me, please. Demons are flying over my bed—banging into the walls and screeching in my ears. All night I hide in my blanket, like a baby afraid of the dark. I see myself in hell with them, being torn apart, like I tore her … and you. *(Pulling at his own hair)* Tearing, tearing, all night long. *(Whispering—to MAG)* Mother, I'm so ashamed now. I don't want to burn in hell. Please, help me. I don't sleep anymore. I'm dying with my eyes open wide … *(A truth)* You know how much I love you; I have loved you all of my life. *(Crawling to her again)* Take this devil out of me … *(Clutching her)* I'm so sorry that I hurt you. Please! I'm so sorry …

please! *(Hesitantly, she places her hand on the top of his head, and he grows still and quiet. After a long silence, softly)* Bless you, Mother.

MAG: *Sister.* I am Sister Margaret.

PACO: Thank you for saving my soul.

MAG: Don't confuse me with God; I cannot save souls.

PACO: I will make this up to you, this terrible thing that I did. We will beat his devil together—it will never hurt you again. I will be so kind, and then my kindness will help you forget—

MAG: Even if I forgive you, there's no way I will ever forget.

PACO: It was just a black, black night. That night is behind us now.

MAG: It will never be behind us. *(Pause, she moves away.)* The morning brought something new.

PACO: *(Pause)* What? What did the morning bring? *(Silence)* What?

MAG: *(Barely able to say it)* A baby.

PACO: *(After a long, stunned silence)* You're pregnant? *(She nods.)* How can that be? You're too old.

MAG: *(Stricken)* Apparently not old enough—

PACO: *(Almost proudly)* A baby? I made a baby?

MAG: How dare you stand there and boast ...?

PACO: I know it was not from an act of love, but I do love you—I do. And I am going to love our baby too. *(He comes to her, takes her hand again, and kisses it.)* Marry me, Sister. Marry me ... I want to marry you. *(She removes it quickly.)*

MAG: Don't you sully me twice, Paco. I'm a nun.

PACO: Yes, I know. It's a miracle!

MAG: *(She slaps him hard across the face.)* What happened was a crime and a sin. You are a sinner. Do you hear me? You have sinned! *(He recoils and cowers on the floor, in true terror of further abuse, and of his own fate. He whimpers. She sees this, and after a moment, she goes to him. She sits and takes him in to her arms, holds him as in the Pieta. She rocks him. They cling to each other. After a moment)* Oh, Paquito. I'm so afraid.

PACO: *(Soothing her now)* No, no, no. Don't be afraid; I'm not afraid any more. Just now I saw my devil leave. He got up and left—he did. I only needed someone to love. And I will worship you—all of the kindness you gave me will come back to you now. I will take care of you, Sister; you and our baby too. Without my father's devil, I am a very tender man. I am never going to leave your side. I will never leave you alone. This has healed me, Sister; you are my angel-on-earth!

MAG: *(MARGARET breaks down and let's herself be held.)* Oh God!

PACO: *(Rocking her)* I will bring you yellow roses and protect you for the rest of your life. We are family now. Please don't cry anymore. *(He kisses her softly on the lips. SISTER UNA appears suddenly and witnesses this kiss.)*

BLACKOUT

This monologue (p. 31) is from the longer work that was commissioned for the St. Nicola Cycle: *a pair of plays suggested by a photograph of a beam of light across an old church.*

Double-Cross
Gail Noppe-Brandon

(SISTER MARGARET, a Caucasian nun in her 40s, is pregnant as a result of being raped by a young man who was schooled in their church. She confesses to her superior, SISTER UNA, that she does not want to raise the child. SISTER UNA, a Caucasian nun in her 60s, tries to persuade MAG to keep the baby by admitting to her own frustrated desires.)

UNA

I have always wanted a child. *(More honest and intimate than she's ever been)* This was the hardest part of my decision to take the vows. *(Pause)* Don't misunderstand ... you know I love my work. And I love my God. But I'm also a woman; I yearned to hold a baby in my arms. Even though we run a nursery school, at the end of the day I have to let them go. If I'm lucky, I get Christmas cards for a few years after they leave. I don't choose their clothes, or bathe them, or cook their favorite food; I don't tuck them in bed or sit up with them when they're sick ... I'll never see a smaller, newer version of myself. *(Pause)* I have not mothered, Sister. Not in the truest sense. *(Her pain is apparent; MAG reaches out and touches her hand.)* I want to tell you something that I've never said out loud. *(Pause, this is difficult.)* When I went through my changes and I knew the chance to make a child was gone, I cried every night in my bed. I felt all of my unborn children leak out with every tear. The crying went on for years; I thought I'd lose my mind. Every time I closed my eyes, I would dream the very same dream ... *(She closes her eyes to conjure it.)* I was all dressed in white, in a bright white room; a child's nursery. I'd see a cradle wrapped in white netting, swaying in the sun. Then I'd hear a baby cry, and I'd reach out my hands. But I couldn't get in through the netting, even though I knew the baby was mine. It was so vivid; I could even smell the lotion on its head. I felt it needing me desperately, crying out more and more, but I couldn't get into the cradle or hold it in my arms. Never once, in all those years, did I get to pick that baby up. *(MAG holds UNA, comforts her.)* I prayed to God to stop my pain—to stop that baby dream. And then I saw that God was helping me say good-bye. *(Pause)* I was grieving for that little baby, the child I would never know. *(She looks MAG in the eyes.)* I have accepted that I won't have *my* child ... but we can still have *yours. (MAG tries to turn away, but UNA holds her.)* God has answered my prayer through this boy, this man, who we all but raised in the church. We gave him the only love he ever really had. And now, we have the only thing we couldn't give ourselves.

The next two scenes (p. 34) are from a play that was commissioned for the Four Views With A Room *cluster, written in response to Andrea Sperling's photograph on the cover of this book.*

The Last Chair
Gail Noppe-Brandon

Characters: LILY   Female, Jewish, 70s, immigrated from
                         Russia as a child
             PAUL   Male, 40s

AT RISE: LILY's apartment has been emptied into a moving van, and she sits in the last piece of furniture left, holding a small houseplant, wearing a robe. PAUL, her son, is moving her—against her will—into a home for seniors. In this scene, he tries to persuade her to get dressed and leave with him.

PAUL: *(Gently)* Mama, the man's waiting. *(No response)* Mom, you've been sitting on that chair for hours. What are you waiting for?

LILY: Leah. *(No response)* Your sister.

PAUL: Yes, Ma, I know who Leah is!

LILY: She's never here.

PAUL: That's because she lives in San Francisco.

LILY: What time will she be here?

PAUL: *(After a pause, he kneels beside her, takes her hand.)* Leah's not coming, Mama. But *I'm* here with you, okay? *(He kisses her hand.)*

LILY: *(She pats his head. There is no apparent sign of tenderness on her face.)* You're a good boy.

PAUL: Come. Let's get the rest of this stuff packed up. It's no fun sitting around in an empty room.

LILY: I'm hungry.

PAUL: Good, because they're going to have lunch waiting for you. A *hot* lunch, so let's finish up now. *(He rises, tries to take the plant from her; she resists.)* Did you want to take this with you, for your new room?

LILY: You take it.

PAUL: Take it where, Ma?

LILY: To Connecticut.

PAUL: Thanks, Mom, but I have two wooded acres around my house—I don't need to take your little plant!

LILY: Take care of it for me.

PAUL: We threw out at least *twenty* apple- and grapefruit-seed plants today; what's so special about this one?

LILY: This one died. *(He stares at her, not comprehending.)* I put it in the transom and forgot about it. For a month, I didn't water it. *(She holds it up to him.)* It had no leaves. The dirt was like rock. *(She returns it to her lap.)* It came back.

PAUL: You always had a way with these things. Remember I called you "Mama Apple-Seed"? *(He laughs, looking for connection.)*

LILY: You were a good little helper. *(Silence)* Play a song for me, Paul. Play that *Fur Elise.*

PAUL: Play on what? *(He is stunned.)* You sold the piano years ago, Mama. To that professor on the Upper West Side.

LILY: I should never have done that.

PAUL: You got a very good price, as I recall. Much more than it was worth!

LILY: I miss it.

PAUL: You don't even play, Mama!

LILY: *(Pause)* I feel like I do. *(He smiles.)* I'm so thirsty.

PAUL: The glasses are packed already; we'll get you something on the way.

LILY: I need a glass of tea.

PAUL: Okay. Let's hurry and pack your little suitcase; we'll get whatever you want on the road.

LILY: I want to make a glass of tea. In my own kettle.

PAUL: They already took the kettle, Ma.

LILY: They stole my kettle?

PAUL: No, they didn't *steal* it. They packed it up. You sat here watching them.

LILY: *(Pause, she scratches at the skin on her arms.)* I'm parched. I can hardly swallow.

PAUL: All right, Mama. I'll run down to the deli and get you some tea.

LILY: Red Rose.

PAUL: One Red Rose. Coming right up! *(He grabs a jacket.)* I'll go get you the tea, and you go in and get dressed—so the man can come up and get this last chair. Okay?

LILY: Lemon.

PAUL: Pardon?

LILY: In the tea.

PAUL: Of course lemon! No sugar, no honey. Right?

LILY: Nice and dark.

PAUL: Nice and dark! You go get dressed now.

LILY: Let him leave the tea bag in the cup.

PAUL: In the cup; you got it! *(Pause)* Your clothes are hanging on the bathroom door. Can you manage alone?

LILY: Where's my kettle?

PAUL: *(Pause, her disorientation saddens him.)* I told you, Mama, it was packed up with all the other kitchen stuff. *(An angry silence)* The Home will make tea *for* you from now on; I'm sure they have plenty of kettles there.

LILY: It takes years to break in a kettle.

PAUL: *(Patiently)* Ma, you can't take your kettle because they don't allow hot-plates in the rooms. It's too dangerous. You'll have tea in their sitting-room, like a queen! And you'll have *company*; it will be so nice for you.

LILY: I like my *own* things.

PAUL: *(Silence)* I know you do, that's why I already brought some of your other things over there, to warm up your room a little. The photos from your bed table, and your yellow quilt … and the collection of lacquered boxes that we brought you from Russia; it's all waiting for you. You won't even need the kettle.

LILY: Which box is it in?

PAUL: I don't know … one of the kitchen boxes. *(She looks at the pile of boxes that remain.)* It's probably on the truck already.

LILY: Your father picked that kettle for me. When I had influenza. The old one was rusty, so I sent him shopping. He was so proud that he picked one with a pleasant whistle. Some of them can be so shrill. This one is very pleasant.

PAUL: Ma—

LILY: Do you remember how your father drank his tea through a sugar cube?

PAUL: Of course I do!

LILY: You always liked it when he did that. He knew you liked it.

PAUL: I never see that anymore—his old-fashioned ways!

LILY: *(A chastisement)* But he was a modern American businessman, too. He was comfortable in both worlds.

PAUL: *(Pause)* Mama, I looked through your dresses, and I chose the black one with the white polka dots. You always look so pretty in it. Is that one okay? *(No response)* It's laid out with a slip and all that other stuff you women wear. Can you get dressed by yourself? *(No response)* Maybe I should have had Miranda stay and help.

LILY: I don't need her help. That was a waste of your money.

PAUL: You should have let us send her more than once a week—

LILY: She burns my toast.

PAUL: Mama, that toaster of yours was decrepit!

LILY: Where is the toaster?

PAUL: Where it belongs—in the garbage.

LILY: *(Shocked)* Just like that?

PAUL: *(Trying to make her laugh)* It was a cheap, fifteen-year-old model; I didn't think it deserved a burial at sea!

LILY: *(Pause)* Is my tea ready yet?

PAUL: No, Mama, I haven't gone yet! And I'm not going, until you promise me that you'll be all dressed when I get back. Promise?

LILY: I'm tired, Paul.

PAUL: *(Pause)* I know you are, Mama. It's been a long day. I should have asked Miranda to stay and help you.

LILY: She pinches my skin in the zippers; I don't want her here.

PAUL: She's *not* here; I let her go. That's why we made a decision to try the Home—

LILY: I didn't make that decision.

PAUL: *(Pause)* You've had two staph infections this year; they can be fatal.

LILY: I'm an old woman, Paul—everything can be fatal.

PAUL: *(Pause)* You can't keep the place clean—

LILY: No one comes to see it anyway!

PAUL: And you call me and Leah every day, to tell us you're lonely.

LILY: I *am* lonely!

PAUL: *(Tenderly)* Well, you won't be lonely anymore; you'll have people around you. For company.

LILY: Strangers aren't company.

PAUL: Mama, if it was up to me I'd take you in with us—

LILY: *(Jumping on this)* You wouldn't even know I was there!

PAUL: But you've never gotten along with Mara; even on our wedding day you fought with her.

LILY: She insulted me.

PAUL: She put you at a table with all your siblings and cousins, a *family* table.

LILY: *You're* my family.

PAUL: We decided to sit with our school friends.

LILY: She was making a point. Your *wife*. The big-shot doctor.

PAUL: She's been very generous to you. She offered to pay for Miranda, without a moment's hesitation.

LILY: She bought me a stand-in daughter because mine lives on the other side of the country.

PAUL: We were trying to make you comfortable, Ma.

LILY: When you had the measles, I didn't hire a stranger to make you comfortable. I sat up all night with a cool rag. Night after night.

PAUL: Mara and I did that for our children, too. That's what parents do; it's their job!

LILY: *(Pause. She considers this.)* Some job. No retirement benefits.

PAUL: *(Pleasantly surprised at her humor)* That's funny, Ma! *(She doesn't laugh; he kneels beside her again, tenderly.)* Mama, I know this is hard for you. I went to thirteen places; I did a lot of research. This Home, it's really nice. They have a beautiful garden. And they play classical music in the dining room. And it doesn't smell like ammonia. *(Silence)* It's only an hour from the George Washington Bridge; we'll be able to visit every month. *(Sees her shudder)* Leah and I talked this decision over for a long time … it's for your own good. *(LILY turns away.)* Mom, I honestly thing it would ruin my marriage if you came. I have to consider the needs of *my* family too.

LILY: When did *I* stop being your family?

PAUL: I didn't mean it like that.

LILY: *(Pause)* I'm so cold. Why is it so cold in here?

PAUL: Because you're not dressed. Please, go put on your clothes; I'll tell the man he can come up and get this last chair.

LILY: This chair was the *first* piece of furniture your father and I ever bought, when his business took off. Before the Depression. *(Silence)* I like a firm chair.

PAUL: I know.

LILY: Your sister always laughed at me for that. *(Pause)* I knew she was laughing.

PAUL: She was just teasing, Ma.

LILY: *(Pause)* Why didn't she come?

PAUL: I told you, she's on assignment in Australia. But she's flying directly to the Home to see you when she's done there.

LILY: She's always flying around. Like a little bird with no nest.

PAUL: *(Talking to her like a child)* Mama, I'll be back with your tea in five minutes, and I don't want to see you sitting in that chair!

BLACKOUT

The Last Chair
Gail Noppe-Brandon

Characters:	LILY	Female, late 70s
	LEAH	Female, 40s

AT RISE: LILY's apartment has been emptied into a moving van, and she sits in the last piece of furniture left. Her son is moving her—against her will—into a residence for seniors. In this scene, she imagines that her daughter (who is on assignment out of the country) comes to be with her. She makes a final plea to escape the fate of the 'Home.' LILY hears the sound of the front door closing as her son goes out to get her a cup of tea.

LILY: Who's that? *(Silence. Yelling)* DON'T BOTHER PACKING ANYTHING ELSE. I'M NOT MOVING. *(She looks back at her lap. LEAH enters; she is a vision in a bright unnatural red—even her hair. She is in LILY'S mind.)*

LEAH: I can't believe you're still sitting on that hard chair!

LILY: *(LILY looks at her, stunned; she blinks hard.)* Leah?

LEAH: How many days did you sit in that chair, waiting for me to get home from school? It used to be in front of the window. Your window seat!

LILY: I moved it. It was drafty. *(Questioning her reality)* Leah?

LEAH: After all those years, you finally felt the draft?

LILY: I always felt it, but I saw you home safely. Every day. Because you wandered.

LEAH: You also waited there when Paul was out on dates; I guess *he* wandered too!

LILY: I waited for all of you.

LEAH: So when did you move the chair over here?

LILY: When your father was dying.

LEAH: You sat *outside* the door? He wasn't contagious.

170

LILY: He slept a lot.

LEAH: And you just sat out here?

LILY: Leah, it's really you?

LEAH: What were you waiting for, outside his door?

LILY: Pill time. If he took a pill himself, he wouldn't use water. He'd take it dry. He'd choke.

LEAH: You're very vigilant.

LILY: I don't know what you mean.

LEAH: Vigilant. You keep *vigil*.

LILY: Your father never had to live alone. Not one day. He had his mama, and then he had me. He was lucky. He went first.

LEAH: I don't think he considered having cancer very lucky.

LILY: Are you moving back?

LEAH: How can I—there's no furniture left here!

LILY: *(Not humoring her)* Back East.

LEAH: You know I don't like the cold.

LILY: So what, I don't like it either.

LEAH: You were born in Russia; you're supposed to like the cold!

LILY: *(Pause)* How many rooms do you have out there, in California?

LEAH: *(LEAH begins to look through the contents of one of the remaining untaped boxes. She sits on the floor the way a little girl would sit and play.)* Same as the last time you asked. Eight, if you include the terrace.

LILY: That's a lot of rooms.

LEAH: They're small rooms. You'd know that if you'd ever, once, come out to visit me during the last ten years.

LILY: I don't fly.

LEAH: We've been over this ground; there are trains. Mighty nice ones too.

LILY: That would be a whole week on the road.

LEAH: What was your hurry; afraid your chair would get cold?

LILY: I'm a home-body. *(Silence)* I thought you'd be moving back. I always thought you'd be back soon.

LEAH: California is where my work is.

LILY: I didn't think you'd keep it like this; there's a whole country between us.

LEAH: Mama, there's always been a whole country between us.

LILY: *(Taken aback)* I don't know what you're talking about.

LEAH: Yes, you do.

LILY: *(Pause)* This is not what I wanted.

LEAH: What *did* you want?

LILY: *(For a moment she studies LEAH, hovered over the box.)* I wanted you here with me, like you used to be. Playing while I did my chores. You were so quiet.

LEAH: I was quiet because you wouldn't tolerate any noise. *(Silence)* Children need to make noise when they play—how come you never played, Mama?

LILY: I had a lot to do around here: cooking; keeping the place clean.

LEAH: It could have been a little less clean—and a lot more fun.

LILY: Fun is for the circus.

LEAH: How would you know? *(No response)* I could never even get you to go to a movie with me; I always had to go with Pop.

LILY: Your father liked that kind of thing.

LEAH: *Everyone* likes that kind of thing, Ma—that's why they call it "entertainment."

LILY: So I'm a loner. *(Silence. She considers what's been said.)* That would have made you happier? If I gave you *entertainment* now and then?

LEAH: It would have made me happier if you gave me a *hug* now and then.

LILY: *(Bewildered)* I hugged you. *(Silence)* Didn't I?

LEAH: You hugged Paul.

LILY: Babies *need* comfort. You were older. *(Silence)* I would have cuddled you plenty, but you were always so self-sufficient.

LEAH: I was just a kid.

LILY: You should spend time with me as an adult; it would be different.

LEAH: Why? What do you imagine we would do together?

LILY: *(Pause, she thinks about this, envisions it.)* You would tell me all about your adventures; you would make me laugh.

LEAH: It's not easy to make you laugh.

LILY: That's not true. Do you know why your father married me?

LEAH: It must have been your looks.

LILY: *(Correcting her)* It was because I laughed at his jokes.

LEAH: I don't remember you *ever* laughing at his jokes.

LILY: Of course I did.

LEAH: Not one. *(Silence)* You were always aggravated.

LILY: *(Genuinely surprised again)* Aggravated? With who?

LEAH: With all of us. *(Laughs bitterly)* Except Paul; he was too afraid to ask you for anything.

LILY: Don't let him do this.

LEAH: Who?

LILY: Your brother. Paul. *(No response)* He would never do this if *you* told him not to.

LEAH: Paul and I made this decision *together;* it's for your own good.

LILY: That's what I keep hearing—

LEAH: How many nights did you forget to eat your dinner?

LILY: Talk to him. I can't talk to him like I can talk to you.

LEAH: Afraid you'll get angry with him? Maybe hurt *his* feelings?

LILY: No more arguing. There's no time; he'll be back soon. Please, Leah.

LEAH: Please what? What is it you want, Mama?

LILY: I was only a girl when I came to this country. I was young and healthy, and even *then* it was so hard for me. Ripped up like a little plant. Everything unfamiliar—

LEAH: Lots of people move when they're children, younger than you were, and sometimes more than once.

LILY: I can't speak for those children. I can only tell you *my* story. I don't change well, you know that. I made a home here with your father. When he died, I was left alone with a lot of ghosts. I'm an old lady, Leah; don't harden your heart to me.

LEAH: *You* hardened my heart to you, Mama. I can't give back what I never got. You're alone now because all your life you've pushed people away, shut them out.

LILY: I never meant to. *(Silence. She sees that LEAH won't yield.)* You've become so cold, Leah.

LEAH: I'm the woman you made me.

LILY: Is it so important to be right? To serve me justice now?

LEAH: I don't serve justice, Mama; I'm a mere mortal. You always liked your privacy; now you have it.

LILY: More than I wanted.

LEAH: Then don't resist going some place where you won't be so alone.

LILY: I've lived in this brownstone for twenty-five years, Leah. I know which steps creak in the hall. I can find a glass in the cupboard in pitch darkness. I know what time to turn the lights on in the winter, so it *never* gets dark. This is my *home*. I do what I like here, how I like it. I watch my shows, I make my tea. I walk around in my nightgown half the day; and that's no one's business. I want to die in my own home. Is that so much to ask? *(No response)* I'm begging you. Talk to him, Leah—you're the strong one. Please. If I have to be alone, without family, then I want to be alone in my own world.

LEAH: This is not the best spot to create your own world in; the neighborhood has changed.

LILY: *(Pause)* Then I'll come be with you in California. We won't even have to talk; I'll just know you're there.

LEAH: I'm *not* there; I'm out on assignment most of the time.

LILY: *You* have to make time for company too.

LEAH: My work keeps me company.

LILY: Then I'll just stay in my room and wait for you.

LEAH It doesn't have to be that austere. This Home you're going to—they have entertainers that come in, and a library.

LILY: I have my TV and my newspapers.

LEAH: But you don't have a nurse to give you your medication, and you don't have maids to keep the place clean, and you don't have anyone to talk to—

LILY: *(Losing control)* I'm talking to *you,* but you don't hear me!

LEAH: *(Meeting her forcefulness)* Oh, I hear you, Mama; I hear you! You want me to say that I'll scoop you up in my arms and rock you and take care of you, and I can't say that.

LILY: *(She cries.)* PLEASE! I DON'T WANT TO DIE IN A STRANGE PLACE, WITH STRANGERS!

BLACKOUT

174

This monologue is drawn from the previous play.

The Last Chair
Gail Noppe-Brandon

(LILY, who is in her late 70s, is in an empty apartment; all her things have been loaded into a moving van, and she sits in the last piece of furniture left. Her son is moving her—against her will—in to a residence for seniors. In this compilation, she imagines that her daughter (who is on assignment out of the country) comes. She makes a final plea to escape the fate of the "Home.")

LILY

I was only a girl when I came to this country. I was young and healthy, and even then it was so hard for me. Ripped up like a little plant. Everything unfamiliar. I can't speak for other children; I can only tell you my story. I don't change well—you know that. *(Indicates her apartment)* I made a home here with your father. When he died, I was left alone with a lot of ghosts. *(Reaches out to her)* I'm an old lady; don't harden your heart to me. I never meant to shut people out. *(Silence; she sees that LEAH won't yield.)* You've become so cold, Leah. Is it so important to be right? To serve me justice now? *(No response)* I've lived in this brownstone for twenty-five years, Leah. I know which steps creak in the hall. I can find a glass in the cupboard in pitch darkness. I know what time to turn the lights on in the winter, so it never gets dark. This is my home. I do what I like here, how I like it. I watch my shows, I make my tea. I walk round in my nightgown half the day, and that's no one's business. I want to die in my own home. Is that so much to ask? *(No response)* I'm begging you. Talk to him, Leah—you're the strong one. Please. If I have to be alone, without family, than I want to be alone in my own world. *(Silence)* If I can't stay here, then I'll come be with you in California. We don't even have to talk; I'll just know you're there. *(No response)* You need family. You have to make time for company too. If you're working, then I'll just stay in my room and wait for you. I have my TV and my newspapers. *(Losing control)* I'm talking to you, but you don't hear me! *(She cries.)* PLEASE! I DON'T WANT TO DIE IN A STRANGE PLACE, WITH STRANGERS!

This scene is from a memory play commissioned for a cluster (of the same name) which was suggested by the image of a wedding ring.

The Ring
Gail Noppe-Brandon

Characters: MAMA   Female, 60
               LIL   Female, 39

AT RISE: LIL and her MAMA sit facing each other, in the living room of LIL's house on Long Island. LIL stares into space. MAMA watches her. The sun is beginning to come into the room. A clock is ticking.

MAMA: What time does Jill get up?
LIL: Around eight.
MAMA: She's going to be up soon. *(No response)* You going to take her to the nursery school?
LIL: Not today.
MAMA: Tomorrow? *(Silence)* You going to take her to the nursery school tomorrow?
LIL: Take her in what?
MAMA: *(Pause)* You need a new car, I guess. *(Silence)* Maybe you should move back near us, in the city.
LIL: We'll see.
MAMA: *(Pause)* What are you going to tell her?
LIL: What do you think?
MAMA: I mean, how are you going to say it?
LIL: I don't know.
MAMA: You better know soon, Lil.
LIL: Just let me sit here.
MAMA: We've been sitting here all night—morning came anyway.
LIL: Please. Don't yammer at me.
MAMA: I'm trying to be a help.

LIL: You're not.
MAMA: What do you want?
LIL: Peace and quiet.
MAMA: The only one who's got that is Rich.
LIL: Leave it to you to make him sound lucky.
MAMA: Who's going to support you? Who's going to help you raise Jill?
LIL: I'll manage.
MAMA: I'm done raising children, Lil. I'm a tired old lady.
LIL: You always have been, and who asked you anyway?
MAMA: Who then?
LIL: I'll take care of my own kid.
MAMA: And who's going to take care of you?
LIL: Same person who always has—me.
MAMA: And the bills?
LIL: They'll get paid.
MAMA: How?
LIL: I'll get a job.
MAMA: What did he leave you? Anything?
LIL: Whatever it is, it is.
MAMA: A grown man should have life insurance.
LIL: Don't you start.
MAMA: I guess artists don't insure themselves.
LIL: I'll jump out of this chair and strangle you.
MAMA: I'm trying to be a help.
LIL: In my whole lousy life you've never been a help.
MAMA: You called us in the middle of the night, and we came.
LIL: Bully for you.
MAMA: I'm not the one you should be angry at.
LIL: You're exactly the one.
MAMA: I didn't leave you.
LIL: You make it sound deliberate.
MAMA: He drove off the road; he must have been drunk.
LIL: You've never driven in your life, now you're an expert? *(Pause)* He didn't drink. He was just tired.
MAMA: They said there was no other car involved.
LIL: His heart might have failed him.

MAMA: Such a young man?

LIL: His father went at thirty-eight.

MAMA: What if Jill inherits that?

LIL: For God's sake, it was an accident, Ma. *(Pause)* He might have swerved for a deer.

MAMA: A deer? He had obligations more important than a deer.

LIL: You keep this up, I'm going to bust.

MAMA: I'm just upset.

LIL: *You're* upset?

MAMA: My head is pounding; I need a cold cloth.

LIL: This is not about you. Don't get a migraine, because I can't take care of you today. I have enough to take care of.

MAMA: *(Pause)* What are you going to tell her?

LIL: *"Your father's dead."*

MAMA: "Dead"? *(Silence)* She's only four—she's not ready for that word.

LIL: She learned it already.

MAMA: What are you talking about?

LIL: In the country last summer.

MAMA: In the country last summer, what?

LIL: She asked what happens to people when they're dead.

MAMA: What made her ask a thing like that?

LIL: Who knows. Maybe she thought about it after we read *Bambi*; or maybe when that old man Keller down the street died. She liked him.

MAMA: What did you tell her?

LIL: Rich told her that when people die, they come back as something else in nature.

MAMA: What did she say?

LIL: "Like a butterfly?"

MAMA: *(Pause)* You want her to think her father's a butterfly?

LIL: There's worse things for a kid to think, believe me.

MAMA: I'm telling you, use that word and she'll have nightmares for two lifetimes.

LIL: She'll have them anyway. We both will.

MAMA: Just tell her he's not coming home anymore.

LIL: She was the apple of his eye.

MAMA: Kids forget.

LIL: She won't forget so quick.

MAMA: A mother's more important. She has her mother; in a few months she'll stop looking for him.

LIL: I wish I could say the same—

MAMA: You're going to make yourself sick, Lil.

LIL: *(She closes her eyes.)* I am sick.

MAMA: You have to pull yourself together now.

LIL: I'm sick with something I'll never get well from.

MAMA: Don't put that curse on yourself, what's wrong with you? My heart is pounding. *(Silence)* Don't sit there like a zombie. You're not the dead one.

LIL: I can't imagine being deader.

MAMA: Get up, you'll feel better.

LIL: I don't want to feel better. I don't want to feel anything.

MAMA: You have obligations; Jill needs you.

LIL: I'll live for her, not for me.

MAMA: You're young yet, Lil; you'll remarry.

LIL: Christ.

MAMA: You'll take off that ring, and someone will grab you up.

LIL: You're asking for it back?

MAMA: Asking for it back? You'll put it somewhere safe, for Jill.

LIL: It's *my* ring. Rich had it reset for me at Tiffany's. *(Silence)* He's not even gone twenty-four hours, you think that's the end of it?

MAMA: That *is* the end of it, Lil. You have to forget him; it's over.

LIL: It will *never* be over. *(Silence)* This is what you wanted all along, isn't it.

MAMA: Why do you say such things to me? *(Silence)* I liked Rich. *(Silence)* In a few months the crying will stop, you'll see. He was never here anyway. *(Silence)* You'll take the ring off, and you'll find someone else.

LIL: *I don't want someone else.* I just want to be alone with my kid.

MAMA: You will be; that's all he left you.

LIL: That's plenty.

MAMA: Kids go away and forget what you gave them; they're not forever either, Lil.

LIL: Mine will be.

MAMA: Nothing's forever. *(Silence)* I could use some coffee. Did you make any coffee, Lil?

LIL: I don't remember. *(LIL rises.)* I'm going upstairs. I don't want her to come down and see you here yet.

MAMA: Wash your face ... she'll see that you've been crying.

LIL: She better get used to it.

MAMA: *(MAMA rises.)* I'm shaking all over. Where will you tell her?

LIL: I'll take her into my bedroom.

MAMA: Then what?

LIL: Then what? Then I'm going to pull the covers over my head and sleep for twenty years. Maybe when I wake up, he'll be back.

BLACKOUT

This scene (p. 34) is from a play commissioned for the Holding Patterns *cluster, written in response to an image of an airplane in the sky.*

Simulating Emily
Gail Noppe-Brandon

Characters: JOAN *(JO)*   Female, 30s
              EMILY *(EM)*   Female, 30s, very pregnant

AT RISE: EMILY and JOAN are seated in airplane seats, in a tight pool of light; there is the sound of an engine humming. JOAN is accompanying EMILY, who is eight months pregnant, on a trip to help her conquer her fear of flying, when EMILY suddenly starts to experience contractions.

JO: I want you to describe exactly what's going on—in detail.

EM: Can't you ever stop being a journalist?

JO: Can you stop being a pregnant woman?

EM: I'm not a *pregnant woman*; I'm a sculptor. It's possible to be both a mother and an artist, Joan.

JO: Emily—

EM: *(Panting)* No! It's important that you see *me*.

JO: I *do* see you; I see you panting. And I'm envisioning you bleeding and writhing in pain—

EM: I've been writhing in pain since we took off.

JO: That kind of pain I can handle—that kind of pain isn't real.

EM: Like hell it isn't! There were times when I would have chosen death over a pain attack. *(She grimaces.)* I guess you just can't fathom that.

JO: I'm beginning to think I can. *(Reaching for her cell phone)*

EM: NO CALLS. *(Restraining her)* This isn't a game, Joan.

JO: No.

EM: *(Short of breath as she talks)* I've been grounded for fifteen years. *Fifteen years!* I'm not like you, Joan. You're never in your home. We're like the clowns in that song: "One who keeps tooling around, and one who can't move."

JO: Tearing.

EM: What?

JO: You said *tooling*—it's *tearing.*

EM: *(Annoyed)* I don't go *tearing* around like you either. I can't grab a map and a ticket and go trotting off to God-knows-where for months at a time. I have *never* sublet my apartment, and I would *never* date a man who lived as far away as Denver. *(Gasping for air)* I can't get off the ground, Joan. And I'm damned if my little Sasha is going to have a mother who can't get off the ground … I have to be the woman she would want me to be.

JO: You wanna be the woman she would want you to be? Go home and sit in a rocking chair. *(EM closes her eyes, grimacing and doubled-up; JO flips open her phone.)* That's it! Tell me your doctor's phone number.

EM: I didn't bring my phone book.

JO: Surely you remember it.

EM: I don't remember anything these days.

JO: Then I'm calling Tom.

EM: No! *(They struggle over the phone in a furious tug-of-war, which builds into a seated wrestling match, until EM bites JO's hand and snatches the phone. JO looks at the mark on her hand, then at EM.)*

JO: Are you fuckin crazy?

EM: Yes I am; I'm a mother bear!

JO: Give me the goddamn phone, Emily.

EM: *(Putting it behind her back)* No.

JO: It's *my phone.*

EM: No outs, Jo. We agreed; no outs. *(Grimaces again)*

JO: Then I'm calling a halt to this whole charade. *(She rises and pulls a chain above her head, which turns on a bright light. The two airplane seats are revealed to be in an abandoned barn, not in a plane. She then crosses and flips off a large white-noise machine; the engine-like noise ceases. EMILY is near tears and doubled up in pain.)*

EM: You promised—

JO: *(Rifling through her purse, looking for a phone book)* Because you begged me; you were desperate: "I need you to come ... I need your courage ... she's going to be *your* godchild ... she needs a fearless mother ..." *(Pause)* Well, you know what? That's bullshit. *(Back to looking)* There's no such thing as a *fearless mother*; and I'm not gonna risk that child's life just so you can prove something to yourself.

EM: You're not concerned about the baby; that's not what this is.

JO: *(Almost to herself)* Sitting out here in the wilds of freakin' Vermont, locked in some damn barn on a dirt road to nowhere ... I should have *my* head examined. Where's that fuckin car-phone number? *(Finds it)* I'm calling Tom.

EM: *(Taking JO's hand)* Please. We'll be landing at 5:00.

JO: The game's over my friend.

EM: It's not a game ... it's a *simulation.*

JO: Okay; this is me *simulating* a call to Tom: *Please come simulate unlocking this fucking barn door and then* simulate *rushing your wife to the nearest hospital.* Now!

EM: Jo—

JO: I'm not a goddamned doctor, Emily. I'm not even a *midwife.* I don't want this responsibility; I don't even like putting Band-Aids on, for God's sake. *(Dials phone listens, presses button, frantically tries again)* Shit. Do you believe this? There's no fuckin' cell tower out here. Shit, shit, shit. *(Practically in tears herself now, she runs to the door, tries to unlock it, rattles it, bangs on it.)* Help! Help! Help us! *(EM watches her, oddly calm now.)* Where the hell are we, anyway?

EM: I don't know.

JO: Well, how far is the nearest neighbor?

EM: A few miles, probably.

JO: A few *miles?*

EM: If we weren't locked up in the middle of nowhere, it wouldn't have fooled my phobia. *(JO shoots her a look.)* I'd still be scared to take a real flight ... this had to be really out there.

JO: Oh, this is really *out there* all right—it's definitely way the hell out there. *(Rattling the door again)*

EM: Please don't leave me, Jo.

JO: Leave you? *(Pause)* How am I gonna leave you? Where the hell can I go? Huh? *(Pause, sees EM's worry)* I'm not leaving, okay? *(No response, comes and sits beside her)* Okay?

EM: Okay. *(Closes her eyes and exhales)* I'm gonna try and relax now. *(JO watches her like a hawk as EM tries to steady her own breathing. After a moment, she grimaces.)*

JO: Jesus. They're getting closer together, aren't they? *(No response)* Christ; I'm gonna be sick. *(Rises and paces)* You have no idea how much I don't want to see this.

EM: Me in pain?

JO: You in labor ... you giving birth ... *anyone* giving birth.

EM: Why, Joan?

JO: Don't make this about *me*.

EM: Why am *I* the only one under study?

JO: I haven't been *studying* you—I've been flying with you. And for my trouble, I may end up having to deliver this poor little kid. *Deliver* her—*me*, of all people!

EM: *(Trying to catch her breath)* Why "you of all people"?

JO: Knock it off. I'm not kidding ... I'm gonna bust in a minute.

EM: You said it was best to keep talking—

JO: Not about *me*, for goodness sake. *(Eyeing her)* And why are *you* so bloody calm all of a sudden? We're still locked in, you know!

EM: I *have* to be calm now.

JO: Oh God. *(Runs to the door again)* TOM? *(Pause)* ARE YOU OUT THERE YET? *(No response)* WE LANDED EARLY; OPEN UP! *(Nothing)* Where is he? How come men are never there when you need them?

EM: Tom is like clockwork—he'll be here at five.

JO: *(Looks at her watch and then notices EM opening her seat belt and squatting down. She loses it.)* What are you doing? *(Pause)* Are you bleeding? *(EM breathes.)* What should I do? *(No response)* Why are you doing that?

EM: It's a pelvic exercise. We learned it in birthing class.

JO: You went to school for this?

EM: *(Smiles)* You'll go too ... when you have your baby!

JO: I'm not having a baby. I don't want a baby, Emily. *(EM shoots her a look.)* I could have had one; I chose not to ... or have you forgotten?

EM: I remember; I held your hand while you cried all night.

JO: Is this payback time?

EM: Fuck you.

JO: *(Crosses to get her purse)* Will it bother you if I smoke?

EM: *(Practicing her breathing)* Yes!

JO: *(Pacing)* Damn it! You know I don't like the sight of blood.

EM: No one likes the sight of other people's blood.

JO: I don't even like my own.

EM: *(Pause)* Is *that* why you don't want kids?

JO: Will you drop that shit? You can have a perfectly fulfilled life without kids, believe me.

EM: Who are you telling? I came late to the party too.

JO: But now you're *unspeakably* glad that you got there before the party ended, right?

EM: Right.

JO: Well, good for you. *(Pause)* I love my freedom. And maybe if you stopped *simulating* freedom, you'd learn to love it too.

EM: That was mean.

BLACKOUT

This scene is from one of the plays commissioned for the Steam *cluster, which had to be set in an all-white steam room. It was commissioned by, and loosely based on, the two actresses who starred in the premiere.*

Somebodies
Gail Noppe-Brandon

Characters: DORA   Female, 40, overweight
             BETHANY   Female, 40, thin, a wannabe dancer

AT RISE: The low-heat steam room at a fitness center in Manhattan. DORA and BETHANY, two strangers dressed in matching white terrycloth robes, have been getting to know each other. BETHANY, who is surrounded by bottles of "product" and water, is in the middle of a marital crisis and wants to talk. DORA sits with her eyes closed, trying to maintain her privacy.

BETHANY: *(Rubbing conditioner into her hair)* So why did you become a librarian?

DORA: *(Without opening her eyes)* For the solitude.

BETHANY: I always knew I wanted to dance; did you always know you wanted to work in a library?

DORA: *(Sighs)* I actually wanted to be an English professor.

BETHANY: A professor! Wow. I could see you teaching.

DORA: I failed student-teaching. *(Turning over)* I'm gonna get a little rest now.

BETHANY: *(Pause)* You failed? *(Silence)* But you seem so bright!

DORA: *(Long pause)* I couldn't get up in front of all those people. *(Sitting up)* Could you spare one of those little waters?

BETHANY: Sure! *(Grabs one and starts to rise)*

DORA: *(Stopping her)* You can just toss it over.

BETHANY: *(She tosses the water, and DORA guzzles it down.)* You seem dehydrated … maybe you should take a break.

DORA: Not until there are ten pounds of me on the floor.

BETHANY: *(Smiles)* I love that image! When I take a dance class in the summertime and we do floor work, I get up, and there's an exact silhouette of me in sweat on the floor. *(No response)* Can you picture that?

DORA: I'll take another one of those waters; stuff is addictive. *(BETHANY starts to rise, but then tosses another. She stares at DORA eagerly.)* So … where do you perform?

BETHANY: Right now I just teach. And take class. *(Sighs)* I don't want to perform until I'm really ready.

DORA: Well, you better get ready soon, before you're too old too move!

BETHANY: *(She is momentarily traumatized.)* How old do you think I am?

DORA: I just meant that dancers seem to have very short work lives. *(Silence)* Arthritis and stuff.

BETHANY: Arthritis! You think I'm old enough to have arthritis?

DORA: No offense was intended. I thought we were the same age ... fortyish.

BETHANY: I am not forty yet!

DORA: Well, sorry. I am.

BETHANY: And are *you* arthritic?

DORA: *(Adamantly)* That's why I'm here. That's why I joined the club; cause I'm getting arthritic ... *and* I'm at risk for a heart attack.

BETHANY: Well, that's not because of your age—that's because of your weight.

DORA: Thank you for noticing. *(DORA pulls her sweatband down over her eyes and turns away. BETHANY turns in the other direction and begins to manically apply her antiwrinkle cream to her face. Steam fills the room. After a moment, she starts to find the silence deafening and crosses to DORA with her hand extended.)*

BETHANY: Let's start over. I'm Bethany Stratton.

DORA: I thought we weren't going to talk. *(Pause. BETHANY stays put. DORA pulls her sweatband up and completes the handshake.)* Dora. Dora Delgrosso.

BETHANY: *(Searching for a memory)* Dora Delgrosso—

DORA: Please; no jokes about alliteration. *(BETHANY stares uncomprehendingly.)* Ninth grade English?

BETHANY: You *should* have been a professor, if you can remember that! *(She returns to her seat and feverishly applies self-tanner to her body.)* I have a terrible memory; I can't even remember last summer, much less junior high school English!

DORA: *(Dispassionately)* I only remember because he was the best teacher I ever had.

BETHANY: Did you stay in touch with him?

DORA: Are you crazy? *(Picks up the water bottle that BETHANY gave her, sees that it's empty. BETHANY pitches her another.)*

BETHANY: Did he give you a bad grade or something?

DORA: I never got a bad grade in my life.

BETHANY: Did he make a pass at you?

DORA: *(Scoffs at this)* I already weighed about one hundred and eighty pounds in ninth grade.

BETHANY: So … what happened?

DORA: Nothing happened.

BETHANY: Something happened!

DORA: *(BETHANY stares at her, demanding to know.)* He read one of my stories out loud in class one day.

BETHANY: *(Not getting it)* And?

DORA: And he knew I didn't want him to.

BETHANY: So …?

DORA: So he read it anyway—anonymously.

BETHANY: *(Silence, BETHANY stares.)* And?

DORA: And the protagonist was an obese girl, so everyone in the class knew that I wrote it. *(Silence. BETHANY still staring.)* It had a lot of private stuff in it. *(Silence)* They all turned around and stared at me. Okay? *(Silence)* Christ. It was one of the worst days of my life.

BETHANY: Didn't they like the story?

DORA: Of course they liked it; they loved it.

BETHANY: Then why was it one of the worst days?

DORA: *(Losing her patience)* Because they all started talking to me after that; asking for help with their writing. *(Snickers)* They called me Shakespeare, for crying out loud. Like Shakespeare ever wrote a short story.

BETHANY: I think it's nice they called you that—

DORA: It's a lot nicer to be invisible. *(She pulls out a piece of licorice from her tote and tears into it. BETHANY stares; DORA offers some)* Completely sugar-free; tastes like shit.

BETHANY: *(Declines candy)* Why would you want to be invisible?

DORA: *(Dismissively)* Because you don't have to worry about what everyone thinks of you. That's why.

BETHANY: But it sounds like you were so popular that year.

DORA: They weren't interested in *me*; they were interested in what I could do for *them*—their homework. And I did it. I did it, and the kid I did it for the most was the one I overheard in the girl's room singing, "Fatty, fatty two-by-four; can't fit through the bathroom door." *(Chomps her licorice)*

BETHANY: That's awful.

DORA: "Popular" … *(Snorts at BETHANY)* That's a word only a cheerleader should use.

BETHANY: *(Pause)* I *was* a cheerleader.

DORA: Well, there you go.

BETHANY: Meaning what?

DORA: Meaning, you were a pretty little center of attention, and now you're stuck trying to keep that shit up. You have a bag full of potions and lotions, and the truth is that you're just fine the way you look.

BETHANY: I'm fine the way I look *because* of the potions and lotions.

DORA: That crap doesn't really change your looks.

BETHANY: Yes, it does.

DORA: And who cares what you look like anyway? If that's the only reason someone likes you, then fuck 'em. Pardon my French.

BETHANY: It's not the *only* reason; it's part of the package.

DORA: You are not a *thing* in a package.

BETHANY: *I* know that, but that's not the way the rest of the world thinks.

DORA: And you're different from the rest of the world!

BETHANY: Yes! I'm a person of passion. I just happen to be in a profession where I'm in front of a mirror all day, and I have too much time to scrutinize myself. I don't judge other people that way, though.

DORA: No?

BETHANY: No. Of course not.

DORA: Do you have many friends who look like me? *(Silence)* Do you have *any* friends who look like me?

BETHANY: The secretary at the Y looks like you; we've become friends—

DORA: Really. Do you go clothes shopping with her? *(Silence)* Do you go to parties with her? Eat lunch with her at the salad bar?

BETHANY: I don't do things like that with anyone. But I really love who she is.

DORA: Sure. I bet she's a hoot. I bet she's got a quick sense of humor, and she's helpful to a fault, and she'd practically kill herself if she made a mistake on something important—

BETHANY: How can you make generalizations like that? Like all … overweight people are the same—

DORA: Fat. You can say "fat people." *(BETHANY looks away.)* I can make generalizations because the world hates fat people; we develop certain common behaviors to compensate for being so detestable!

BETHANY: The world does not hate fat people.

DORA: No?

BETHANY: No. *(Pause)* You just make us nervous. *(Silence)* What's that saying? "There but for the grace of God go I?" *(DORA stares.)* Really. You're like a wake-up call … and it makes us nervous.

DORA: You're not nervous—you're jealous! "How come that bitch gets to eat all the cheeseburgers she wants, and I can't!"

BETHANY: *(Excited)* Or maybe it's: "How come she gets to be invisible, and I have to be judged all day long?"

DORA: No one told you that you have to look great.

BETHANY: You don't know what anyone told me, Dora.

BLACKOUT

This monologue is drawn from the previous play.

Somebodies
Gail Noppe-Brandon

(DORA, an obese 40-year-old woman, is in the low-heat steam room at a fitness center in Manhattan. She recently met a long-lost childhood friend here, whom she didn't recognize at all because she's had so much plastic surgery. Here DORA reacts to her friend's assumption that she could never understand her need for male approval.)

DORA

Why can't I understand—because I'm fat? You think I never wanted attention? Everyone wants attention. I bury myself in a big body, but I don't think of myself as fat; I've never thought of myself as too fat. I think of myself as a normal-looking woman—it shocks me that I'm seen as fat. I haven't always been this way. I lost a huge amount of weight in college. I got so slim I landed a lead in the campus operetta;

I even wore a merry-widow. *(Smiles)* I looked fabulous! I got more attention from men in that one year than I did in the rest of my life put together. *(Pause)* And I hated it. I never wanted *that* much attention. I felt completely exposed. Naked. Like the world was staring at me. Like they all wanted to take a bite. Like I had to give them all a piece of me, just to show how grateful I was that they noticed me at all. Even the director of the operetta started coming on to me. *(Laughs bitterly)* He was older; so I thought he was different. He said he was going to coach me on how to be sexier—for my role. He taught me how to kiss … and a few other things. I actually thought he loved me. *(Pause)* He gave me a case of crabs and stopped calling. So … I decided my father was right—sex *is* dirty. *(Sees her friend's reaction)* He's Catholic. His idea of a woman is the Virgin Mary! *(Pause)* I lost my virginity and got bugs from the guy. Then I gained all my weight back.

This play was written as part of the Invincible Summer *cluster of plays, the first-ever FYV summer master class. The trigger was a quote from a poem by W. B. Yeats.*

This Little Light
Gail Noppe-Brandon

| Characters: | ELLIE | Female, Caucasian American, 18, a runner |
| | KENYA | Female, African-American, 43, a trainer |

AT RISE: A locker room. The day of the pre-Olympic Trials, Nashville, Tennessee. KENYA is giving ELLIE a leg massage. They are listening to music; the lights have been dimmed. ELLIE wears a bath towel and a tank top.

KENYA: Breathe. *(She rubs.)* It's just nerves.
ELLIE: No.
KENYA: It's normal to be nervous. *(Silence)* Everyone gets nervous before a big meet, and this is the big one!

ELLIE: It's not nerves.

KENYA: What, then?

ELLIE: Something's wrong.

KENYA: Nothing's wrong. This is the company you belong in. You're the best. The *best*.

ELLIE: *(She starts to get up from table.)* I'm gonna be sick again.

KENYA: You want me to help you?

ELLIE: *(Running to a bathroom offstage)* I can puke without being coached. *(She slams the door. KENYA turns off the music and follows, talking to ELLIE through the door.)*

KENYA: I used to throw up every time too. It was a regular thing with me! *(Silence)* It got so I worried if I *didn't* throw up! *(She laughs.)* It was like my sacrifice to the God of running. *(Pause)* Mercury, I guess that would be. Wasn't he the one with wings on his feet? *(Silence)* I know what you're thinking in there; I can hear you thinking it. *(Pause)* "I should be praying to a *Goddess*, not a God. Diana the Hunter, or some such." *(Silence)* Surprised I know that? *(Silence)* I took Greek mythology in school. I'm not just a jock, you know. This girl knows some things! *(Silence. KENYA knocks on the door.)* How ya doing, Ellie?

ELLIE: I can't wretch with you babbling out there. Go away.

KENYA: *(Moving to the bench and sitting)* I went away.

ELLIE: *(From offstage)* Why don't you wait upstairs?

KENYA: You planning on running out the back door?

ELLIE: I can't run anywhere.

KENYA: You can run. You *will* run. This is what it's all been for. *(Looks at her watch)* You have thirty minutes.

ELLIE: Please go away.

KENYA: Okay. I'll go upstairs and get you a coke, settle your stomach. *(Silence)* I'm going now. *(She walks to a second door, opens it, and then closes it again, hard. She remains inside the locker room. After a moment, we hear the sound of ELLIE coughing and gagging. We hear a toilet flush. We hear water running. Then we hear ELLIE sobbing. KENYA has been listening to all of this. She approaches the bathroom door. Hesitates, then knocks softly)* Ellie. *(The crying stops abruptly.)* Ellie?

ELLIE: Did you get the coke?

KENYA: The machine was broken.

ELLIE: Figures.

KENYA: Why were you crying?

ELLIE: I got sick.

KENYA: Yes?

ELLIE: I don't like the feeling.

KENYA: Don't cry anymore … you don't want to dehydrate yourself.

ELLIE: Kenya—

KENYA: Come on out now.

ELLIE: I never throw up; I must have some kind of virus or something.

KENYA: I told you already, it's the nerves. And this Tennessee heat. Come out, and I'll give you some Gatorade.

ELLIE: I'm dizzy. I feel like if I stand up, I'll fall over.

KENYA: Let me come in and help you. *(She tries the door, but it's locked.)* Open up, Ellie. *(The door knob turns, and ELLIE emerges, looking pale and disheveled.)* Girl, you look like hell.

ELLIE: I look better than I feel. *(KENYA puts ELLIE's arm around her own shoulder and walks her back to the bench. They both sit.)*

KENYA: You want me to rub you some more?

ELLIE: No.

KENYA: I want you at your best today. You gotta keep those muscles warm. *(She gets up and brings ELLIE's gym bag.)* Here. *(She pulls out some sweat pants, holds them out.)* Put these sweats on.

ELLIE: I don't need sweats; I'm burning up with fever. *(KENYA feels her forehead.)*

KENYA: You're as cool as I am.

ELLIE: I know you're disappointed, Kenya. Sorry.

KENYA: Sorry my ass. *(She gets some Gatorade out of the gym bag, hands ELLIE the bottle.)* You're gonna drink this to replace your fluids; you're gonna stretch out again. I'm gonna rub you a little more, and then you're gonna wash off your face and go up to the blocks to take your rightful place among these fine athletes. We've worked too hard and too long for this. You're not gonna crap out on me now, cause if you place today we're going to the Trials Friday. The *Trials.* Now drink up.

ELLIE: *(She turns and stares at KENYA, right into her soul.)* You'd have me out there half dead, wouldn't you?

KENYA: Where's that coming from? I'm the one sitting here keeping you warm, rubbing your legs—

ELLIE: I thought you cared about me—me, the person. But it's just me, the runner, isn't it.

KENYA: There's no separation. The person and the runner are one.

ELLIE: What if I stopped running? Like you.

KENYA: I retired, but I'm still a runner. I *ran* the race. When I say I'm Kenya Martin, people say, "Oh, the runner!" I'll *always* be the runner. I have different dreams now, different passions. I don't live for the race anymore—my prayers have changed. But I'll always have the soul of a runner. It's only my prayers that have changed.

ELLIE: Now you pray for *me* to get the medals.

KENYA: Don't flatter yourself. I have love for you, but I don't squander my prayers for someone else's dream. I'm your coach, and I give all I've got when we work together. Cause that's my work. And I believe you're very talented. I think you could go Olympic, and that's exciting for a coach. But I have a life—I have children, and *grandchildren*. And I have a waiting list of runners who'd kill to train with me. You get my meaning?

ELLIE: Are you threatening to dump me because I'm sick?

KENYA: You're not sick. You've got nerves, that's all. But I'm really starting to wonder if you've got what it takes. *(Silence)* Being a competitive athlete isn't just about long, strong legs. It's not just about working hard. It's about wanting to win. To *win*. To beat out of the field. *(ELLIE turns away, but KENYA gets in her face.)* You get me?

ELLIE: My head is pounding; can't you cut me some slack here? I've won a lot. *(They stare at each other—a challenge.)*

KENYA: You've won a lot, yeah; but you've also missed a lot you should've won.

ELLIE: Don't start questioning everything because I'm out of it this once.

KENYA: Do I need to remind you of the twisted ankle before the last State finals? Which was twisted in a bowling alley the night before? It's not just this once.

ELLIE: Twice, then.

KENYA: Or the fainting spells before the Mid-Atlantic games, for which the judge disqualified you? Brought on, I might add, by not eating for two weeks.

ELLIE: I wasn't hungry—

KENYA: Need I go on? And on?

ELLIE: We've been together a long time—there's bound to be some bad health. And some plain bad luck.

KENYA: That's very true. But, you know, it's never during practice. It's always right before the competition.

ELLIE: Stress is higher.

KENYA: Yes.

ELLIE: I thought it was *supposed* to be higher. I thought that was all part of it.

KENYA: Yes, if you can *use* it. If you can get into the high-stakes rhythm and go with it. If it excites and feeds you. Not if it cripples you.

ELLIE: *(Turning on her)* I'm not crippled, goddammit.

KENYA: Then get out there and run. *(Silence)* You run, or I walk.

ELLIE: It's not that easy.

KENYA: Who you telling? *(Silence, then she pushes ELLIE.)* Why'd you want to be a runner anyway?

ELLIE: Because I was the fastest kid in the neighborhood.

KENYA: That's not enough. Why? *(Silence)* Why, Ellie?

ELLIE: I don't know ... I feel free when I'm running. I feel like I'm flying. I feel invincible.

KENYA: *(She smiles.)* I know that feeling! How 'bout winning? How do you feel about that?

ELLIE: It's not as important to me. I just want to keep on running.

KENYA: Bull. *(ELLIE stares at her.)* If that's all you wanted, you'd get up every day and jog around the reservoir. You'd enter some local marathon and feel good about just finishing. No. You need the *race*. *(Silence)* Why? *(Silence)* Why do you need the race?

ELLIE: *(Pause)* I like being the fastest, okay?

KENYA: Okay. Everyone who's ever won a race won it cause they like to be the fastest. Even yours truly. Especially yours truly! Being fastest will put you on the map. And if you're lucky, it will put you through college. *(Pause)* The medal stands are right in front of the VIP box, Ellie, right in front. When I looked out and saw my mama sitting there crying—it was the finest view on this earth.

ELLIE: *My* mama won't have that view.

KENYA: I know ... but from where your mama is, she can see everything. Everything. *(Silence)* I had a mama, and you have a papa. You gotta see what *is* there, Ellie.

ELLIE: He won't be there either.

KENYA: But I saw his name on the list. *(Silence)* Don't tell me he's working again.

ELLIE: He's always working.

KENYA: Not this time. Not these races. No one misses the Trials. Gimme his number.

ELLIE: I don't need him here; leave it alone, Kenya.

KENYA: *(She studies ELLIE.)* Isn't he proud, Ellie?

ELLIE: Of course he's proud. He wanted to be an athlete himself. *(KENYA stares at her, waiting for an admission of some kind.)* Why wouldn't he be proud?

KENYA: He's never come to watch.

ELLIE: He watches on TV.

KENYA: They weren't all televised. *(No response)* You *do* need him here, today of all days. Couldn't he take the day off? Everyone gets *one* day of vacation; I mean he's not the president of the goddamn country, Ellie. He should be here.

ELLIE: He can't be here, all right? The track is below ground. *(KENYA stares, not following.)* There's no elevator.

KENYA: You lost me, baby.

ELLIE: There's no handicapped access, for God's sake. *(Silence)* He's in a wheelchair.

KENYA: *(After a moment)* How come, all this time I didn't know that.

ELLIE: Because you've never met him.

KENYA: The tracks weren't *all* below ground.

ELLIE: There were reasons—

KENYA: How come it never came up in conversation?

ELLIE: I don't know. We mostly talk about running.

KENYA: *(After a moment)* What happened to him?

ELLIE: M.S. *(Silence)* That's multiple sclerosis.

KENYA: I know what it is. *(Pause)* How long's he been in a chair?

ELLIE: Since I was three.

KENYA: And he was an athlete once?

ELLIE: He did gymnastics in college ... before he started getting sick. *(Pause)* He sells insurance now, all the time.

KENYA: *(She takes Elli's hand.)* I would hate to compete without my family here to watch me. I don't think I could have done it.

ELLIE: *(Without sentiment)* I've had *you*.

KENYA: I'm your coach, not your family—it's not the same. It's not enough.

ELLIE: It's been fine.

KENYA: Let's try to get him here for the Finals Friday.

ELLIE: I'm not running—

KENYA: I'll make a stink; I'll have them put in a ramp. It's probably illegal not to have one anyway. Hell, they can *carry* him down if they have to. *(She jumps up.)* I'm on it.

ELLIE: *(Grabbing her) No!* Are you nuts? I don't want that. I don't want a whole big commotion ... everyone staring at him; he'd hate that.

KENYA: *He'd* hate it, or *you'd* hate it? *(Pause)* Are you ashamed of his weakness?

ELLIE: He can do more chin-ups than you can! It's just his legs that are weak. *(Pause. She glances at her own strong legs.)* Ironic, huh?

KENYA: You've never invited him, have you.

ELLIE: He wouldn't *want* to come. Don't you understand? *(No response)* All these athletes who can run faster than most people can drive. Men primping all over the place. He's not much older than you are. How do you think it would make him feel?

KENYA: I guess he'd have a lot of feelings, not the least of which would be pride, Ellie—pride. *(Silence)* Listen, whether you run or not, he's gonna be in that chair. That's a fact. Don't you think he'd like to see you on that medal stand, while his family name is being announced? *(Pause)* Why do you think he *watched* it on TV?

ELLIE: I don't know. *(Reflects)* He couldn't come to the first State-wide I ran, so he asked me to call him after. When I told him I won, he said, "Yes, I was watching." That's all he said. He'd never really seen me run full-out before. He was very quiet; he sounded like he'd been crying. That was only the second time I ever heard him cry—

KENYA: I imagine he was feeling moved.

ELLIE: *I* imagine he was feeling impotent. *(Silence)* He told me I was moving too fast for him to even see me go by. He said he couldn't keep up with me anymore, and he was gonna have to let me go. *(She swallows back tears.)* He asked me if I remembered the little red wagon he used to tie on his wheelchair, to pull me around the block in. He said he should have tied his chair to my waist and had *me* pull *him* instead. He didn't know he'd had a "speed demon" on his hands. He said it must have been frustrating for me in that little wagon, moving along at a snail's pace. He understood, because he'd been an athlete once, too. He asked me to forgive him. *(She can no longer speak.)*

KENYA: Did you like it when he pulled you in that wagon?

ELLIE: No. *(Pause)* I loved it.

KENYA: Then maybe you *better* slow down, cause you've been moving so fast, you're missing the obvious.

ELLIE: I know he loves me—

KENYA: Ellie, if God has seen to it that you have to do the running for both of you, than you damn well better use your gifts to do that.

ELLIE: I don't believe in God.

KENYA: Ever read the Bible?

ELLIE: Never.

KENYA: Well that's too bad, cause there's actually some wisdom there. Jesus said "do not hide your light under a bush." God gives us our lights, Ellie, and if we all hid them—the world would be dark. Running is your light. And your father's, through you. *(Pause. ELLIE stares at the floor.)* Now get out there and run, or you and me are through.

ELLIE: I'm telling you, I'm sick.

KENYA: And I'm telling you, running is the cure. So get yourself quiet, and psych yourself up. *(She holds out ELLIE's running shoes to her. They stare at each other, in checkmate.)* It's downright arrogant to throw away a gift. Only God decides who can walk and who can run—and who can fly.

ELLIE: *(Pause. ELLIE is trying not to reach for the shoes.)* But my father's stuck on the ground; and everyone he's ever loved has flown away from him.

KENYA: Then don't fly away from him—fly toward him.

BLACKOUT

This compilation is drawn from the previous play.

This Little Light
Gail Noppe-Brandon

(ELLIE, a female athlete in her late teens, who is too afraid to go out and compete in the big race she's come to run, tells her coach why she never invites her father to watch.)

ELLIE

My father couldn't come to the first State-wide I ran, so he asked me to call him after. When I told him I won, he said, "Yes, I was watching." That's all he said. He'd never really seen me run full-out before. He was very quiet; like he'd been crying. That was only the second time I ever heard him cry. *(Pause)* I think he was feeling impotent. He told me I was moving too fast for him to even see me go by. He said he couldn't keep up with me anymore, and he was gonna have to let me go. *(She swallows back tears.)* He asked me if I remembered the little red wagon he used to tie on his wheelchair to pull me around the block in. He said he should have tied his chair to my waist and had *me* pull *him* instead. He didn't know he'd had a speed demon on his hands. *(Laughs sadly)* He said it must have been frustrating for me in that little wagon, moving along at a snail's pace. He understood, because he'd been an athlete once too. He asked me to forgive him. *(Pause)* My father is stuck on the ground, and everyone he's ever loved has flown away from him.

> *This monologue is from a play that was commissioned for our first Main Stage cluster, entitled* Nothing You Can Say. *Each of the plays dealt with breakdowns in communication.*

When Language Fails
Gail Noppe-Brandon

(KATE, a woman in her late 40s, has been trying for days to get her daughter, LEE, to talk to her. LEE has been brutally raped by a serial rapist who murdered all of his other victims; she is in the hospital. LEE has not spoken to anyone—not the policewoman on the case, JENI, or the police psychiatrist—since this attack. Although KATE is very concerned about her daughter's mental state, she also feels that there is some spite in LEE's unwillingness to open up to her. KATE enters the room where LEE has been being observed. LEE is alone; KATE is holding a teddy bear in her hand.)

KATE

Lee? *(No response)* Your friend Samantha called! *(Silence)* I told her you were in the hospital. I said you had pneumonia ... no one needs to know. *(No reaction. After a moment, KATE holds the bear out to LEE.)* She sent this—do you want it? *(No response. After a moment, KATE retracts it.)* I didn't think you would. I told her that you were a little beyond stuffed animals, but she insisted that I bring it; should I leave it? *(She circles LEE's chair—observing her—and then sits in the chair beside her.)* Lee? *(Pause)* What are you doing, Lee? *(Silence)* I'll tell you what you're doing; you're breaking my heart. *(KATE starts to break, and then takes a deep breath and recovers.)* I want you to stop this, this reign of silence. It's very childish, and it's accomplishing nothing. Lee? *(Silence. KATE pulls her chair closer, gets into LEE's face.)* If you talk to anyone, it should be *me*. You don't have to talk to that cop if you don't want to. I'd like to see the bastard that did this to you fried, but that's *her* problem. She can do her lousy job without you. I *need* you. I'm sitting here in the dark, and you're all I have. *(She reaches out and touches LEE's cheek; LEE recoils.)* What is this, Lee? What kind of game are you playing here? *(Pause)* Are you punishing me? *(Silence)* A mother's just a human being. We can't keep our children safe from every terrible thing that might happen to them in this world. We like to think we can, but we can't. *(KATE twists the teddy bear's legs nervously, unconsciously.)* Lee, you're frightening me. I don't know what to do here. You weren't even willful like this as a little child—you were my sturdy little helper! *(Silence)* You're a grown woman now, Lee. *(Pats her hand)* You're starting college in a few months. College! *(Pause)* You think this is how a college student behaves? *(Long pause)* You don't want to be a grown woman anymore, is that it? *(LEE blinks; KATE softens a bit.)* It's not easy, Lee. I know. But you can't go backwards. That's why I raised you to be a strong woman. You screamed, just the way I taught you to, and he ran away. *(LEE begins to rock herself back and forth.)* Stop that rocking, Lee. *Please! (LEE doesn't.)* Lee, do you want to end up in the booby hatch? You want to throw your whole life away over this? You've got to pull yourself together, Lee, that's the name of the game. *(LEE keeps rocking; KATE puts the teddy bear down, rises, and then tries to pull LEE up out of her chair. Unbeknownst to them, JENI has entered the observation booth and watches them.)* I'm taking you out of here. *(LEE pulls away and stays in the chair; KATE stares at her.)* Don't you want to come home with me, Lee? *(LEE turns her head away. After a moment, KATE sits again.)* Do you know what men used to do to women after they raped them? *(Silence)* They cut their tongues out. So that they couldn't talk; so that they couldn't tell anyone who did it. *(Silence)* You want to go back to the Middle Ages, Lee? *(No response)* I thought you were a modern woman. I thought you were a feminist. I thought you were my little warrior. *(Silence)* You have to be strong now, Lee. I need you to tell me that you're okay. Just tell me you're okay. *(LEE turns away, stops rocking; KATE leans in.)* Lee-Lee, remember after Daddy died; you made me a lamb chop once? You cooked it so long that it was black—like a piece of charcoal! But I ate it. All of it. And I told you it was delicious. Cause that's what you needed to hear. *(No reaction)* Sometimes you have to say what someone you love needs to hear. I need to hear you say something right now. *(Closes her eyes, waits to hear LEE's voice. LEE picks up the teddy bear, clutches it.)* Just three little words, Lee. "I'm okay, Mom." That's all I'm asking for. It's not a lot to ask. *(LEE starts to rock again; KATE opens her eyes and sees LEE holding the bear. KATE grabs the teddy bear, starting to break down.)* Stop this nonsense! *(LEE looks away. After a moment, KATE takes a deep breath, wipes her eyes, and composes herself. She reaches over and smoothes LEE's hair.)* I'm tired, Lee. *(Pause)* I'll see you tomorrow. *(KATE exits. After a moment, LEE opens her mouth wide in a silent scream. JENI, who is still watching from the booth, buries her face in her hands.)*

Sarah Paulson

I first met Sarah when I held an audition at LaGuardia High School (my alma mater), looking to cast a fourteen-year-old girl in the new play [by Michele Lowe] that I was directing. Sarah stood out from all of the other young women who auditioned, not only by dint of her talent but because of her utter passion for the work. After she was cast, Sarah impressed every adult in the company with her capacity to memorize the entire script quickly, as well as with her maturity off stage and her vulnerability on stage. All of these qualities seemed dramatically at odds with her academic record at school. At the conclusion of the run, by which time I had determined to "adopt" her for life, I invited Sarah to continue working with me as a student in the FYV afterschool workshops—on the condition that she maintain high grades in all of her academic subjects. She agreed to both, and that was the start of a journey that would take us through the writing and performing of over twenty original plays. Sarah's innate ear for dialogue served her well in both pursuits. The following play was written when Sarah was fifteen years old, and it reflects her sophistication with language and her courage with feelings, as well as the academic discipline she was developing within the context of the relationship-based teaching. The monologue that follows was taken from a play that she wrote for a cluster entitled Does Anyone Hear Me *and reflects these qualities. After graduating from LaGuardia, Sarah landed a Broadway show the following year, and she has not stopped working since. Credits include Wendy Wasserstein's* The Sisters Rosensweig, *and Tennessee Williams'* The Glass Menagerie *on Broadway, Beth Henley's* Crimes of the Heart *and Tracy Letts'* Killer Joe *off-Broadway, films like* What Women Want *and* Down With Love, *and television series* Jack and Jill *and* Studio 60. *Sarah brought the same professional intensity that I had first encountered to every role that she was cast in during the years that she participated in the FYV teen workshops, and she credits FYV with having planted the seeds of her success.*

This play was written as part of a cluster entitled Gallery, *for which each participant selected a painting as their point of departure. Sarah selected Vincent Van Gogh's "Starry Night."*

Brown-Eyed Girl
Sarah Paulson

Characters: SUMMER   Female, 16
                  DAD   40s

AT RISE: SUMMER sits on a small hill, gazing toward the trees in the distance. Beside her are a book and a cassette player.

SUMMER: *(Looking up at the sky. It is dusk; a few stars are starting to appear.)* "Starlight, star bright, first star I see tonight, I wish I may, I wish I might, have the wish I wish tonight." *(She closes her eyes and silently makes a wish. SUMMER'S DAD enters. He stares at her, trying to figure out what she is doing, then figures it out and sits beside her. He is watching her intently. She finishes her wish, opens her eyes, startled.)* Dad! What are you doing?

DAD: Watching you. What did you wish for?

SUMMER: If I tell you, it won't come true. *(Pause)* How did you know I was making a wish?

DAD: I do it all the time!

SUMMER: Really? I never saw you do it.

DAD: You aren't always here.

SUMMER: True. *(She looks at the sky.)* I wish I *could* live up here. *(Silence)* It's so beautiful. You can always see the stars. It's too polluted in the city to see anything.

DAD: I wish you could live here, too.

SUMMER: *(She lays back)* And I wish I didn't have to go back to school on Monday.

DAD: Have you talked with Mom?

SUMMER: Yeah. She's going to pick us up at 5:30. She wants to take Alexis shopping for an outfit to wear on Monday for school pictures.

DAD: She's buying your sister an outfit for one school picture?

SUMMER: Sad, isn't it?

DAD: God, she's changed. She used to be such a hippie—wild hair, always carefree. She would fly to the moon on a moment's notice.

SUMMER: I wish that was the mom I knew.

DAD: *(Pause)* We were really good together.

SUMMER: Why did you get a divorce, if you were so good together?

DAD: She divorced me.

SUMMER: And you don't know why?

DAD: *(Pause)* It had to do with my inability to stay in one place. I was always moving to accommodate my work schedule, wasn't home. She said I wasn't there for her enough.

SUMMER: Was it true?

DAD: *(Pause)* Yeah.

SUMMER: Oh.

DAD: Does that bother you?

SUMMER: It was a long time ago. *(She leans herself on her elbow, sees her book, thumbs through it.)*

DAD: What's that?

SUMMER: My poem book. Robert Frost, he's my favorite.

DAD: What's your favorite poem?

SUMMER: "The Night Light."

DAD: Read it to me? *(She puts the book down.)* No book?

SUMMER: I've memorized it.

DAD: Impressive.

SUMMER: "She always had to burn a light
Beside her attic bed at night
It gave bad dreams and broken sleep
But helped the lord her soul to keep.
Good gloom on her was thrown away.
It is on me by night or day,
Who have, as I suppose, ahead—

DAD: The darkest of it still to dread."

SUMMER: You know it?

DAD: In photography class in college we had this project once, to find a poem to fit the picture we were assigned. That was the poem I chose.

SUMMER: *(Pause)* Did you always know you wanted to be a photographer?

DAD: Yeah. *(Pause)* You want to follow in my footsteps, don't you?

SUMMER: No, photography is not for me.

DAD: *(He hits her)* Oh no?

204

SUMMER: *(She hits him back) No!*

DAD: Too good to follow in your old man's path? *(He gets her in a headlock.)*

SUMMER: That's right. *(She gets out of the headlock and attacks him.)*

DAD: *(He tickles her.)* This used to be a form of torture.

SUMMER: Let me go! Dad … help! *(She is laughing so hard she can't breathe.)*

DAD: *(Still holding her)* So you want to join me in the business?

SUMMER: Okay! I'll be anything you want, just get off!

DAD: Promise?

SUMMER: *Yes! (DAD gets off)* I had my fingers crossed. *(She jumps up; DAD chases her. She picks up tape player.)* Don't make me use this.

DAD: To throw at me?

SUMMER: Uh-huh.

DAD: Don't you want to dance instead?

SUMMER: Do I have to be a photographer?

DAD: No.

SUMMER: All right. *(Puts down recorder)* Ready?

DAD: Ready. *(SUMMER pushes 'Play.' "Brown-Eyed Girl" comes on. They dance around wildly, laughing, joking. After awhile SUMMER gets tired, she sits in the grass.)* Tired already?

SUMMER: Extremely—aren't you?

DAD: Not in the least! *(Reaching out to her)* You're young; you're filled with energy—your bones need to keep moving!

SUMMER: Yeah, and you're old, so pop-a-squat and relax.

DAD: You talked me into it. *(He sits.)*

SUMMER: Always do. *(She lays back.)*

DAD: *(He looks at the sky. After a moment)* Summer?

SUMMER: Yeah?

DAD: I need to tell you something.

SUMMER: What?

DAD: I don't know how to say this.

SUMMER: What is it? *(She sits up.)* Dad, are you okay?

DAD: I got offered a job.

SUMMER: A job?

DAD: Yes.

SUMMER: You already have a job.

DAD: This job is better, at a bigger company, with a bigger salary.

SUMMER: What's the job?

DAD: It's chief photographer for a magazine called *Style*.

SUMMER: *Style*? Never heard it.

DAD: That's because it's in LA.

SUMMER: LA., California?

DAD: Yes.

SUMMER: Oh.

DAD: Summer, you can come and visit any time you want.

SUMMER: You mean you're taking the job?

DAD: I accepted three weeks ago.

SUMMER: *(Pause)* When do you go?

DAD: Next Saturday—

SUMMER: That's *our* weekend.

DAD: I know. I meant to tell you right away, but ... I couldn't do it. I've got to go out there and meet the head of the company.

SUMMER: So you knew this was our last weekend together, and you just let it fly by like any other weekend?

DAD: Like I said, you can come and visit me any time.

SUMMER: I *can't* come and visit you any time. I have school and friends and things to do. It won't always be convenient for you either. And who's gonna pay for it?

DAD: Summer, I need this job.

SUMMER: You have a job.

DAD: Yeah, for a small-time paper that will always be a small-time paper. *Style* has grown into a major magazine in a matter of months.

SUMMER: *(She turns away.)* I should have expected it. You did it once, you'll do it again.

DAD: What are you talking about?

SUMMER: Just what I said. You did it to Mom, so why wouldn't you do it to me? Do you not like seeing me? Is that it? It's me, isn't it? *(Moving away)*

DAD: *(He grabs her.)* Honey, it's not you. I'm doing this for *me*. It's best for me.

SUMMER: Why are you being so selfish? You, you, you.

DAD: You're being just as selfish. You're saying that I should stay here for you. I'd only be holding myself back.

SUMMER: I love you. I'd never let anything come between us.

DAD: Nothing will come between us.

SUMMER: You'll leave and never come back.

DAD: I'd never leave you. Our visits will just be less frequent.

SUMMER: You don't know how much I love seeing you. I get away from the city, away from Mom, away from everything. The only time I'll be able to see you is on holidays. Dad, that's four times a year, five at the most.

DAD: Summer, you gotta trust.

SUMMER: I want to, but—

DAD: Then do it.

SUMMER: I don't think I can. *(Pause)* I need to be alone for awhile.

DAD: Listen—

SUMMER: Please, Dad, I don't want to talk anymore.

DAD: *(Pause)* I'll be inside if you need me. *(He gets up, looks at her, kisses her head, and exits.)*

SUMMER: *(To herself)* I do need you. *(She looks up at the sky.)*

BLACKOUT

This monologue is from a cluster of plays entitled Does Anyone Hear Me?, *all of which dealt with breakdowns in communication.*

Too Many Walls
Sarah Paulson

(JULIANNA, a teenage girl who has begun to drink heavily, reluctantly tells her therapist about the death of her best friend and admits that she needs help to cope with it.)

JULIANNA

She used to say: "There are too many walls. Too many walls to climb in one lifetime. Too many walls that keep getting higher." *(Holding up a small empty flask, she addresses the bottle.)* I'm scared. I'm scared that I'll *never* see what's beyond those walls. *(Closes her eyes, laughs bitterly to herself.)* Adults always tell you that this is the best time in your life! That you're not supposed to worry. But I do. I worry all the time.

(Addressing therapist) When you're seventeen, people don't think you know what love is. What pain is. But I do. *(Pause)* It's like they think teenagers come from a different planet—but we don't. We just want to find out what's on the other side of the wall. Maybe it's dark and gray; maybe it's not a place where the sun always shines, and the sidewalks aren't made of candy. *(Silence)* Just for a minute I want to see a place where there's love, but every time I get one leg over, I fall back down. *(Addresses bottle again)* Can you help me get over those walls? *(Silence)* I just need a little help. Hello? *(Silence)* Do you hear me? *(To herself)* Does anyone hear me?

Susan Peters

Susan and I first met when we were studying acting together at the Charles Kakastakis studio in NYC. Because we shared a technique that highlighted authentic connection, I cast Susan in several of our main stage productions, (including Simulating Emily *and* Double-Cross, *selections of which are featured in this collection). As she became familiar with the goals of FYV, Susan expressed an interest in doing some teaching. I invited her to participate in a teacher training workshop, as preparation for the FYV classroom. Susan was very well trained for the work that was being done in the acting sessions. However, it was an eye-opening experience for someone who had originally trained as a singer and musical theatre performer, to witness the kinds of communication blocks that the other adults in the room were struggling with and the ways in which the FYV coaching style enabled them to move beyond the blocks. The opportunity to write a play also offered Susan a new personal challenge. "When our pieces were presented, I was much more nervous watching my piece being performed than I was performing myself." Although it took several rewrites for her to find her story, the resulting first play proved my theory that people who have been trained as actors in the "pursuit of wants" and who have learned to really listen become naturally good writers. Note how full a sense of the marriage you get in such a short piece. Susan went on to assist several of our teacher participants through the process of leading their own middle school students toward enacting monologues and developing plays of their own. At the time of this writing, Susan was working part-time in the publishing industry and raising three children.*

Susan wrote this, her first play, as part of a cluster entitled Moving On. *It was suggested by the photograph on the cover of this book.*

Secrets
Susan Peters

Characters: MICHAEL   Male, late 30s
              MARY   Female, his wife

AT RISE: Late afternoon, in the home of MICHAEL and MARY. MICHAEL is seated at the table, waiting for MARY to return from shopping. He has something he needs to tell her. MARY enters with shopping bags. There is real tension between them.

MARY: Where's Jason?

MICHAEL: In his room—I told him he could have some computer time before dinner.

MARY: It's a beautiful day. Couldn't he do that later?

MICHAEL: It was a reward for helping me in the garden.

MARY: Okay. Whatever. *(Starts to leave)*

MICHAEL: What did you buy?

MARY: *(Somewhat impatient)* Remember? His birthday? I found that Game Boy he wants. Think we can keep it a secret for a month?

MICHAEL: What?

MARY: What do you mean "what"?

MICHAEL: Keep what a secret for a month?

MARY: *(Impatient)* The Game Boy. What did you think I meant?

MICHAEL: Nothing. *(Pause)* It's just—

MARY: *(Pause)* Just what?

MICHAEL: I don't know … the whole birthday party thing. You really think it's a good idea?

MARY: What do you mean? He's been looking forward to it.

MICHAEL: Well, come on, Mary. The way things are going and everything—

MARY: Yeah? And how are things going, Michael? *(Silence)* How's Connie? Does she ask about Jason when you're together? Is she at all interested? Or do you even talk to her about our son?

MICHAEL: *(Angry)* For heaven's sake, Mary. Leave Connie out of this. I've told you a million times this isn't her fault.

MARY: That's supposed to make me feel better about your leaving me? Leaving Jason?

MICHAEL: Dammit, Mary, I'm not leaving Jason. I love our son. Just because it's over between us, doesn't mean I stop being his father. *(There's a scrape of a chair leg in the corridor. MICHAEL and MARY react to the noise.)*

MARY: *(Almost whispering)* God, Michael. How could you be so careless? Do you think Jason heard you?

MICHAEL: *(Going to check)* No ... no. I don't think so. *(Stops. Looks directly at Mary)* Though maybe it wouldn't be such a bad thing.

MARY: What do you mean?

MICHAEL: What do you think I mean? How long do you think we can pretend? He's going to be ten years old. He knows things aren't right.

MARY: You promised me. You swore to me. Nothing until after his birthday. He's been looking forward to it for months.

MICHAEL: Pretending is better? Living a lie is better? We need to tell him, Mary. He may already know.

MARY: Know what? Know that his father is a sleaze? That his father wants to leave him?

MICHAEL: You won't have it any other way, will you? You say you want to protect Jason, but this is all about your hurt. Your anger.

MARY: You're damn right, I'm angry. All the time I thought you and Connie were just working on that stupid building project.

MICHAEL: Telling you was the hardest thing I ever had to do. But as difficult as this is, we have to get past it and think about our son.

MARY: Jason is my son, and I am going to let him keep a little more childhood before you destroy it.

MICHAEL: I don't want to destroy him, Mary. I love him. And because I love him, I want to be honest. Look, things happen in life that we don't plan. I didn't plan to fall in love with Connie. But it happened. You don't believe it, but this is hurting me, too.

MARY: Good. I want you to hurt. Like you've hurt me. But I want to keep that hurt from Jason a little bit longer. And I don't give a damn how much pain that gives you.

MICHAEL: *(Quietly)* What if Jason did just hear us? How much pain do you intend to give him pretending everything is well? *(Silence)* And how do you suppose he'll feel when he does find out? Don't you think he'll realize that we've been lying to him?

MARY: *(Grabs front of his shirt)* Sweetheart, you owe me. You are going to pretend right along with me. And if you don't ... *(Trying to keep upper hand)*

MICHAEL: *(Holding her hands. Quietly)* What? You'll keep Jason from me after the divorce? An angry, vengeful ex-wife using her child as a weapon? I thought you were smarter than that. How could that ever help?

MARY: *(No more fight left in her)* I don't know. I don't know what's going to help.

MICHAEL: Mary. We have to face it. All of us. Jason too.

MARY: *(Honestly. With no rancor)* Not right now. I know he is going to need us both, but I'm not there yet. I need time. And we need to give Jason this time. Just a little more time. That's all I'm asking of you.

MICHAEL: *(Long pause—MICHAEL reaches for shopping bag.)* I'll put the Game Boy away. He's going to love it. *(MARY gives him the shopping bag.)*

BLACKOUT

Felicia Reymont

This, Felicia Reymont's first play, was written for a FYV workshop for seniors, piloted at The Caring Community, an agency that provides services to the elderly in the Greenwich Village area. It was the clinical director's hope that a workshop of this kind would serve several purposes: reduce isolation, boost social and cognitive skills, and alleviate depression. It is fair to say that all of those results were achieved over the course of the months we worked together, and, as has been the case with every other group, some real talent emerged. Felicia already had a love of writing, but she claims that "this wonderful workshop pulled it out of me and helped me write with focus, flow, and confidence." Felicia's natural humor was immediately apparent to the group, and she struggled hard to shift what were originally one-dimensional caricatures into three-dimensional characters. And as she moved beyond sitcom format, we began to see Felicia's own range of feelings as a human being. The seniors in the audience at the final presentation all appreciated seeing this delicate and often unspoken subject, senior sexuality, handled with such care. Felicia continues to write on a regular basis.

This play was in response to Andrea Sperling's photograph on the cover of this book.

Friends To The End
Felicia Reymont

Characters: LOUISE   Female, late 60s
             MARGOT   Female, late 60s

AT RISE Margot and Louise, two friends, sit side by side in a doctor's waiting room. No one else is there. Louise is attractive and conservatively dressed. Margot is a flashy blonde bombshell. Margot is very agitated, covering her face with her hands.

LOUISE: *(Trying to console her)* Come on now, take deep breaths. You do *not* have AIDS. You'll see.

MARGOT: I'm gonna drop dead of a heart attack when they call my name. Look at me. *(Holds hands out in front of her)* I'm shaking.

LOUISE: I'm telling you, you do *not* have AIDS.

MARGOT: How do *you* know? *(Before she can answer)* You saw the letter. From the Board of Health! Imagine some guy with AIDS naming *me* as one of his partners!

LOUISE: But you don't even recognize the name.

MARGOT: It had to be that Jim who never called again. *(Shakes her head)* I had a weird feeling about him, like he was giving me a phony name. *(Thinks)* Probably married.

LOUISE: Going around having sex, knowing he has AIDS.

MARGOT: He's a murderer.

LOUISE: He should be strung up by the balls. *(Pause)* I don't want to start preaching now, but—

MARGOT: Believe me. If I get away with it this time, I'm never having sex again, ever. I swear.

LOUISE: Hmmm. Where have I heard that song before?

MARGOT: Get off my back.

LOUISE: How many times have I had to talk you off the ledge over some low-life creep?

MARGOT: I know, I know. *(Bows her head)* I don't deserve your friendship.

LOUISE: *(Rising)* You know what? You're sucking the life out of me. All those wasted hours listening to you cry over losers. And for what? *(Silence)* You never learn. Unwanted pregnancies. Abortions. Herpes. And now *this*. *I'm* having the nervous breakdown.

MARGOT: Fine then, just leave me here alone. Go somewhere and relax. Get something waxed. I can face the music without you.

LOUISE: Shut up. *(Sits)* You drive me nuts.

MARGOT: *(Pause)* Oh, God, I'm such a mess.

LOUISE: You just don't love yourself enough.

MARGOT: No kidding.

LOUISE: Well, it's no wonder. As far back as I can remember, your father was always putting you down.

MARGOT: And when my mother tried to defend me, boy, would he let her have it.

LOUISE: He was a real woman hater, which is probably why you have no self-esteem. And why you blow money you can't afford on every cosmetic out there.

MARGOT: Anything else?

LOUISE: Well, now that you ask, there's the clothes.

MARGOT: You don't buy clothes?

LOUISE: Yes, but everything you buy is either too short, too tight, or too low cut.

MARGOT: *(Looks at her)* That's nice to know.

LOUISE: Can't you see you're give off the wrong vibes?

MARGOT: Meaning?

LOUISE: Look what you attract. *(Silence)* Empty-headed pretty boys half your age who only want one thing. And they have nothing to offer but trouble.

MARGOT: *(Getting angry)* Easy for you to point a finger. You have a husband who loves you.

LOUISE: You could have had the same thing. Phillip was crazy about you, and he was a real catch.

MARGOT: He bored me to tears, and you know it.

LOUISE: Tell me those muscle-bound jerks from the gym are better. *(Snickers)* They don't even care enough about you to use a condom.

MARGOT: It's not always just the guy's fault.

LOUISE: Sure. Miss Eager-to-Please over here. No condom? No problem.

MARGOT *(Fighting back)* Seems to me you've gotten carried away once or twice yourself.

LOUISE: I was no angel, I admit it. But I stopped living dangerously a long time ago.

MARGOT: *(Pause)* If I had another chance, I'd run the other way. No matter how hot the guy was.

LOUISE: I should get this in writing.

MARGOT: The saddest part is, it wasn't even worth it. *(She hurriedly stands)* Let's just get out of here before I jump out of my skin.

LOUISE: *(Pulls her down)* No. You need to know for sure or you'll always worry.

MARGOT: *(Long tense pause)* I'd give anything to take it all back.

LOUISE: Coming from someone who loves living *la vida loca*, I wonder.

MARGOT: How can you be sarcastic at a time like this?

LOUISE: Once we get through this, you're going into therapy. I mean it.

MARGOT: Listen to yourself. Making plans for someone who's doomed.

LOUISE: *(Rubs her forehead)* I've got a splitting headache.

MARGOT: *(Jumps up again)* I can't take any more. I'm gonna scream.

LOUISE: *(Pulls her down and holds her)* Shhhhh. They're gonna call you any second.

MARGOT: *(After a silence)* You have the patience of a saint. *(No response, she is fighting tears.)* I do all these stupid things, and you never give up on me.

LOUISE: Don't give me so much credit. I've almost dumped you a bunch of times.

MARGOT: Thanks for sharing that.

LOUISE: But just when I'm ready to walk, the good Margot comes out, and I'm back on the rollercoaster again.

MARGOT: "Good Margot?" There's a good Margot?

LOUISE: Yes, there's a good Margot. I'm not a total masochist, you know.

MARGOT: Tell me about the good Margot, quick. Because when that door opens, it's gonna be all over.

LOUISE: *(Looks at her)* Listen. The good Margot is fun, kind, and generous to the core.

MARGOT: *(No sarcasm)* I can't believe you feel that way when all I do is bring you down.

LOUISE: Honey, I don't forget things. Who stayed by my mother's side until I could make it back from my honeymoon?

MARGOT: It was the least I could do. The poor thing couldn't even move with that broken hip.

LOUISE: She'd have died for sure if you hadn't found her lying there. You saved her life. *(Pause)* And who dragged me from doctor to doctor when I had that breast scare? *(Margot is wiping tears away.)* Don't cry, sweetie, you're making *me* cry. We're gonna get through this. Together. *(Margot dissolves in tears, and Louise gets out a tissue.)* Here. Blow your nose. *(Louise flinches.)*

MARGOT: Did you just pull your hand away? *(Shocked silence)* Oh my God, you did. You're afraid to touch me.

LOUISE: Now you're hallucinating.

MARGOT: Hell, I don't blame you. No one's ever going to touch me again.

LOUISE: Stop it. *(Offers her hand)* Now hold on to me. I won't let go. *(Margot takes her hand.)* Whatever happens, I'm with you all the way.

MARGOT: Friends til the end. *(Louise puts her arm around Margot. No smiles)*

BLACKOUT

Molly Rhodes

Molly began her FYV training when she was fourteen and continued throughout her teen years. Always a "good girl," Molly was an articulate and high achieving student academically; she attended one of the most prestigious specialized public high schools in NYC. She needed to "find her voice" in a different kind of way, because she was hampered by the persistence of a stutter. Although I never addressed the impediment directly, because the acting training focuses so intensely on "the person you are talking to," rather than on the way actors say what they are saying, Molly moved from a position of self-consciousness to one of "other-consciousness." And because the process also allowed her to voice her darker emotions, like anger, in the service of fighting for what her characters wanted, she overcame her perfectionism and stopped fearing what would come out of her mouth. There was comfort, too, in knowing that someone in the class was holding her script and would help her out if she forgot a line. As she got out of her own way, Molly became a moving and authentic young actor, and she no longer stuttered! Her writing also became increasingly more emotional and less intellectual as she got out of her head and into her body. Although the voices of her characters were still cerebral, they also voiced the adolescent fears and confusions that she was grappling with. For her this play was a "Blast from the past! Rereading it brought back all the issues I was struggling with at the time. Having the forum to explore those issues was invaluable, both as a writer looking to get in touch with what I truly cared about and as a human being wanting to express what was important to me. The FYV emphasis on using theatre to explore issues and ideas that were complex and central to our lives has had a deep effect on the topics I'm attracted to as a playwright. I am drawn to stories that are complicated, current, and that have no pat, easy answers. As I continue to grow as a writer, I keep in mind the tenets of theatre that Gail passed down to me: that the essence of what we are trying to get across is not in the big, pretty words we use but in the relationships between the people who are saying them." At the time of this writing, Molly was pursuing playwriting in San Francisco, where she was awarded a PlayGround fellowship to develop The Singularity of We. *She was also raising money for a counseling-based outreach program for youth and young adults.*

> *This was the last play Molly wrote with me before she began college. It was written as part of the* If I Knew *cluster, which featured fantasies taking place in the minds of students at their high school graduation ceremony.*

Fourteen B (14B)
Molly Rhodes

Characters: ALICE   Female, 21, has a slight British accent

                LINDA   Female, 16

AT RISE: ALICE hears a knock on the door of her studio apartment; the floor is strewn with papers. She crosses and opens the door.

ALICE: Hi, can I help you?

LINDA: Yeah; I live upstairs. In 14B? *(No response)* My mom called you earlier about using your copy machine?

ALICE: Oh, right. Let me just get myself organized, and I'll show you where it is, okay?

LINDA: Okay. *(LINDA enters and stands awkwardly by the door as ALICE quickly collects her stuff on the floor.)*

ALICE: *(Still cleaning up)* Please, come inside. Make yourself at home— as much as possible in all this mess! I suppose you wouldn't believe me if I told you it was the maid's day off? *(LINDA smiles.)* My mother always told me I'd end up living like this.

LINDA: My mother tells me the same thing!

ALICE: I think all mothers secretly yearn for the day when we'll come back, in tears, with a year's worth of laundry and dishes, begging mercy and forgiveness for not heeding all their wonderful advice when it was given!

LINDA: Is that what you do?

ALICE: Oh, no! I have yet to swallow my pride. *(Still cleaning)* I prefer to convince myself that cultivating rare forms of fungi in my bathtub is a fair price for independence! *(She rises.)* What do you want to copy?

LINDA: *(Handing ALICE a large stack of papers)* They're applications for summer programs.

ALICE: Are you hoping to attend *all* of these?

LINDA: No, but my parents didn't want me to be short of choices.

ALICE: *(Looking through pile)* I'll say.

LINDA: I'm sorry there are so many. If you think it's too much to print—

ALICE: It might take a couple of minutes, but I'm sure it's nothing my copier can't handle.

LINDA: Could you show me where it—

ALICE: Why don't *I* just put them in the machine? Save you the trouble of having a battle with its mood swings.

LINDA: I don't want to inconvenience you.

ALICE: I wasn't planning to work much longer anyway. Wait here for a moment; I'll be right back. *(ALICE exits for a few moments, as LINDA stands awkwardly in the middle of the apartment, not knowing where to sit. ALICE sticks her head back in.)* You can have a seat if you want to … anywhere that you see space is fine.

LINDA: Thanks.

ALICE: Would you like something to drink? It won't be more than ten minutes, but if you're thirsty—

LINDA: No. I'm fine, thank you.

ALICE: Okay. *(ALICE exits again, as LINDA finds herself a seat. A few moments later, ALICE enters.)* It shouldn't take too much longer. *(Pause)* Are you sure you don't want something to drink?

LINDA: Positive.

ALICE: Suit yourself. *(She sits, studying her.)* I couldn't help noticing some of the places you're applying to: foreign exchange programs, laboratory internships, drama courses … makes my summers spent on Jones Beach seem absolutely mundane!

LINDA: It wasn't my idea. My parents think it will "broaden my horizons" or something. *(Pause)* What?

ALICE: Nothing. You just remind me so much of myself when I was your age. God, did that sound really corny?

LINDA: I know what you meant.

ALICE: I couldn't wait to get out from under my parents' overprotective wings.

LINDA: If I had my own way—

ALICE: I guarantee you it's a lot scarier when you do. You almost begin to miss having someone there to lay it all out for you.

LINDA: *Almost*, but not quite, right?

ALICE: There are good days and bad days. I only graduated from college a few years ago, so I'm still having more of the latter than the former.

LINDA: College must've been great, though. I have another year of high school to go after this, and I'm already yearning for all that freedom, that opportunity to finally find out who I really am.

ALICE: Yeah; I tried that route. Went searching for the college where I would "discover myself." *(Pause)* Can I let you in on a secret?

LINDA: What?

ALICE: I didn't find it. Not that I regret going, because it gave me a lot, but so has everything else I've done before and since then. It's not the be-all and end-all of your existence.

LINDA: At least you're free to decide what you want to do with your summers, instead of having it dictated to you by your parents.

ALICE: Are you kidding? I'd give a vital organ to be able to do some of the things you're applying for. I only *dream* about taking off the entire summer to go to an exotic foreign country.

LINDA: Couldn't you do something like that? You must have friends from college who live all over the country; you could hitchhike—travel around and visit them.

ALICE: With what money, and what time? I've got all my college loans to pay off. This summer I'll probably fill in for all the people in my company who are taking short vacations with their families.

LINDA: What company?

ALICE: The name will mean nothing to you. I'm basically a fact-checker there. People from other departments give me their reports and presentations, and I back-check all the facts and statistics they use. The facts can range anywhere from the number of dead after a revolution in South America to how many former US presidents liked vanilla ice cream!

LINDA: Oh.

ALICE: Yeah, exactly; "Oh." Not where I thought my BA in English would get me.

LINDA: If you don't like it, why do you do it?

ALICE: You've got to live somehow.

LINDA: What about doing something you enjoy? *(ALICE smiles at her.)* I'm reminding you of you again, aren't I?

ALICE: It's a good thing! I hope you keep your thirst for enjoyment; I've come across too many adults who have sacrificed it to *get by*. Including myself. *(Laughs at herself)* Did you hear that? I called myself an *adult*. The future sure has a way of creeping up on you.

LINDA: But there's so much you could do, so many choices open to you.

ALICE: When I graduated from college I thought I could conquer the world; now I spend half my time praying it doesn't flatten me first.

LINDA: You sound so jaded. What on earth happened to make you dislike your life so much?

ALICE: That would make it easier to accept, wouldn't it—if I had some great monumental event to put all the blame on and purge over at a group therapy session. Then maybe I wouldn't just sit around waiting for my life to start. All throughout high school, four years that no one could pay me enough to relive, I kept reminding myself that my future still lay before me. Even in college, as I searched for my major and the career that would fill my void, define my life, I never stopped believing in the great day when I would "find myself." Now, here I am; with all this freedom and responsibility. I'm supposed to be at the point where I've *discovered* who I am. *(Shakes her head)* But I can't help thinking there's got to be something more.

LINDA: I'd hate to think my life was over before I even reached twenty-five.

ALICE: I'm sorry. God, I didn't mean to depress you. I don't want you to think this is all you have to look forward to. I just think you shouldn't underestimate all that you're being offered now. Those programs your parents want to send you to may seem like nothing but a bore, but I guarantee you that you'll look back on them and be grateful for the carefree summers you had. Don't waste a minute that you have worrying about what your future will hold, or what you'll do with yourself when you're older. There's enough of that later in life, believe me.

LINDA: Maybe.

ALICE: "If only the young knew; if only the old could"?

LINDA: Sounds like a motto my mother would have.

ALICE: Yes, I was afraid you might say that. *(Rises)* I think your applications are probably done. I'll go get them. *(She exits.)*

LINDA: *(Yells to her)* I hope it wasn't too much for your copier to handle. *(ALICE enters, carrying the applications.)*

ALICE: Don't worry. I used to feed this thing whole manuscripts to print.

LINDA: Manuscripts? Like screenplays?

ALICE: Usually compilations of short stories, to send to various publishers.

LINDA: So your BA in English wasn't a complete waste after all!

ALICE: I didn't mean to imply that it was a waste; I'll never stop writing, no matter what else I do.

LINDA: That's what you always wanted to do?

ALICE: I imagined myself in some secluded section of the French Alps, overlooking the Riviera, bathing my throat in Gordon's and tonic as I completed the final chapters of my novel!

LINDA: Is that still your dream?

ALICE: It's one variation of my dream. To tell you the truth, I'd accept a cramped apartment on the Lower East Side, overlooking the FDR, if it would afford me the chance to write.

LINDA: Then why are you analyzing the presidents' ice-cream habits, when you could have a career you really enjoy?

ALICE: I wish it was that simple. I wish I didn't have to worry about paying bills or meeting deadlines for reports I really couldn't care less about. But that's not what they call *reality*, is it?

LINDA: Reality is what you make it.

ALICE: Right now I'm just trying to make ends meet. *(Holding the pile out to her)* I still hold on to the dream of establishing myself as a writer. But it's hard, you know? What I wouldn't give to have all the freedom you have.

LINDA: What freedom? *(Takes pile)* To choose between my parent's variations on how my life should run? What I wouldn't give for *your* freedom, the ability to make my own life.

ALICE: It's not as easy as it looks.

LINDA: At least you can decide what you *want*.

ALICE: At least you don't have to *know* what you want.

LINDA: How can I know what I want? I haven't even begun to discover myself.

ALICE: Neither have I.

LINDA: Well … I guess that's what tomorrow's for.

ALICE: Well then, I propose an imaginary toast to tomorrow, and our futures. Never stop living. *(Raises an invisible glass)* Or learning. Or growing! *(Silence)* That was too corny, wasn't it? I know I have a bad habit of saying corny—

LINDA: It's okay. I know exactly what you meant. *(Returns the imaginary toast)*

BLACKOUT

Melissa Rocha

I first met Melissa when she participated in a FYV professional development workshop. She did so along with all of the other seventh grade teachers at the middle school for children of recent immigrants where she was teaching. Melissa was initially terrified to stand up and speak in front of her peers in the workshop, and she did not think of herself as a writer. Moreover, she was still finding her own voice as a new educator. However, Melissa rose to the challenge with tremendous courage and good grace. Following her own training, I worked with Melissa and her five colleagues to bring the same acting and writing experience to her bilingual students. Focusing the energy of these rambunctious and recently uprooted tweens was quite a challenge, but because Melissa was herself bilingual, she was committed to enhancing their confidence about communicating in a new language and in a new country. And she did. Over the months that we worked together in her classroom, Melissa began to exert "tough love" in helping her students to maintain their focus, an ability that she discovered by "fighting for" someone else during her own monologue work. The youngsters really responded to the study of published monologues (in English). They became comprehensible, and they lost their self-consciousness about their accents as they became increasingly other-conscious. They also loved writing the plays and were able to improve their usage and grammar significantly by listening to their drafts being read aloud by classmates each week. Melissa ran successful workshops in her school for several years. Sadly, the teachers suffered an unfortunate change in leadership that deteriorated the tenor of teacher/student communication in the school, and all of the teachers I had trained there eventually sought employment elsewhere. Like several of the others, Melissa decided to leave the school system altogether, and she pursued what she felt to be more holistic work as a private tutor. Melissa participated in a second FYV Workshop; after many re-writes, Breaking Away *was the expression of her newfound voice. I included it in my* Find Your Voice *book as an example of excellent teacher work. Her dramaturgical skill became so sophisticated, in fact, that I subsequently asked Melissa to assist me in the teaching of several teen after-school workshops. "I remember Gail's direction to develop characters who fight for their wants and needs, both emotional and physical. I've learned to* listen to my students' wants and needs more closely and to better identify and fight for my own as well." Melissa is currently teaching English as a Second Language to adults and preparing students for their GED exams. In addition, she privately tutors students in grades 3 through 12.

This, Melissa's second play, was written for the cluster Beneath It All, in response to a photo of shoes beneath a bed.

Breaking Away
Melissa Rocha

Characters: ROSA   Latina, middle-aged
               ANA   Latina, mid 20s

AT RISE: ANA is in her bedroom in San Juan, nervously packing her suitcase for New York.

ANA: *(Talking to herself while pulling things from underneath her bed and putting them in a suitcase)* I haven't seen these shoes in years! *(Looking around at the pile)* I can't take all of these things to New York.
ROSA: *(Enters quietly and looks at suitcase)* Ana, what are you doing?
ANA: *(Startled that her mother has come into the room and nervous that she may have heard her)* Nothing, I'm just cleaning.
ROSA: You don't need to do that now. Why don't you help me pack your father's overnight bag, we have to leave for the hospital soon.
ANA: Can't you take him by yourself?
ROSA: You're better at talking to the doctors.
ANA: I need to get some things done.
ROSA: You promised you would come. Take out some extra shirts for your dad.
ANA: *(Going to the closet and pulling out some shirts)* Which do you want?
ROSA: Give me both; it doesn't hurt to pack a little extra. *(Silence while she packs)* He's getting sicker, Ana.

226

ANA: You're just convincing yourself of it by saying that. He'll be fine.

ROSA: That's not what the doctors said. Anyway, I don't have time to argue—we're running late. *(Starts to leave)*

ANA: Ma, I can't stay.

ROSA: *(Stops)* You don't have to stay. I just need you to talk to the doctors. You're the one with the college education. They listen to you.

ANA: I mean I can't stay here.

ROSA: *(Pause)* What?

ANA: I'm getting on a plane to New York tomorrow.

ROSA: When did you decide this?

ANA: At the last minute, because I knew you'd try to convince me out of it.

ROSA: You can't.

ANA: I've been saving money for a year.

ROSA: You have a responsibility to your family, starting with this appointment.

ANA: I have to go.

ROSA: Finish packing his bag, and I'll meet you outside. I'm not discussing this. *(Heading for the door)*

ANA: *(Grabbing her)* Listen to me.

ROSA: You don't care if your father gets sicker? You'll leave when he needs you the most? He's going to the hospital so that they can clean his kidneys. His diabetes could kill him if he doesn't take care of himself—

ANA: That's just it—if he doesn't take care of himself, then there's nothing we can do. If he'd taken care of himself to begin with, he wouldn't be where he is now.

ROSA: If he hadn't worked as hard as he did to make sure you went to college, you wouldn't be where you are either. Have you thought about that?

ANA: A million times. But how long do I have to keep paying him back?

ROSA: As long as he needs us, and until he's healthy again. *(Turning to leave)* We have to go.

ANA: He should have thought about his health when he was drinking too much.

ROSA: Don't be disrespectful. *(Turning back angrily)* He's your father and my husband. We're all part of the same family. This is where you belong, not in New York.

ANA: I have to live my own life.

ROSA: Now, when I don't have anyone else to help me?

ANA: You have to let go.

ROSA: You're father is going to the hospital overnight!

ANA: They're keeping him overnight just to be safe, not because they think he's gonna die. Don't guilt me into staying.

ROSA: What do you think you're gonna find in New York, anyway? Your family's here. New York is someone else's dream, not yours.

ANA: I think I'm the one who should decide my own dreams.

ROSA: Be realistic. Where would you stay?

ANA: Cousin Julia's.

ROSA: Is she paying for your food, getting you a job?

ANA: I'm twenty-five years old.

ROSA: I have enough troubles here. Now you want to make me sick worrying about you being in New York?

ANA: New York is a chance to have my own life. *(Pause)* You took a risk when you moved away from home too.

ROSA: You have a good job here; you don't need to leave like I did.

ANA: I have a good job, but it could be better.

ROSA: Your father won't understand. *(Silence)* You'd be splitting our family apart.

ANA: He already took care of that with his drinking.

ROSA: Don't insult me.

ANA: *(Pause)* I know what I'm doing doesn't make sense to you. And I don't know what I'll find in New York, but I know that if I stay here I'll find nothing.

ROSA: What do you want to find?

ANA: *(Taking her hands)* The same things you wanted when you left your family.

ROSA: My family had no money, I *had* to find work. You're leaving a decent job.

ANA: Didn't you want more?

ROSA: Yes, but you're alone. You're a young woman alone, going to New York; at least I had your father with me.

ANA: I can take care of myself.

ROSA: But I can't take care of your father alone. What am I supposed to do without you?

ANA: You'll be fine without me. Dad will be fine, too.

ROSA: *(Pause)* When were you going to tell him?

ANA: *(Takes an envelope out of her pocket.)* I wrote him a letter.

ROSA: *(Takes it)* He may never forgive you.

ANA: Will you?

ROSA: Why do you have to leave so suddenly?

ANA: You knew that I would leave one day. I'm not doing it to hurt anyone.

ROSA: *(Puts the envelope in suitcase)* Get the extra blankets from the top shelf in the closet.

ANA: He doesn't need extra blankets; they'll have those in the hospital.

ROSA: They say it's cold in New York in the winter.

BLACKOUT

Phillip Schiller

Phil participated in the FYV training during his senior year, when we were in residence at his NYC high school. He was a charming and outgoing young man who demonstrated terrific courage in exploring his darker and more sensitive sides during the acting classes. This was the first play that Phil ever wrote, and it caught his lovely sense of humor, as well as his nascent efforts to explore angry feelings. Recalling the photograph (of an old stone wall), Phil remembers "being inspired to write about an experience someone would have in Italy, having visited the country that summer. It was my second attempt at writing a scene and, rereading it now, I find it excellent! I still enjoy writing comedy to this day. If FYV hadn't exposed me to the world of theatre and writing, I would have had much more difficulty in finding myself. The program made me into an outgoing, creative, team-playing person. I am reminded of that every day when I use the talents I began to develop back then." At the time of this writing, Phil was studying film at the Zurich University of the Arts.

This, Phil's first play, was part of a cluster entitled Unexpected Obstacles. *It was written in response to a photograph of light on a marble wall (p. 38).*

Lost In Italy
Phil Schiller

Characters: BETH   Female, 17
               ANTONIO   Male, 18

AT RISE: BETH, a high school student who is abroad in Italy, walks into an alley with a marble bench. She looks lost, but admires the pretty art on the walls and ceiling. She takes a picture and looks around to see where she is. She hears footsteps, gets up with her Italian language book. A young man approaches.

BETH: Hello! I mean … *Buon giorno!*
ANTONIO: Si.
BETH: Okay. Communication. Umm. Dove i?

ANTONIO: *(With heavy accent)* American?

BETH: Yes. Do you speak English?

ANTONIO: No. Well, little bit, si.

BETH: Alrighty. *(Speaking as though he's deaf)* Where … am … I?

ANTONIO: *(Pause)* I no understand.

BETH: I am looking for the Ufizzi. *(ANTONIO takes the phrase book and goes to the Italian/English; points to "I don't know.")* Okay! You don't know. An Italian who's lost in Italy—

ANTONIO: You American. I like America!

BETH: Have you been to America? *(ANTONIO looks clueless.)* Oh brother. Hold on. *(Looks in her book)* Siete stati mia prima la?

ANTONIO: No. *Soltano nei movies.*

BETH: That's why I came to Italy! I saw the movie *Only You* and fell in love with the scenery! Did you see it? *(Silence)* It was with Robert Downey Jr. and Marisa Tomei?

ANTONIO: I loving movie.

BETH: It was very funny.

ANTONIO: Si, funny. *(A pause—there is an awkward silence. Both look around.)*

BETH: So … oh … hold on. *(Checks book)* Che cosa e il vostro nome?

ANTONIO: Antonio. And … you?

BETH: I'm Beth. *(They shake hands.)* Nice to meet you. So, why are *you* here?

ANTONIO: I here vacation. I living Voltera.

BETH: Oh. Voltera; where is that?

ANTONIO: *In e nel mezzo di Tosacana.*

BETH: Middle of Tuscany! It must be beautiful there. *(He shakes his head no, she laughs.)* If *you'd* lived in Rhode Island all your life, you'd think any place in Italy is nicer.

ANTONIO: *(Trying to pronounce it)* Rhode Island? In America? I love the America!

BETH: *Niente di speciale. (Another pause, then ANTONIO points to the art.)*

ANTONIO: America art so beautiful?

BETH: None that I've seen. This art is so pretty. So white, yet the naked people look great!

ANTONIO: Don't look naked, look art. *Capite? (BETH looks up and looks at the art; ANTONIO studies her.)*

BETH: So ... it's not that they *are* naked, but that they *appear* naked.

ANTONIO: You having amico?

BETH: A boyfriend?! *(Shy laugh)* No. I haven't found him yet. *(Wondering)* Do you have a girlfriend?

ANTONIO: *(His accent abruptly changes to perfect American English.)* No. I'm single.

BETH: *(Beth looks up stunned, doesn't know what to think.)* You're American!

ANTONIO: Surprise!

BETH: So you're not—

ANTONIO: Italian? Nope. I saw you walk in here and followed you. I figured if I was Italian, you'd find me more interesting!

BETH: Well, I *did.*

ANTONIO: *(Flirty)* So you find me interesting?

BETH: *(Quickly)* No! Yes. No!

ANTONIO: Confused?

BETH: Well, yeah! I'm mad—and embarrassed too. I thought you were Italian, different from the guys back home. At home, everyone is so ordinary; they take you to the same places, tell you the same things. I wanted to meet someone who was different. *(She starts to walk away; he stops her.)*

ANTONIO: I *am* different. Just not in a *foreign* sense. *(Beth takes a moment to think. She is mad but studies him.)* If it's difference you're looking for, how many guys from Rhode Island can pull off being Italian?

BETH: Yeah, but—

ANTONIO: *(In an Italian accent, trying to get BETH to smile)* I lika your hair.

BETH: Stop!

ANTONIO: *(Back to English)* You're still mad?

BETH: How would you feel if a great-looking girl pretended to be French but really was American.

ANTONIO: Great! I wouldn't have to move to France to see her.

BETH: How can I know if you're telling the truth?

ANTONIO: I just went all-out to get your attention; it's not like I lied about everything.

BETH: You pretended to be Italian; that's a pretty big lie.

ANTONIO: Look, I wanted to meet you. I was just being creative.

BETH: *(BETH looks down at her book.)* God. Three minutes ago I drooled all over you, thinking you were this nice Italian. And now ... you're American.

ANTONIO: I just played a little joke. Come on. *(Charming)* Didn't you think it was the least bit creative?

BETH: *(BETH looks away.)* Yes.

ANTONIO: *Te che bella.*

BETH: *(Pause)* You really think I'm beautiful?

ANTONIO: Si. *(They look at each other, and he speaks in normal English.)* Listen, I'm sorry. The Ufizzi is right around the corner. *(He gets up and offers his arm.)* May I take you?

BETH: *(Pause, then she hooks his arm.)* I'd like that.

ANTONIO: *Bene.*

BLACKOUT

Nora Scott-Simpson

Nora began her FYV training when she was still a pre-teen attending a private Catholic school in Greenwich Village. Always sweet and pleasant, she was perhaps the shyest and most reticent young communicator I worked with during the last twenty years. She was barely audible when she spoke, possessed two left feet in the movement exercises, and shook with terror when she sang. No matter how small a role she undertook during our term-end presentations, she could be found praying and agonizing in the wings beforehand. And then everything began to change. After a few terms, Nora finally agreed to try writing a play. The result was really two parallel monologues, and it was one of the darkest and saddest pieces ever written in the program. The other members of the workshop were shocked, as was her family, to hear the voice that was emerging, but we praised her for her courage—and we worked to ensure that the piece was as authentic as possible. She survived the reaction, and the following term Nora returned with an entirely different affect; she was both buoyant and outgoing and sported lots of gothic clothing and jewelry. She seemed to be entirely in her own body and was able to dance beautifully during a performance of one of our clusters at the American Museum of Natural History. She also developed a lilting soprano voice and became one of the more imaginative and adventurous actors I have ever trained. In fact, she went on to attend LaGuardia High School for the Arts—as an acting major! She proved my long-standing belief that the shyest people, once connected to the power of their own voices, often make the greatest actors and writers. Nora is now doing something she never would have predicted or thought would have brought fulfillment to her life: "I am a stay-at-home mom to three lovely boys, living in the Midwest and driving a minivan. It is interesting for me to remember how terribly shy I was as a pre-teen and to see how outgoing and exuberant my kids are. I think back to the person I was and remember her, but she is so far from who I am today. Before I had children, I was in the music business, working as a promotional independent. As a liaison between record labels and radio stations, it was necessary for me to have confidence and a secure sense of self-worth. Being in FYV was such a motivating experience for me." This, Nora's first complete play, was written for the cluster Ashes, Ashes, We All Fall Down, *which was based on interviews of teenagers* in recovery at the Phoenix House rehabilitation program. Note the bold courage of the confrontation and the depth of the feelings she captured in the short piece. It was performed to thunderous applause by fellow workshop members Bobby Lopez and Sarah Paulson (also featured in this collection and pictured on p. 35).

Ashes
Nora Scott-Simpson

Characters: LAYLA Female, 17
CHRIS Male, 20

AT RISE: LAYLA enters apartment, gets a cigarette, then sits on the floor. She sees her boyfriend CHRIS watching her. He approaches and squats beside her.

CHRIS: Where'd you go?
LAYLA: I needed some air fresh. I mean fresh air. Just a little air. It's really stuffy. Stuffy. Stuffy, you know? *(Silence)* That's a cool word, I like it. But that's what it is. It's stuffy. That's why I went out. You know? *(Silence)* Stuffy, I like that word. Stuffy, stuffy, stuffy, stuffy.
CHRIS: *(Looks in her face)* What is wrong with you?
LAYLA: You wouldn't understand cause you're so uptight.
CHRIS: What are you on? *(Silence)* Layla, you promised.
LAYLA: You have something on your face. *(Rubs his cheek)*
CHRIS: *(Pushes her hand away)* You're coked up. I don't believe you.
LAYLA: I am not ... coked up. I don't ... I told you I didn't, so I wouldn't ... do it. Or the other way around. You know what I mean. I'm not. I don't do it anymore, Chris. Chris, I do not do coke. I did, but I stopped. Quit. Past yes, present no. I do not, me, as in I, do not do it now. Not coke.
CHRIS: Are you done making an ass of yourself? *(Silence)* You went out with Claire. She's sold it to you in the past, so why not in the present?
LAYLA: We just went through this. No present. No, no, no, no present. *(To herself)* I'm not on coke, bastard. *(Stands)*

CHRIS: *(Stands)* I thought you believed in honesty? You want an honest relationship with me, and you're lying.

LAYLA: You don't believe me?

CHRIS: Great. Honesty at its goddamn best.

LAYLA: What is the big deal, Chris? I knew you'd be a dick. I know, I ... knew. What is the big deal?

CHRIS: What's the big deal? This is what almost broke us up the last time. We're goin' in goddamn circles.

LAYLA: This is the first time I've ever done heroin, so just chill, geez.

CHRIS: *(Indicates the door)* That's it. Out of my house. Get ...

LAYLA: What are you, my daddy? Screw you. *(Goes to get another cigarette)*

CHRIS: *Out of my house! (She closes the door.)* Damn it, Layla. How could you?

LAYLA: Shut up! You are giving me a huge headache. Just shut up!

CHRIS: *(Grabs her)* I'm giving you a headache? You're breaking my heart; you're killing yourself.

LAYLA: Come on, I'm fine, see. Babe, I'm fine. Relax. I won't do it again. Just relax. *(She tries to kiss him; he pulls away.)*

CHRIS: That's what you said last time.

LAYLA: I'm sorry. I'm so sorry. I don't want to lose you.

CHRIS: *(Pause)* I don't want to lose you either.

LAYLA: Let's relax. Okay? *(Kisses him all over his face)* I love you. *(Kisses him passionately. He doesn't respond much.)* Want a beer?

CHRIS: No thanks.

LAYLA: Music?

CHRIS: That would be nice. *(He sits while she goes to put on music.)*

LAYLA: *(Puts in a tape—Eric Clapton is heard)* It's our song. "I see everything in your eyes." Remember when you said that to me?

CHRIS: I remember. *(She sits on his lap; his arms are around her; they kiss.)* Promise you'll stop.

LAYLA: Yes, I promise. I'll stop. Promise. I love you. I don't want you to leave me.

CHRIS: I couldn't leave you.

LAYLA: Promise. Do you promise?

CHRIS: Yeah.

LAYLA: Say it.

CHRIS: I promise. *(She cuddles into him.)* Where did you get the money, Layla?

LAYLA: What?

CHRIS: The money. How did you pay for the heroin?

LAYLA: Oh … well … Claire just gave it to me, as … an early wedding gift.

CHRIS: Oh?

LAYLA: As a gift, for free, you know? Nice, right?

CHRIS: *(Pushing her away from him, looking into her face.)* Claire never gives anyone anything for free. She wouldn't give her own mother an aspirin for free. Why are you lying again, Layla?

LAYLA: You don't believe me again? Chris, I could never just … you know—

CHRIS: *(Throws her off and stands)* What are you doing? *(Silence)* Where did you get the money?

LAYLA: *(Sits on chair)* I'll tell you, but you gotta promise not to be mad. It was all I could do. I needed a pick me up, and it was all I had.

CHRIS: *(Bends to her)* Where did you get the goddamn money?

LAYLA: *(Softly)* I gave her my engagement ring.

CHRIS: *(Stands up, walking around kicking things)* I don't believe you. Holy shit. I don't believe you. I don't mean anything to you. I mean nothing to you at all.

LAYLA: *(Crying)* I'm sorry.

CHRIS: You can't explain this. I don't care how bad your mother treated you; you can't just treat me like dirt and expect me to say, "Oh, it's okay, her mommy used to ignore her when she was younger." Grow up, Layla. I saved for that damn ring for two years, and you traded it for heroin.

LAYLA: *(Covers her ears)* Don't yell at me.

CHRIS: *(In her face)* Yell at you? You better hope I don't touch you; I could kill you.

LAYLA: *(Cowering)* Screw you. I want to go home.

CHRIS: *(Rises and slowly walks away)* Sure—damn it. Go home.

LAYLA: *Take me home!*

CHRIS: *(Turns and looks at her)* I can't get near you.

LAYLA: Take me home. Please. *(Crying, dropping to the floor)*

CHRIS: Get off the floor.
LAYLA: *No!*
CHRIS: Get up.
LAYLA: No, leave me alone.
CHRIS: No problem—good night. *(HE exits and turns out the lamp light.)*
LAYLA: *(In the darkness)* I want to go home. *(Silence)* Chris? *(Silence)* Chris, answer me. *(Lights and music fade)*

BLACKOUT

Elizabeth (Liz) Skollar

Liz participated in the FYV training for several years, while we were in residence at her NYC high school. She was an extremely shy girl whose voice crackled with anxiety, and she often hid behind her long hair during the acting classes. Over the terms that she studied with us, Liz became increasingly confident and comfortable being the center of attention. She also began to take herself, and her own words, more seriously. This was the first complete play that she wrote, and many times rewrote, and it really packed an emotional punch in performance. In it, she explored adolescent pain and peer pressure—as well as the courage to avoid that pressure—and the other high school students in the audience responded very favorably, despite the fact that the female character takes a position that might not be seen as cool. "I just remember looking at the image of a broken window and writing about what that meant to me." Liz went on to graduate from Hunter College; at the time of this writing she was doing crew work for an off-Broadway play.

Birthday Bash
Elizabeth Skollar

Characters: SARAH   Female, 18
              TONY   Male, 18, her boyfriend

AT RISE: SARAH and TONY are standing in front of a broken-down looking door.

TONY: Come on. You have to see. *(TONY tries to hold SARAH as she shrugs his hands away.)*
SARAH: *(Holding back)* Just tell me what it is.
TONY: What's the problem?
SARAH: I don't want to go in.
TONY: It's just an empty apartment.
SARAH: Why do you want me to go in there?
TONY: Because I want to show you something. *(He pulls her again, but she breaks away.)*
SARAH: Can we just sit here and talk?
TONY: About what?
SARAH: I wanted us to celebrate my birthday ... sober.
TONY: I am sober.
SARAH: Don't bullshit me. I can smell it all over you.
TONY: Sarah, why do you always have to be so difficult?
SARAH: Your drinking is a problem!
TONY: I don't want to do this now.
SARAH: Then when?
TONY: I really want you to see this. Let's go in! *(Reaching for her)*
SARAH: *(Withdrawing)* Don't you understand? You're not only hurting yourself. You're hurting me.
TONY: How am I hurting *you*?
SARAH: By not respecting my wishes. You know I'm totally against drinking. You know my mom was an alcoholic. You know all this. I shouldn't even have to say it. You never drank before, this isn't the Tony I knew.
TONY: My drinking has nothing to do with you, so stop trying to be so controlling. It's *my* life!
SARAH: Yes, it *is* your life, but I'm in it. The things you do affect me. How can you be so selfish?
TONY: I'm not selfish, and I'm not an alcoholic. I had *one* beer. *(Taking her hands)* We can work this out.
SARAH: It's not about working anything out. I know you're hurting. I know you have problems living alone with your mother, and you

miss your dad—

TONY: *(Letting go)* That's enough, Sarah!

SARAH: But you were always against alcohol, too. I know you're upset—just don't hurt yourself because of it.

TONY: *(Turning away)* You don't know everything, so stop acting like you do.

SARAH: *(Yelling)* You're not responsible for your father's death. He had a heart attack—it happens.

TONY: *(Yelling back)* We had a huge fight the week before he died.

SARAH: *(Pause)* I'm sorry, but that fight didn't kill him. *(Coming around to face him)* Your father loved you, and I love you, too. I'm your *girlfriend*. I'm not with you just because you're cute. I care for you. We've both lost a parent, and I'm here for you to talk to. *(No response)* I mean, what are we doing, Tony? Is this the relationship you want? *(Silence)* We're not getting any closer lately. Every time I'm with you, you're drinking. You make excuses and lie about where you're going and who you're going with, just so I won't get on your case. Do you think I don't see what you're doing? *(Silence)* It's all wrong for you, and it's not fair to me.

TONY: Could we just stop arguing and go inside?

SARAH: No, it's always what *you* want. I can't do this anymore. I can't, and I won't. *(Starts to leave, he grabs her.)*

TONY: Look at me. It's your *birthday*. Let's have fun.

SARAH: *(Yelling)* How can I have fun? I'm not happy. *(Screams at him)* Can't you see your problems mean more to me than my birthday?

TONY: *(Struggling to hold on to her)* Let's go inside. I've got something waiting for you—

SARAH: Like what? A bed?

TONY: Gee, thanks. Is that what you think of me?

SARAH: I don't know what to think of you.

TONY: Think of me as your *boyfriend*, who's trying to make the best of a hard time.

SARAH: If you're trying to make the best of it, then why are you drinking?

TONY: It makes me feel good.

SARAH: Listen, Tony, this relationship can't go on unless you stop drinking. Is that clear?

TONY: I have to choose?

SARAH: *(Starts to clap her hands)* You're catching on—

TONY: You just won't stop with this whole drinking situation—

SARAH: It's not a situation, it's a *problem*!

TONY: And a minute ago, you accused me of trying to sleep with you. What is it you want? What did I do?

SARAH: Wow. If you haven't gotten it yet, you never will. *(Starts to walk away)*

TONY: *(Runs in front of her)* Sarah—

SARAH: I don't want to give up on you, but—

TONY: Please, you're making everything harder on me.

SARAH: *(Angrily)* It's me or the drinks.

TONY: You can't make me choose.

SARAH: It's either your fucking beer or me!

TONY: I'm not choosing!

SARAH: Are you sure?

TONY: *(Shrugs his shoulders)* I can't.

SARAH: Fuck you and your beer!

TONY: What the hell?

SARAH: Well, "Happy Birthday," huh? Did I thank you for the marvelous birthday this turned out to be?

TONY: You started this whole big mess!

SARAH: You would say that—

TONY: Sarah, I have a surprise party for you inside!

SARAH: *(Pause)* Is that supposed to make up for everything? I guess *I* have a decision to make now, right? *(SARAH holds her hands out and looks at each one at a time.)* Party with you ... or with my family, who wanted so badly for me to spend today with them. Hmmm. My family. Want to know why? *(Silence)* Because *they* will never let me down. *(She leaves.)*

TONY: Sarah!! Where are you going? *(No response. He yells out to her.)* HAPPY BIRTHDAY! *(The broken down door opens and everyone at the party yells from inside, "Surprise!" (To the crowd)* She left me.

BLACKOUT

Lucy Thurber

I first became aware of Lucy Thurber's work when her agent submitted one of her plays for our consideration. She was subsequently invited to participate in the Steam *cluster for our Main Stage, which asked four playwrights to imagine what might happen if two people were alone in a steam room. Lucy opens the play that this scene is excerpted from, with her female characters fully clothed in the steam room (p. 37). One of them is playing a violin! This opening is representative of the bold and offbeat choices made throughout the piece and was what attracted us to her unusual and (at the time) not yet widely heard voice. Lucy remembers, "Having such a good time, and the challenge of working from a prompt (the steam room) that conjured the idea of luxury and trying to find longing within that luxury. Using a prompt is such a doorway to each individual writer's biases and excitement at that moment." At the time of this writing, Lucy Thurber was the author of seven plays, and the Atlantic Theater Company had opened their 2007 season with her play* Scarcity. *She then received a commission from Playwrights Horizons.*

Laura and Wendy
Lucy Thurber

Characters: LAURA   Female, 50s
              WENDY   Female, 20s

AT RISE: LAURA, who is struggling with middle age, is in a steam room at a New York spa. She is wearing an expensive dress suit and pearls. The atmosphere is surreal; steam envelops the stage creating the feeling of fog. Her daughter, WENDY, a woman in her early twenties, has agreed to meet her there and plans to tell her mother that she is moving away to attend a conservatory in California. WENDY is fully clothed, sweating and holding a violin. Her skirt is long; in fact everything about her seems to hide her body. Her mother has asked her to undress and promised not to watch.

WENDY: Don't look at me.
LAURA: What?

WENDY: Don't look at me while I'm changing.

LAURA: I'm your mother.

WENDY: I said stop looking at me!

LAURA: Don't be childish.

WENDY: Stop looking, stop looking, stop—

LAURA: All right, all right! *(LAURA turns away and begins to take off her clothes. They both get down to bra and underwear. She glances at Wendy.)*

WENDY: You never keep your promises. *(She sits and plucks the strings of her violin.)*

LAURA: I always keep my promises. I just didn't promise. *(Smiles)* Your butt is so much like your father's—

WENDY: No, it's not.

LAURA: Sure it is; just minus all the hair!

WENDY: God—stop it.

LAURA: *(Putting on a robe and sitting down)* I love this. I could come every day.

WENDY: You do.

LAURA: Not *every* day; besides, somebody has to spend your father's millions. *(Silence)* It's so liberating to talk about money, don't you think?

WENDY: No. *(She puts on robe.)*

LAURA: I never talked about money till I met your father. I was surrounded by it and never knew its value. He taught me the value of what I had, because he showed me what it was like *not* to have it. *(Pause)* You don't remember your father's mother, do you?

WENDY: Of course I do; what are you talking about?

LAURA: Yes, of course you do. *(Pause)* You and I used to come here every week; do you remember? Back before you were always so busy—

WENDY: Yes—

LAURA: Always so busy—

WENDY: Yes.

LAURA: I would love for us to have a real adult relationship. Like we did when you were little, I mean, but all grown up. We can come and just tell each other everything. Once a week maybe, on Wednesdays?

WENDY: Maybe.

LAURA: Why not Wednesdays? Is there a better day then Wednesday? I want so much—

WENDY: I know, Mom.

LAURA: *(Looking at WENDY'S violin)* My mother played the piano, did you know that?

WENDY: Of course.

LAURA: You probably got your musical talent from her.

WENDY: Yes, maybe.

LAURA: She was always playing that piano, my mother.

WENDY: Yes.

LAURA: Always alone, my mother.

WENDY: No, she wasn't.

LAURA: After her accident.

WENDY: That was before you were born.

LAURA: What?

WENDY: Mom, she had that accident before you were born.

LAURA: I know that; she is *my* mother after all.

WENDY: Yes.

LAURA: She was going to be a concert pianist.

WENDY: Yes.

LAURA: That terrible accident destroyed all her plans.

WENDY: Sure.

LAURA: Terrible accident; lost her pinky. Can't be a concert pianist without a pinky. Instead, she had me. I never quite made up for her losing her music. *(Pause)* I loved the way you always used to play for me when you were little. Do you remember?

WENDY: Yes.

LAURA: Play something for me. Are you still writing music? Remember those wonderful little songs you used to write for me on Mother's Day?

WENDY: Of course.

LAURA: I thought you forgot.

WENDY: Why would I forget?

LAURA: I think you wanted to show off for me.

WENDY: What?

LAURA: Just like my mother. She always wanted to show off all the things she could do. *(Pause)* Do you have any boyfriends?

WENDY: Not at the moment, Mother.

LAURA: Why not? You must. I always had tons of boyfriends.

WENDY: No. No boyfriends at the moment.

LAURA: Men you fuck?

WENDY: I hate it when you swear.

LAURA: I love to swear. Your father taught me to swear; it was so exciting. I'd never heard swearing before your father.

WENDY: I find that difficult to believe.

LAURA: You have no idea how sheltered I was. "Hells Bells." That was the worst I ever heard. *(Pause)* Come on; tell me about your romances.

WENDY: I don't have any.

LAURA: A pretty girl like you—

WENDY: I'm not pretty—

LAURA: Beautiful—

WENDY: No—

LAURA: Yes—

WENDY: I am not—

LAURA: Yes you are, you are, you are—

WENDY: Okay, Mom, I am. I'm the most beautiful girl that ever lived—

LAURA: To me you are. Actually, it's convenient that you're not seeing anyone right now; I have someone I want you to meet.

WENDY: No.

LAURA: Why not? You'd like him. He looks a lot like that blond boy you used to see.

WENDY: I don't think so—

LAURA: Of course he does. I met him the other day playing tennis, and I told him all about you.

WENDY: I'm sure you did.

LAURA: What was that blond boy's name again?

WENDY: Clyde.

LAURA: That's right, Clyde. Weren't you crazy about him?

WENDY: Yes.

LAURA: So where is he?

WENDY: It didn't work out.

LAURA: It didn't work out? What did you do, sweetie?

WENDY: Nothing.

LAURA: Come on, tell me what happened—

WENDY: *I don't want to talk about it!*

LAURA: Of course you do.

WENDY: It's always the same with you; we never talk about anything—

LAURA: I try, don't I? It's you who won't talk, not me—I always talk—

WENDY: Of course you do. You never shut up.

LAURA: Well, I'm sorry I'm not brilliant, like you—

WENDY: Don't—

LAURA: I'm sorry that all I ever was, was just a wife and mother—

WENDY: Don't—

LAURA: There was a time when that was enough for you and your father—

WENDY: I'm not my father—

LAURA: You're just like him—

WENDY: I'm not—

LAURA: Of course you are. There was a time, when we were young, that he loved me—

WENDY: He worships you.

LAURA: No. I was just a symbol to him, of all the things he wanted to accomplish in life. He was crass, uneducated, unrefined, and so brilliant. And he got me. Fought my whole family for me. And look at him now—rich and famous. And me, I'm nothing. He has all those other educated women to talk to—

WENDY: You are *highly* educated. You speak four fucking languages and have been to every civilized country in this world; you are the most—

LAURA: But not *real-life* education. Not like you and your father. I bet you wish he'd married someone with a real-life education. Some nice girl from his neighborhood. Someone more like his mother; she always hated me—

WENDY: No, she didn't—

LAURA: Yes, she did.

WENDY: No; you hated her.

LAURA: You have no use for me any more. Neither of you. Do you remember when you were young and you worshipped me?

WENDY: Yes, Mother, I remember.

LAURA: How you worshipped me—

WENDY: Yes—

LAURA: All your little secrets—

WENDY: Yes—

LAURA: And you used to pray at night to grow up and be beautiful just like me.

WENDY: I remember; and none of those prayers worked, did they?

LAURA: Don't start; you know that you're—

WENDY: Listen, Mother, I'm a very plain girl. I'm not interesting or flashy. I don't fill up a room when I walk in, and people don't talk about me after I leave. I'm nothing like you. You have always been the kind of woman people talk about.

LAURA: Darling.

WENDY: I know the truth. I do *one* thing well. I'd like to play you something, Mother.

LAURA: Well I've been asking you to, haven't I?

WENDY: I want you to try and listen.

BLACKOUT

This monologue is taken from the previous play.

Laura and Wendy
Lucy Thurber

(LAURA, a woman in her mid-fifties—and struggling with middle-age—is in a steam room at an expensive New York spa. She is wearing an expensive dress suit and pearls. The atmosphere is surreal; steam envelops the stage creating the feeling of fog. Her daughter, WENDY, a woman in her early twenties, has agreed to meet her there and stands fully clothed, sweating. Her skirt is long; in fact everything about her seems to hide her body. She is playing the violin—very well—though her mother doesn't seem to notice. LAURA tells WENDY the facts of life ... for women.)

LAURA

Wendy, you have such a cute little body; I don't know why you dress like that. *(No response)* You really take after the women in your father's family. All the women in my family are tall and thin. Of course, I'm not saying you're *fat*. It's just that you're more … *round*. But lots of men like that sort of thing. *(Snickers bitterly)* Men like your father. He always complained about my *flat ass*. *(Studying WENDY)* You don't have a flat ass. *(No response)* What happened to all the clothes I bought you? You look like you got your wardrobe at the Salvation Army. *(WENDY ignores LAURA and continues to play.)* Though it seems everybody's kids are going to the Salvation Army these days. I guess I can understand an obsession with poverty—having married your father. Your father … savage, disturbing, and exciting! There will never be another man like him: hard in business, soft in bed. It's because he's Catholic. *(Shakes her head)* Oh, how my father hated that! A *Catholic* in the family. *(Pause)* Do you know why I named you Wendy? *(Silence)* It's because of *Peter Pan*; Wendy from *Peter Pan*. *(WENDY keeps playing.)* When you were born I looked at you and thought: "I'm going to steal her away to Never, Never Land! We'll live with the fairies and elves. *I* will be her Peter Pan … and neither one of us will ever grow up." *(WENDY plays on.)* Wendy; the girl everybody wants. And the girl everybody wishes she was. Magic comes flying through your window. *(Pause)* Your father was like that for me. But eventually even magic turns stale; the real world always creeps in. *Nobody* is young forever.

Jayson Torres

Jayson first encountered FYV when a Lower East Side middle school teacher took his class to see one of our term-end performances; that same teacher eventually took the training herself and then joined our board of directors. Following the Q&A, he and one of his classmates both enrolled in an upcoming workshop. Jayson was an incredibly sweet and loving boy who smiled at everyone and elicited smiles in return. It took him several terms to find the courage to "fight for" things and to take his own intellectual power seriously. Once he did, his work began to soar. This play was written in a master class that he attended during college, and it beautifully captures the conflict over assimilation that he and many of his friends were coping with. Jayson remembers seeing the picture of the Statue of Liberty, and "wanting to make it funny, but it was too sensitive a topic. I remember wanting a not-so-happy ending! Because of FYV, I was provided a safe haven as a teenager. I got a chance to act and write and to be around theatre twice a week. I don't think I'll ever find such a joyous feeling again. What tools Gail has blessed me with!" Currently, Jayson is a day habilitation specialist for developmentally disabled adults; he works with them in a classroom setting. "I feel so fortunate in helping a population who generally are seen as having no voice. I hear and see their potential every day."

This play was written as part of a cluster entitled Liberty, *in response to a photograph of the Statue of Liberty.*

Mi Hija Latina, the American
by Jayson Torres

Characters: IVY   Latina, 18
                  CONSTANTINO   Latino, 40ish, her father

AT RISE: CONSTANTINO is watching television in the living room. IVY enters.

IVY: What are you watching?

CONSTANTINO: *(Not looking up)* It's the last episode of that novella, *Macarena*. She just found out that her maid is her mother and that her husband is really a woman! Ay, Ivy, the Café Bustelo is *riquisimo*.

IVY: Papi, you have no life!

CONSTANTINO: Niña, Channels 41 and 47 *are* my life. *(Finally looking at her)* So where were you?

IVY: Hanging out with Jessie and Erica; we were talking about our plans for tonight.

CONSTANTINO: Hija, I know you didn't forget about your cousin Marisol's *Quincenera*.

IVY: Ay, Papi, did you really think I was going? That whole *spending time* thing, getting drunk on coquito, and dancing salsa is not appealing to me. Anyway, Webster Hall is the spot tonight. *(She starts to exit)*

CONSTANTINO: Quien es Webster?

IVY: Daddy—

CONSTANTINO: No, Ivy. *(Stopping her with his voice)* I want to know why you'd rather go to someone's hallway, than enjoy what will be one of your cousin's biggest days. *(Silence)* She went to yours.

IVY: *(Turning to him)* Please!

CONSTANTINO: Stop talking back to me. You sound just like an American. When are you going to finally acknowledge that you are a Latina? *(Silence)* Your mother would be so disappointed.

IVY: Mami would have accepted me for who I am and accepted any decision I were to make. *(Pause)* I decided I am not going tonight.

CONSTANTINO: *(Rising)* You are going nowhere but to your cousin's party, and that is final. I told you how I feel about you hanging out with those gringos.

IVY: What did my friends ever do to you?

CONSTANTINO: It's your cousin's party tonight, her Sweet Fifteen— the closest thing to her wedding. You know what this celebration means; Marisol will finally be gaining her independence. The same independence that you were given. The same independence you have taken advantage of by not living according to my expectations.

IVY: That independence is getting me ready for my future.

CONSTANTINO: But where is all I've taught you about being Latino? *(Silence)* All I am trying to say is … stay with your own people, hija.

IVY: Are you trying to imply that I am too *white*?

CONSTANTINO: No, Niña, I'm saying that you are too … *American.*

IVY: I *am* an American. We've had this conversation before. I didn't even want a Sweet Fifteen; none of my friends had one. Just let me live an American life without the third degree.

CONSTANTINO: *(He sits, heavily.)* To me, if someone is not helping to preserve *my* culture and beliefs, then the hell with them. The hell with all of them. *(He turns back to his television program.)*

IVY: *(Coming between her father and the TV)* So the hell with me?

CONSTANTINO: *(He pulls her close to him. She drops to her knees.)* Why are you doing this to me, hija? I love you. *(Kisses her hands)* I just want you to hold your heritage close to you. I have tried to teach you everything there is to know, and you know that your mother tried, too, before she died. And now, it is like we have never taught you anything. It is important to me that you represent who you really are in everything that you do and to respect what your mother and I have endured. *(With difficulty)* I miss her so much, Ivy. And that is why I want you to follow in her footsteps. I want you to be the strong Latina she was, to make your mother proud. Is that so much to ask?

IVY: Just because I don't want to go with you tonight and I hang out with white people, that does not make me less of a *Latina*. I have all that you taught me right here. *(Placing his hand on her heart)* Don't you think that's what counts?

CONSTANTINO: It does count, mija. If you'd only allow me the chance to teach you—

IVY: *(Rising)* A chance to teach me what? A chance to teach me to be subservient? A chance to teach me that a man's backhand is the "tool of discipline"? Or maybe to teach me how to push out five kids in four years? Well, Papi, I have news for you—I am my own person; you have done all that you can do. I have my own goals. I have my own future ahead of me. You are not going to teach me to walk around a house doing chores like you had Mami—

251

CONSTANTINO: *(Rising, in her face)* What kind of daughter speaks to her father like you do? I have never taught you such things. I have tried to be a good father, Ivy. God knows that I have tried.

IVY: Daddy, I will never be what it is you want me to be.

CONSTANTINO: *(Takes a step toward her)* Don't make me say it. As God is my witness, don't make me say it.

IVY: Say it, Daddy! If you are supposed to be that typical macho Puerto Rican father, then say it.

CONSTANTINO: When I look at you everyday, I regret it. I regret ever coming into this country. As soon as your mother and I stepped off of that plane from San Juan, we were cursed.

IVY: How could you say such a thing? Do you hear yourself? If Mami were alive, you would never speak like this. I know that you don't mean any of it.

CONSTANTINO: *(Pacing wildly)* I meant every word I said. Do you know what it feels like to see your culture slowly disappear in front of you? You barely speak Spanish. You choose to hang out with those gringos. You refuse to visit your brothers back home in Puerto Rico—

IVY: *This* is my home, Daddy.

CONSTANTINO: *They* are preserving who we are; *you* are denying who we are.

IVY: America is where it all began for me, and America is where it will end for me—

CONSTANTINO: Your mother and I didn't raise you like that.

IVY: You raised me to be open-minded and independent.

CONSTANTINO: And to use these qualities to help your people; not to hurt your father.

IVY: I'm not trying to hurt you, Daddy. I'm trying to make something of myself, because when you are gone, I will have to depend on myself. And I wouldn't be able to do that if I weren't educated or if I didn't have positive people by my side.

CONSTANTINO: There are tons of positive Latinos around us, especially in our family. Look at your Titi Evelyn—she has her own talk show dealing with Latino issues. And your childhood friend, Luis Ruiz, has his own chain of Spanish restaurants. *They* are around. And being with them would remind you of who you really are.

IVY: I know who I am, Daddy, and I know that you don't want me to hang out with the no-good Puerto Ricans from around our block.

CONSTANTINO: It's a start.

IVY: *(Starting to exit again)* You just don't think when you talk.

CONSTANTINO: And you have no regard for me, or for your mother's efforts. We *had* to come here. *(She stops and listens but doesn't turn around)* I was out of work for years, and everyone around us was doing badly; they were robbing each other until there wasn't anything left. We knew it was time to go, but all I had was the English I learned in grammar school. When we heard from neighboring pueblos that New York City was where the Puerto Ricans were, your mother and I came here with sixteen dollars, our one-way plane tickets, and our fingers crossed.

IVY: *(Turning)* I have always respected the fact that you came here so that we could lead better lives. And *this* is who I am. This is who I turned out to be.

CONSTANTINO: *(Defeated)* That's nice, hija ... that's nice.

IVY: Do you want me to ruin my life just so that I can know my culture? I'm sorry, Daddy, I want to go to college, and I am not about to put my future on hold so that I can learn to be your perfect Puerto Rican daughter. *(Picks up her coat)* I'm leaving now. Maybe when I come back, I'll have Ricky Martin's arm around me. Maybe then, you'll accept me.

CONSTANTINO: If you're going to leave, leave. *(Takes a moment, fighting tears)* It is hard for me to say this, but you are the daughter I never wanted.

IVY: *(Also fighting tears)* And it is even harder for me to say that you just lost that daughter. *(She exits.)*

CONSTANTINO: *(To himself)* Hija, I lost you the day you were born into this country—

BLACKOUT

Celine Valensi

Celine participated in the FYV training during her senior year at the high school where we were in residence at the time. A beautiful and unusually sophisticated girl, Celine exhibited tremendous courage in the acting classes by gradually dropping the detached affect that initially turned the characters she was portraying into caricatures. She began to allow herself to appear vulnerable and authentic, as she moved from a concept of acting as posing to one of interacting. And, as she developed the craft of truly listening, as is always the case the craft carried over into the dialogue that she developed in her writing as well. As she worked and reworked this play, it became less and less sarcastic, more and more poignant. It took tremendous fortitude for her to write this, just as it took tremendous fortitude for two of her fellow workshop members to perform it before other teenagers. The audiences enthusiastically rewarded all three for their magnificent work—further evidence that when people speak authentically, others will listen authentically. Celine remembers the photograph that inspired the piece as "A play on shadows. I went on to college with a full academic scholarship that FYV helped me get." At the time of this writing Celine was managing a staff of one hundred in a restaurant located in New York City's Bowery Hotel.

This, Celine's first play, was written in response to a beam of light traveling across a wall, which she saw as a balcony (p. 38). It was written for a cluster of plays entitled Unexpected Obstacles.

Intermission
Celine Valensi

Characters: MICHELLE   Female, early 20s
                LEYLAH   Female, early 20s

AT RISE: Intermission at a theater. LEYLAH comes out and rests her elbows on a marble balcony; she has been crying. Shortly afterward, MICHELLE follows.

MICHELLE: It was a natural reflex.

LEYLAH: *(Peering into crowd)* You're dying for them to find out.

MICHELLE: Can you blame me?

LEYLAH: *(Now turning to MICHELLE)* I can blame you for trying to make the decision for me.

MICHELLE: Well, maybe if you stuck to this decision every time you made it, I wouldn't have to do it for you.

LEYLAH: God, you don't let up. We'll tell them when it's right. *(Looking around the room)* And I guarantee you; this is neither the time nor the place.

MICHELLE: I was just trying to be subtle.

LEYLAH: Holding my hand in front of my parents is not subtle.

MICHELLE: Can you think of a better way?

LEYLAH: Look, it's my birthday; I'm not going to spend it fighting with you.

MICHELLE: Exactly—it's your birthday, and we can't even spend it with each other.

LEYLAH: We are with each other.

MICHELLE: Not the way we should be. Seriously, what do you propose? That we go back into the theater, sit with your parents, and make small talk about the lines for the bathroom?

LEYLAH: Whatever happened to being understanding?

MICHELLE: Don't give me that. I understand just fine. Don't you think my parents have the same dreams for me as yours do? My dad wants to walk me down the aisle; my mom's anxious to spoil her grandkids rotten. *(Pause)* But I've made a decision; I'm ready to give it all up for you.

LEYLAH: *(Pause)* They watched us grow up together, Michelle.

MICHELLE: Don't pretend you're not telling them for their sakes. You're protecting yourself.

LEYLAH: Is that a crime?

MICHELLE: *(Pause)* The more we try to protect ourselves, the less we're gonna recognize each other. Secrets eventually consume people.

LEYLAH: I just don't want to hurt them.

MICHELLE: That's inevitable.

LEYLAH: It's different for you; your parents are more accepting.

MICHELLE: I still have to face *your* parents. What are they gonna think of me?

LEYLAH: What I think is more important.

MICHELLE: Then how can it be that you still won't hold my hand in public?

LEYLAH: *(Pause)* It's just so natural in our little cocoon, but so wrong to everyone outside of it.

MICHELLE: Why do you find us so shameful?

LEYLAH: I don't … but that's only because I know we're a miracle. If I had never met you, I'd find it wrong too. *(Pause)* I must've played the scenario out in my head a hundred times. Every time, my parents either laugh cause they think I'm kidding, or they tell me they never want to see me again.

ANNOUNCER: Please take your seats.

MICHELLE: We better go in. *(She begins to walk. LEYLAH is reluctant.)*

LEYLAH: I can't go in there. God, Michelle, what am I gonna tell my mom?

MICHELLE: Tell her what feels right.

LEYLAH: Nothing feels right.

MICHELLE: *(Clearly very insulted)* I'm glad you find us so wrong.

LEYLAH: That's not what I meant.

MICHELLE: This is gonna tear us apart. I know it. We need to announce it soon.

LEYLAH: This isn't a sale at K-Mart. You don't announce it.

MICHELLE: It's what we need to do.

LEYLAH: I need time.

MICHELLE: Deja vu. We're runnin' out of rope here, Leylah.

LEYLAH: *(Suddenly very defensive)* What difference does it make how long our rope is? It's not like "the sooner, the easier."

MICHELLE: What do you plan to tell them when they come to visit us in the new apartment and we only have one bed? *(Silence)* Is that how you want them to find out? I can see it now—your mother's all, "Honey, where's Leylah's bed?" And you're all, "Well, Mom, we save on heating by sharing a bed. You know, body heat and all."

LEYLAH: If we did it your way, there'd be a picture of us kissing on every billboard from here to Nantucket.

MICHELLE: At least we'd be honest.

LEYLAH: Is it so hard to accept that I'm afraid?

256

MICHELLE: I'm scared too.

LEYLAH: Then how do you know that telling them is the best thing for us right now?

MICHELLE: Leylah, look at me ... *(takes LEYLAH's face in her hand)* We have two choices; either we live in secret and it rips us apart for sure, or we take the risk and hopefully end up living happily ever after.

LEYLAH: *(Looks at MICHELLE)* It's worth the risk, isn't it.

MICHELLE: Yeah. Yeah, it is.

LEYLAH: *(Pause)* Okay.

MICHELLE: Are you sure?

LEYLAH: *(Pause. Putting hands over MICHELLE'S hands)* Yeah. You're right. You're right about the whole thing. I'll tell them. *(Their hug is interrupted by the announcer.)*

ANNOUNCER: Final call. Please take your seats.

LEYLAH: *(Breaking away)* Soon.

BLACKOUT

Charles Watson

When Charles submitted a play for our consideration, it became clear that although he had not yet been widely produced, he was a writer of great emotional depth. We invited him to participate in a cluster for our Main Stage; it was entitled Four Views With a Room. *The trigger photo that the writers responded to was one that I subsequently used often in the FYV Workshops—Andrea Sperling's magnificent hand-tinted photo of a chair in front of a door, which is pictured on the cover of this book. This image has evoked hundreds of varied responses over the years, and there are often echoes from one response to another. This particular cluster was comprised of several artists whose work is included in this collection: Linda Faigao-Hall, Charles Watson, Gail Noppe-Brandon, and Franck Ramirez de Las Mercedes. When we got together to share our first drafts, it was fascinating to see that, although we were of different races and genders, Charles and I had both envisioned this chair as a last piece of furniture left in the living room of a home that someone was being forced to leave against their will. We even had some similar lines of dialogue! It is a wonderful example of the kind of echoes that come up when several people respond to a single trigger. Charles created a wonderfully original and endearing character in the guise of a mentally challenged middle-aged woman. He remembers, "sharing with Gail and the other writers my memory of a mentally-challenged relative I grew up with. I learned [during the workshop collaboration] that the way others view my work is not always easy to hear, but it's important to hear. And that their input can and will improve it." Charles continues writing plays and working to get them produced.*

The Lonely Room
Charles Watson

Characters: JACKSON   Male, African-American, late 30s
                      SHIRLEY   Female, African-American, late 30s, his
                                          mentally challenged sister

AT RISE: JACKSON and SHIRLEY have just buried their mother, in whose home SHIRLEY has lived all of her life. JACKSON tries to convince

SHIRLEY that she will now be better off in a group home; he wants to earn some rental income on his mother's apartment, and his wife doesn't want to take SHIRLEY in with them. SHIRLEY has just had a tantrum and now sits in a chair, rocking back and forth to comfort herself.

JACKSON: *(Squatting beside her)* You okay now, Shirley?

SHIRLEY: *(Not looking at him)* I'm always okay.

JACKSON: This is what I was talking about before; you can't start screaming just cause you don't want to hear me.

SHIRLEY: I don't need to go.

JACKSON: Remember what I told you, Shirley?

SHIRLEY: About what?

JACKSON: About the apartment. About the furniture.

SHIRLEY: When?

JACKSON: After the funeral.

SHIRLEY: My head wasn't right then.

JACKSON: I was with Missy.

SHIRLEY: Don't remember.

JACKSON: It was important.

SHIRLEY: There was only one thing important that day.

JACKSON: *(Pause)* With Mama gone and all, Shirley, what are you gonna do?

SHIRLEY: Do?

JACKSON: How you gonna live?

SHIRLEY: Like I always have.

JACKSON: There's nobody to take care of you.

SHIRLEY: Mama always told me I was a big girl; I could take care of myself.

JACKSON: How you gonna get by?

SHIRLEY: I get money. You know, my disability. And Carmine at the supermarket said I could maybe work there, cleaning and stuff.

JACKSON: Is that gonna pay the rent?

SHIRLEY: Mama said this place is cheap.

JACKSON: But by yourself? How can you live all by yourself?

SHIRLEY: I got you, Jackson, don't I? *(Silence)* I mean you're always visiting, and Philly can. *(Pause)* I know Missy don't visit, but—

JACKSON: Even with us visiting, you need help.

SHIRLEY: I don't need no help. Mama used to help me, but she got old, and then I helped her.

JACKSON: You can't be alone.

SHIRLEY: *(Looks into his eyes)* Then what can I be?

JACKSON: This place seems so lonely now.

SHIRLEY: I ain't never asked for anything. *(He turns away.)* Listen to me, I ain't askin' for nothing I ain't already got. I just want to *be*. Mama said I'd always have someplace to live. That's what she told me. Now, you folks makin' her out to be a liar. This is my *home*— always been. Mama said always would be. This is *my* home. Didn't she tell you that, Jackson? You heard her.

JACKSON: There were things she didn't need to know.

SHIRLEY: She knew *me*. *(Hugs herself)* I miss her so much. Every room in this place smells of her. There ain't nowhere I can go that she ain't laughin' or telling me what a good girl I am! *(Looks at him again)* You can't take that away. *(Silence)* Can you tell me I can't live on my own?

JACKSON: Can you pay the bills?

SHIRLEY: *(Pause)* I might need help with that. Isn't family supposed to help each other? I ain't askin' for the world.

JACKSON: No, you ain't, but you're looking for a part of it that's not there. *(Pause)* Besides, it's more than just me and you, Shirley. I got a family—

SHIRLEY: I'm a part of it.

JACKSON: But things can't stay the same. I got a family in a small place. I … we got problems now. And we … I have to tell you this. *(He rises, paces.)* It's more than just you and me. Missy found someone who's interested in this apartment. They'll give us good money. Next week's the first. That's when they move in.

SHIRLEY: *(She begins rocking again.)* But Mama said—

JACKSON: I know what she said! And I know she's gone. I've barely slept since she died. But it's a fact; an ugly, definite fact that we need the money.

BLACKOUT

Emily White

Emily, a professor of Education at Bank Street College, participated in a FYV professional development workshop along with ten other members of their Leadership Center faculty. The goal was to bring aspects of this approach to the way teachers are trained—especially those who will eventually reach students at the point of their earliest exposure to school— by introducing it to the professors who train the teachers. Throughout the workshop, despite the fact that Emily had not written a play "since third grade" and had no prior experience with acting, she was consistently courageous about the study of performing a monologue and the writing of a play. In fact, she provided an enormous sense of equilibrium to a group that was very resistant to the notion of adhering to any imposed structure. While the FYV methodology works with each individual participant at his or her own level, it most definitely imposes a universal structure in an attempt to surpass the many fears and inner censors that keep people from expressing themselves. Ultimately, some great work, and some important educational epiphanies, emerged from the members of this workshop, most notably regarding the amount of fear engendered when one is asked to share ideas or perform in front of peers. After many rewrites, Emily's moving play, though initially long and unfocused, reflected the warm and emotionally intelligent voice of the woman who wrote it. When the Find Your Voice *text was published, Emily's positive review of the method was featured on the cover. She still recalls the original writing prompt, a photograph of a tea bag on a countertop, which gave her a jolt. "I was in the midst of a transition, or recognition. Tears came. I wrote my play."*

The cluster was entitled Offerings.

Dusk
Emily White

Characters: MURIEL   Late 80s, widow
               DELIA   Middle-aged, her daughter

AT RISE: A small, orderly, 1950s-type kitchen in the suburbs. MURIEL perches at the small table, lost in thought. She just got home a while ago.

Her coat is on the back of the chair; her purse is still on the table. MURIEL has lived in this house for sixty-five years. Widowed a decade ago, she has been managing things just fine. Her daughter, DELIA, visits her twice a week. Outside the frosty kitchen window, the last of the late afternoon sun glints off the half-frozen river.

DELIA: Hi, Mom. *(Enters, taking her coat off. After a moment, she approaches MURIEL.)* Rosa called me. She told me about the assessment test at the rehab center; she said you failed it. *(Sits beside her)* I'm so sorry, Mom. But I'm not surprised.

MURIEL: *(Looks offended) You* pushed for this: set up the appointment for today, hired Rosa to come and drive me there. It's not fair, putting me in a position like this. I've never had an accident in my life.

DELIA: Mom, two weeks ago a cop saw you idling in the middle of Palmer Avenue.

MURIEL: I was listening to the engine. *(Delia gives her a look.)* You have to do that after you get a car from the repair people. You can't trust them.

DELIA: People don't stop and listen to cars in the middle of a four-lane road. The doctor said you probably had a mini-stroke; that's why you had to start taking those pills.

MURIEL: Lots of people have those. Younger than me. They drive. My sister is blind in one eye, and they let *her* pass the test. Ninety-one years old! And *she's* had an accident.

DELIA: A driving test isn't just about vision; it's about reflexes, too.

MURIEL: *(Changing the subject)* Make some tea. It's cold out there.

DELIA: *(Stands up, goes to stove)* I know that your freedom and privacy mean everything to you, but it's time for some help now. You have to hang up your keys. Put them away. Give them to me.

MURIEL: I never use that kettle. Put it back. I use the saucepan—

DELIA: *(Mostly to herself)* It figures. Why use the nice "Good Grips" Mother's Day tea kettle? *(To MURIEL)* Don't change the subject; I know you're worried.

MURIEL: I'll tell you what's really worrying me right now—

DELIA: What?

MURIEL: The cat! He's never out this long. *(Gesturing to the window)* It'll be dark soon.

DELIA: Max always comes back. Let's talk about getting you a driver.

MURIEL: I'll have to sit here half the night waiting for him. His schedule was thrown off, me being out all afternoon. See what you started? *(Looks over her shoulder at the pan on the stove)* Your water is boiling.

DELIA: Nothing ever happens to a cat. What are you worried about?

MURIEL: *(Wringing her hands)* I just hate it when animals are out in bad weather.

DELIA: *(Pause)* Does this have anything to do with that dog we had when I was little?

MURIEL: Misty. *(She remembers)* You were only eight or nine; no one else was home with us. The river was mostly frozen over, and the dog went out in the middle of it. Just walking along. I saw her through the window. The ice gave way, right out from under her; it was thinner than it looked. First she was walking—then she fell through. She clung on with her front paws, trying to pull herself back up on the ice; her hind paws were in the water, kicking madly. The ice kept breaking away beneath her. The more she tried, the more it broke up … but only right where *she* was. She was trapped.

DELIA: I don't remember.

MURIEL: I threw that damned canoe in and slid it out on to the ice. When I reached for her, she almost lost her footing completely. I couldn't grab her. She was too scared and heavy for me; I would've fallen in myself. I was making it worse. Finally the police came. The officer got in the far end of the canoe and made a path to her through the ice. It was clever. He see-sawed through the ice using the boat. Misty managed to see the path, a way out. She dog-paddled out on her own, following the boat.

DELIA: I can't believe she didn't freeze to death.

MURIEL: I have to find Max. *(Stands up)*

DELIA: *(Stopping her)* No, Mom. It's freezing out there. I'll go.

MURIEL: You? The cat won't come to you. You'll make it worse. You've done enough for one day! *(Tries to pull away)*

DELIA: *(Holding her)* It's called *help.*

MURIEL: It's called *interference.*

DELIA: It's called keeping people safe.

MURIEL: I won't have it. It's not what I want. *(In desperation she breaks free.)* Everything has changed.

DELIA: No, no. *(Sits her mother down)* The driving has changed. What else?

MURIEL: Nothing's the same. *(Slowly, turning away)* Nothing.

DELIA: You're still here. We still have the house. You're okay. We can hire Rosa again to drive you in the mornings. *I'm* around.

MURIEL: But what am *I* going to do? What am I going to *do?*

DELIA: *(Pause, then directly but tenderly)* You'll be like this for years: mobile, telling us all what to do. Maybe five more years, ten years. Not like Dad with the wheelchair, the adult diapers. This is different. I don't think we'll see that around here again.

MURIEL: *(Pause)* The morning your father died, Rosa tried to call 911.

DELIA: She wanted to save him.

MURIEL: I grabbed the phone out of her hand.

DELIA: *(Puts her hand on her mother's leg)* Good for you, Ma.

MURIEL: That's one of your jobs, Delia.

DELIA: *(Tenderly, taking her mother's hand)* I'll stay on the far end of the boat. No dramatic rescues. No pulling at you. No drowning myself. You'll swim your own way out.

MURIEL: That's it. *(Sighs)* Now move a chair over to the window so I can watch for Max. *(DELIA starts to rise, MURIEL grabs her)* I'm holding you personally responsible. For everything.

DELIA: That's some job, Ma; and the pay is great! Do we get to talk about car keys now?

MURIEL: I'll put them in the drawer, and I won't use them again. *(Lets go)* Pour your tea.

DELIA: What about more help during the day?

MURIEL: *(Silence)* It already boiled.

DELIA: *(Moves to the stove, looks at pan)* I just realized why you use this lousy little saucepan. It's for when you don't have your hearing aid in. You use it so you can see the bubbles. *(Grabbing handle of the saucepan)* Ouch!

MURIEL: You'll get the hang of it.

BLACKOUT

This monologue was drawn from the previous play.

Dusk
Emily White

(MURIEL, a woman in her late 80s, is being pressured by her daughter, DELIA, to give up her keys and some of her independence. Here she recounts a moment from the past, when her dog almost drowned, which captures her desire to age and die with dignity.

MURIEL

You were eight or nine. No one else was home. The river was mostly frozen over, and the dog was out in the middle of it. Just walking along. I saw her through the window. The ice gave way, right out from under her. It was thinner than it looked. First she was walking. Then she fell through. She clung on with her front paws, trying to pull herself back up on the ice. Her hind paws were in the water, kicking madly. And the ice kept breaking away beneath her. The more she tried, the more it broke up, but only right where she was. She was trapped. I threw that damned canoe in the river, and it slid out. When I reached for her, she almost lost her footing completely. I couldn't grab her. She was too scared and heavy for me. I would've fallen in myself. I was making it worse. Finally someone, maybe me, called the police. When the officer came, he got in the far end of the canoe and made a path to her through the ice. It was clever. He see-sawed through the ice using the boat. Misty managed to see a path—a way out. He let her dog-paddle out on her own, following the boat.

Dante Williams

Dante began his FYV training while attending a private high school in New York City as an Oliver scholar. An extremely bright young man, Dante was also extremely shy and often hid his genuine feelings behind self-deprecating humor. During his several years in the workshops, Dante grew more confident, both as an actor and as a writer. The play that this monologue is taken from featured a series of monologues, which built to a crescendo of voices reflecting various aspects of the main character's identity crisis. For many adolescent males, the FYV training provokes a shift from laughing at oneself, before others can, to taking oneself more seriously. Although infused with Dante's wonderful sense of humor, it also treated with poignancy and vulnerability, the real racial and emotional tensions with which African-American males must contend. "The childhood story of the sandbox is very much true, except my mother was much older when she had me. I wanted the pieces to be fun and playful, with serious undertones, and what better way to do that than to relate to childhood antics and experiences? I learned that people listen to and watch you when they find something interesting. Once that attention is lost, it takes a lot to get back. FYV taught me how to keep people's attention and infuse color and excitement into the ordinary. I also learned the value of timely, specific feedback and that dialogue is a powerful unit of human drama." Dante returned for a master class during his college years, and, after many years with a large media company, he began to turn his keenly observant eye toward a career in photography. At the time of this writing he planned to open his own studio.

The following three monologues are from a play that was part of a cluster entitled, Does Anyone Hear Me?, *all of which dealt with breakdowns in communication. The protagonist was played by Shadeed Elliott (p. 35) who, at the time of this writing, fifteen years later, was training to become a Find Your Voice facilitator!*

The Sandbox
Dante Williams

(ADAM, an 18-year-old African male who recently graduated from high school, is trying to encourage RICARDO, his childhood friend, to pursue the only choice that would make sense—a career in basketball—rather than going off with his girlfriend for a year abroad.)

ADAM

Are you trying to tell me, Adam Little, that you wouldn't enjoy spending your life playing basketball? *(No response)* Let me introduce you to my version of the course Basketball 101. Adam Little is now presiding! *(Puts his arm around RICARDO)* Basketball all starts when we're babies and our moms hang those little rings over our cribs; we see how many times we can toss our pacifiers through the hoops. Then we move into high school, perfect our skills, and display them for the college scouts. Then college scouts enroll us into their fine institutions, and we're seen by thousands of viewers via television broadcasts. *(Slaps his back)* Then the pro scouts come marching into town. They realize how desperately they need our young talents, and they pick us up in the draft so that we become instant millionaires who are idealized by everyone. In no time at all our paychecks are the size of Luke Perry's—we're talking *humongous!* *(Looks into his face)* We will be raking in the dough, the moolah, the cash, the dinero, the crazy ducats, cars, yachts, gold, Nike endorsement, contracts. *(No response)* And with the money you're making, you can buy yourself another girl like dat' one over there. *(Points)* Just look at Wilt Chamberlain!

The Sandbox
Dante Williams

(DON, an 18-year-old African male, tries to strong-arm his cousin RICARDO—who recently graduated from high school—into forgetting his plans for college and backing him in avenging his father.)

DON

Rico, come here. *(No response)* Rico, come here! *(Still no response; DON comes up and grabs him by the scruff of the neck.)* What's your problem, Cuz, huh? *(Silence)* Who took care of you while your mom was in the crazy house? Who changed your diapers when you were a baby? *(Pause)*

Who made sure you went to a decent school, with decent clothes on your back? And who was gunned down because he was mistaken for a member of a rival gang? *(Shakes him)* You know who it was; it was my father—your uncle. And you're gonna let them get away with that? *(RICARDO tries to rise; DON pushes him back down.)* It ain't over til the fat gunman sings. Then it's over. You wanna go to college? Nah, you're not going to college. And you're not gonna get to marry a classy girl like Tina either. *(Pause)* You expect her family to let her marry a ghetto kid like you? *(No response)* And you're *not* thinkin' basketball, are you? Cause we all know that your chances would be one in a million. *(Snickers)* You expect to have a wife, two kids, a dog named Rover, and a little white picket fence in the suburbs? Get up in the morning and have your cup of coffee before you get in your Lexus and drive to your big office in a high-rise? *(Smacks the back of his head)* Is that what you expect? People like us don't get chances! Our future was decided for us the day we were born. You can be coming home from college and still get your ass shot down in the ghetto simply because you have a couple of dollars in your wallet. *(Gets in his face)* Unless you were born with a silver spoon in your mouth or a family history of success, you don't have a chance. Life ain't fair, Rico. Believe it or not, you're just like me, only you don't want to admit it. I'm fighting to make someone proud of me, too—my father. Why can't you? *(Silence)* Let's go, man. *(Tries to pull him up)* Don't be a sellout.

The Sandbox
Dante Williams

(RICARDO TYSON, an 18-year-old African male, recently graduated from high school. Everyone in his life is telling him what he should, and shouldn't, do next. In this monologue he reacts to his mother's admonition that, based on her experience with his father, RICARDO should not go off with his girlfriend unless he is prepared to commit to her for life. He addresses the audience.)

RICARDO

When I was eight years old, I remember going to the sandbox every day after school. It was *my* sandbox; nobody could enter without my permission. *(Smiles)* One day I let in this girl who rode her bicycle around my sandbox every day; her name was Desiree. We decided to play house. I was the daddy, and it was my job to pick the mommy. My best friend Adam told me to pick Desiree because she wore a bra. How could I pass up the opportunity to have a wife who wore a bra? So, she and I got married and had a son named Adam. *(Snickers)* Unfortunately, we had a few disagreements along the way. Within two hours we were getting a divorce! The very next day after school, I entered *my* sandbox to find Desiree and her new husband—Douglas—the school bully. My son Adam and I were then thrown out of my sandbox on our asses! *(Pause)* When you really think about it, the same thing happened to my mother. She was only fifteen when she got pregnant by her high school love. He didn't want anything to do with her—or me—after that. *(Pause)* Two people can be in love one minute and then never have anything to do with each other the next.

Marilyn Williams

I met Marilyn when she participated in a FYV professional development workshop with a group of other inner-city teachers. Marilyn immediately struck me as a very emotionally rich and imaginative person; her colorful personality enabled her to explore the acting work with more abandon than most teachers. I had worked with many teachers like her— that is, they had a melodramatic idea of acting and struggled with the concept of authentic connection. When she began to understand the concept of pulling for a response rather than just talking and simultaneously conquered her fear of forgetting lines (which also benefited from her growing ability to remain fully engaged), a real craft emerged. As is always the case, though Marilyn was not particularly confident in her abilities as a writer, her growing sense of dynamic interaction and the notion of fighting for things bled over into the play she was crafting. The early drafts needed a lot of dramaturgy for clarity, but the underlying story was so powerful that when the technical problems were cleared up, it resulted in this raw and deeply affecting play. "I vividly recall that while I was creating the piece, the conclusion both stunned and surprised me. Now that I have a more concise understanding of my writing voice, I am able to challenge myself, and I have the comfort of writing with ease and freedom." At the time of this writing Marilyn was working on a collection of vignettes that describe her childhood memories of growing up in the South Bronx.

This, Marilyn's first play, was written for the cluster Beneath It All, *which used a photograph of objects hidden under a bed as the trigger.*

The Trade-Off
Marilyn Williams

Characters: AJ   Male, African-American, 40s
             LUREEN   Female, African-American, 40s, his
                       wife

AT RISE: The couple's bedroom; LUREEN finds AJ half under the bed searching for something.

LUREEN: If you're looking for the dope that you hid in your shoes, I have it. *(He emerges and looks up at her.)* How long?

AJ: Where is it?

LUREEN: The question is not *where*, but *why*? *(No response)* Why the hell are you doing drugs, after twenty years of sobriety? *(Pause)* Is this the reason we haven't been the same in bed? *(Laughs bitterly)* Stupid me, thinking it was the cancer medication ... or another woman. *(Approaches him)* You've been cheating on me with *heroin*. That was always your first love; wasn't it?

AJ: It's not my first love, *you* are, but I can't be your *everything*. You should have had our baby.

LUREEN: Don't bring that crap up.

AJ: You had to have an abortion—scared you would lose your shape.

LUREEN: You never really wanted a baby.

AJ: You'll be sorry and childless when I'm dead. *(Rising)* Now, where are my drugs?

LUREEN: We're talking about your issues, not mine. And you're not dying tomorrow. *(He starts turning things over all around the room.)* I understand you being afraid, but has the cancer impaired your thinking too? *(No response)* I thought it would've brought you closer to understanding what really matters in life: our love, our families, our friendships, and our relationship with God.

AJ: *(Looking in bureau drawers for the drugs)* I just want to enjoy the time I have left. That's what matters; the time I have left. My dope is not like your Jesus; I can touch it cause it's real—and you better give it to me.

LUREEN: When I thought you had another woman, I started working out more, buying new clothes; trying to keep my man. Stupid me. You had another woman all right—the "white bitch." How do I fight her?   .

AJ: *(Looking frantically in different spots for the drugs)* Where did you hide the dope?

LUREEN: *(Taunting him)* Maybe I flushed it ... like I did your child— not because of my shape, but because I couldn't trust you. No, you enjoyed stopping by the dope dens too much, telling get-high stories, keeping contact with those half-ass junkie friends of yours, you piece of shit. Once a junkie, always a junkie, huh?

AJ: *(On his knees)* You never got high, baby. You can't begin to understand. H takes you to a place where there's no cancer pain, no past to deal with, no future to plan, and no death to care about. *(Studying her face)* It's just like the peace you claim you get from loving that Jesus of yours. *(She turns away.)* I don't have time for your shit, Lureen; we're all gonna die some time. Just give me the dope.

LUREEN: *(Standing over him)* My Jesus brings families together; your drug is separating us.

AJ: *(Reaching for her hands)* It doesn't have to.

LUREEN: *(Pulling away)* Just like it did to my mom and dad.

AJ: It really doesn't have to.

LUREEN: They once partied together. Made love till dawn. Sang Nancy Wilson and Dinah Washington songs. Traveled up and down the East Coast. But once the drugs got out of hand, the rent was always overdue, food was scarce, and rubber-soled shoes didn't last. My dad became vicious.

AJ: *(Grabbing her)* I don't give a damn about your stupid father! He couldn't shelter and clothe all of you and get high too. He didn't know how to get high without getting hooked.

LUREEN: You *can't* get high without getting hooked. *(He starts to exit.)* Where are you going?

AJ: *(Putting on jacket)* To buy something.

LUREEN: Here. *(Reaching in to her pocket, throwing a package of dope to AJ)* You're already dead. *We're* dead.

AJ: *(Opening the package)* Like I said, we're all gonna die some time. This just makes it easier. As long as you don't let it get out of hand.

LUREEN: How do you not let it "get out of hand"?

AJ: I do things.

LUREEN: Like what things?

AJ: *(Opening bag of dope)* Like drinking goldenseal tea, skin-popping instead of mainlining, snorting instead of skin-popping; I switch up, baby. Switch the way I get high and then clean my system with tea and vinegar.

LUREEN: Why didn't that work before?

AJ: I didn't know what to do back then.

LUREEN: So you were *stupid*, like my dad.

AJ: *(Taking a snort and then looking at her earnestly)* I'm not trying to hurt you. Getting high is a way for me to cope with *leaving* you, my first and only love.

LUREEN: *(Trying not to break down)* Then take one damn minute and give some thought to my life without you. *(Takes his face in her hands)* I won't have you to laugh at my jokes, or to watch those dumb comedy shows with me, or to make sexy catcalls while I stroll around in my bra and thong sets. *(He looks away.)* You know what I mean, when you sound like a fresh old man flirting with a young girl? Shit, don't think you're the only one around here dying. *I'm* dying too, and I gotta live. And I'm scared to live without you.

AJ: *(Takes another quick snort)* Why do you think I get high? You have no idea how much I love you. *(He pulls her onto his lap.)* I'm scared to be without you too.

LUREEN: *(Giving in, leaning against his chest)* Remember our first date? *(Laughs through her tears)* You were so broke we had to split a slice of pizza! My dad was so jealous of your sobriety. He knew you were smart and going somewhere, and so did I. *(Looks into his face)* In the time we have left together, I don't want to end up like my mother—sad and lonely, even though my dad was right there. They were in different worlds, AJ. They shared nothing.

AJ: *(Slurred voice)* You won't be like your mom, baby. I promise. We can share everything. *(Putting the drug to her nose—encouraging her—she snorts deeply.)*

LUREEN: It won't get out of hand … right?

BLACKOUT

Andre Zucker

My history with Andre goes back a long way and charts a path that, he likes to remind us, saw me through two pregnancies! There was a third birth as well during those years, and that was Andre's. He began his FYV training when we were in residence at his high school, and like hoards of other school children today, Andre was a freshman afflicted with the label of ADD. He was a source of continual distraction in the studio, from constantly swinging and clanking the chain on which he wore his house keys to talking constantly with his classmates. There was a perpetual level of chaos around him, one that detracted from the experience that everyone else in the room was having. His efforts to learn and perform a monologue were hampered both by his inability to stick with anything long enough to memorize it and his inability to allow himself to look at—and be looked at—by another person. He was, however, able to complete a short and very abstract play about two boys who get locked in a meat freezer. It was clear from his writing that Andre's was an intellect of a higher order and that perhaps his perpetually zoned-out affect had developed, in part, to protect himself from boredom! Although we were inclined to "invite him to leave the workshop" after that first difficult year, we decided to persist. Over the next three years as Andre (who had spent many years on Ritalin, to no avail) continued to work at connecting through the acting and writing work, he morphed into a focused and responsive actor. He also became a writer whose wonderfully surreal aesthetic was now married to a deep and authentic sense of humanity; Ode to Joy *was written in his senior year. Andre had not only become an artist, he had become a respectful citizen of the workshop. Andre went on to study playwriting at Purchase College, and he continued to participate in FYV summer master classes, during which he wrote* Future Children of a Lost Generation. *His understanding of the methodology was so profound that he was asked to teach writing in our after-school and summer-school programs several times, and he has been a guest actor at the final performances of many of our educational workshops. He also performed in several plays in a Young Voices workshop, all of which were written by the participating eight-year-olds—including my own son, Jesse, with whom I was pregnant the year that I met Andre! "When* Ode to Joy *premiered, the audience was only kids from my high school.*

They felt very obligated to react to the play as loudly as they could. At first, I thought they were being discouraging, but I soon realized they were caring about the characters in their own loud way! Through this training, I learned that I was capable of long-term projects. I never believed before I came to the training that I could sustain myself for long periods. I learned through FYV that I actually was able to, and that is a skill I use every day." Andre is still writing and acting, and in the summer of 2007 he completed Camino de Santiago de Compostela, walking almost 100 kilometers across northern Spain. At the time of this writing, he was working on a play about the camino.

This play was written in a master class during the summer after Andre's freshman year in college. It was triggered by a photograph of a wrapped gift box.

Future Children of a Lost Generation
Andre Zucker

Characters: JESSICA   Female, 16
             RICHARD   Male, 19

AT RISE: There are two chairs that face each other. In between the chairs is a wrapped present. RICHARD and JESSICA are standing behind the chairs and looking at each other. The room is dimly lit.

JESSICA: Baby, I'm pregnant. *(RICHARD screams like a little girl.)* Richard!
RICHARD: *(He sits.)* I'm going to die.
JESSICA: *(She sits too.)* We need to talk about it.
RICHARD: You're really pregnant?
JESSICA: Yeah, I said it; I'm pregnant.
RICHARD: *(He looks away.)* Sweet Jesus, you're hardly sixteen.
JESSICA: And you're nineteen; age is only a number.
RICHARD: Yo, I'm gonna go to jail for this.
JESSICA: No, you won't.
RICHARD: Look at me; I could get gang-raped for this.
JESSICA: These things can be worked out.

RICHARD: *(Writhing)* Dead, I am so dead. *(Pause)* Can we do something about the pregnancy?

JESSICA: Abortion?

RICHARD: Perhaps.

JESSICA: I don't believe in abortion. Jesus Christ; I'm a fucking Catholic.

RICHARD: *(Face in hands)* Oh my god, you're a Catholic!

JESSICA: Yeah, church every Sunday. *(RICHARD screams like a little girl again.)*

RICHARD: So we have to get—

JESSICA: Yeah.

RICHARD: No.

JESSICA: I don't know what pagan-ass religion *you* belong to, but I'm not going to hell.

RICHARD: I'm Episcopalian.

JESSICA: So?

RICHARD: I hardly know you.

JESSICA: And?

RICHARD: We met less than a month ago.

JESSICA: So?

RICHARD: We're not getting married. *(She pushes him with her foot; the chair falls over, and Richard lands flat on the floor with his face next to the gift box.)*

JESSICA: You irresponsible motherfucker. What are you going to do? *(Silence)* Do you know the penalty for premarital sex? Do you? I'll get murdered. My father is not an easy-going man.

RICHARD: *(Still lying on the floor)* I am in hell's land.

JESSICA: You're damn right.

RICHARD: You curse a lot for a Catholic girl. *(He sees box.)*

JESSICA: *(Kicks him again)* Pay attention.

RICHARD: What's this gift doing here?

JESSICA: You have no balls. Get off the floor.

RICHARD: How long has this been here?

JESSICA: What are you talking about?

RICHARD: *(Sits up and shows her the box)* This gift. Did you bring this here?

JESSICA: You're not even paying attention.

RICHARD: *(Rises)* I've been here all day; when did this get here? Who put this here?

JESSICA: *(She rises too.)* I'm *pregnant*.

RICHARD: I know … but this is really weird.

JESSICA: You are so irresponsible.

RICHARD: No one except you has been here today. *(Looks at her)* Did you bring this here?

JESSICA: You have some real serious problems you have to deal with.

RICHARD: What?

JESSICA: I said: the shit has hit the fan and you ain't doing anything about it.

RICHARD: I'm opening it. *(He takes off the silk wrapping paper and hands it to JESSICA.)*

JESSICA: *(She feels it.)* It was wrapped in silk.

RICHARD: Are you sure you didn't bring this?

JESSICA: It was here when I got here. *(Suspiciously)* No one else lives here, right?

RICHARD: Just me. *(He opens the box.)*

JESSICA: What's in it?

RICHARD *(Richard sits and is silent.)* Oh my god!

JESSICA: What is it? What is it? Fucking tell me what it is.

RICHARD: *(He looks into the box again.)* This isn't funny. Are you sure you didn't bring this here?

JESSICA: *(She grabs the box and pulls out a Paddington Bear. In shock, she drops the bear.)* I didn't bring it.

RICHARD: What the hell does this all mean? *(Silence)* What's happening? I don't understand. I don't get it.

JESSICA: How the fuck are we going to raise a kid?

BLACKOUT

Ode to Joy *was written in Andre's senior year of high school for a cluster entitled* Leaps of Faith. *It was written in response to a photograph of an airplane in the sky (p. 33).*

Ode To Joy
Andre Zucker

Characters: JOE   Male, 16
               REBECCA   Female, 18, his sister

AT RISE: An airport waiting area. A young woman sits in a chair, holding a carry-on and a book bag. She sits down and opens her bag, pulls out a magazine, and starts to read. Her brother JOE walks in carrying a bottle of iced tea.

JOE: Here, Rebecca. *(He hands her the bottle.)*
REBECCA: I asked for diet.
JOE: This tastes better.
REBECCA: Joe, if I drink this I'll get fat.
JOE: Toothpick girl, you look fine.
REBECCA: I have to watch my weight for what I do.
JOE: One non-diet beverage will not make you a porker. You'll still be
    able to dance.
(All of a sudden a voice rings out.)
VOICE: Flight 609, this is your third boarding call.
REBECCA: *(Getting agitated)* Listen, we're going to Seattle for
    Christmas, which I'm not too thrilled with. At dinner I wouldn't
    be surprised if we ate lard right out of the can, so I can't stay on my
    diet for Christmas … but you can return this.
JOE: I don't have a receipt. Just don't drink it.
REBECCA: I'm thirsty.
JOE: You have money; I'll drink it.
REBECCA: This is just like you, always thinking of yourself.
JOE: I just went and got you a drink!
REBECCA: Look, I can't smoke in here. All of a sudden it's a high
    crime against the state and her people to smoke in a building, so
    I'm a little edgy.

JOE: Yeah, cigarettes, a dancer's lunch.

REBECCA: Shut up, Joe. Just cause I happen to watch what I eat, unlike you, who considers pork rinds healthy, doesn't make me like those anorexic ballerina girls.

JOE: I hardly ever eat pork rinds. *(Silence)* Just forget it. What flight are we?

REBECCA: Flight 204.

JOE: We should be getting on in about ten minutes.

REBECCA: I hate airports and airplanes. *(Looks around)* Let's skip this; we'll call Mom and Dad and tell them that we're both sick with the plague or something and that we're not making it to Seattle.

JOE: Look, if we don't get on this plane, heaven help us, cause Mom will have our heads.

REBECCA: I truly and honestly don't want to go.

JOE: That's too bad, because we are going. *(Looks at watch)* In about nine minutes.

REBECCA: *(Losing it)* Yeah, onto a plane that will transport us to rainy, stupid Seattle. And in rainy, stupid Seattle, we'll be with our weird family. That weird family will criticize us at every turn. So let me tell you something, Joe, I'm ready to kill.

JOE: Hey, hey, chill, ok? Don't worry about it. I'll go get you another iced tea. This time it'll be diet.

REBECCA: It better be. *(He walks away.)*

VOICE: Final boarding call for flight 609. Final boarding call for flight 609. *(REBECCA sits shaking her foot nervously; after a moment, he comes back empty-handed.)*

JOE: Sorry, they ran out of diet.

REBECCA: This is all your fault.

JOE: You're right, I should have called the iced tea company and commanded them to move the diet assembly line much faster.

REBECCA: You should have gotten the diet when you first went, so we wouldn't have this non-diet problem.

JOE: I'm not having this non-diet problem, *you* are having this non-diet problem. *(He sits.)* Look Rebecca, I was nice enough to stay here in New York with you. You said, "Joe, please stay, I only have three more shows in my school performance." So I stayed, to show you that someone in the family cares about your art. I really wanted to leave, but I also know that you're terrified to fly. So how about I get you a Diet *Coke*?

REBECCA: *(Yelling)* I want iced tea.

JOE: *(Quieting her)* You have iced tea.

REBECCA: It's not diet. They won't have diet iced tea on the plane either. I'm going to have to go a ridiculous amount of time with only soda and no cigarettes.

JOE: That's a bummer, but it isn't my fault.

REBECCA: Yes, it is.

JOE: How? *(Silence)* It ain't my fault. There is no way this is my fault. Try to prove it's my fault. Try, come on, I dare you, try. See? You can't, so stop trying to scapegoat me.

REBECCA: *(Turning away)* You're not making this whole airport waiting experience pleasant.

JOE: Oh, so that's what this is about?

REBECCA: Not only that.

VOICE: First boarding call for flight 202.

JOE: *(Starts to rise)* That's us, we better go.

REBECCA: No, idiot, we are flight 204, not 202.

JOE: You don't have to be so incredibly rude to me.

REBECCA: Look, today you have put me through hell. This morning you weren't even finished packing. I had to *help* you pack.

JOE: Oh, I'm sorry you had to help someone else for a change.

REBECCA: Shut up.

JOE: No. You only think of yourself and how it's possible to eat less than two grams of fat a day.

REBECCA: So I watch my weight, what's it to you?

JOE: Mom worries.

REBECCA: About what?

JOE: About the fact that you're getting too skinny, and all you talk about is how you eat too much. A carrot is all you eat for dinner, and for breakfast all you eat is a microscopic bowl of nonfat yogurt. And your lunch—your lunch isn't even solid, it's smoke.

REBECCA: So you think I am anorexic.

JOE: You're not anorexic … yet, but you will be if you keep up this way of eating. Can't you eat more stuff that's not fat-free?

REBECCA: I'm a dancer; dancers are skinny. The other girls are much skinnier than me.

JOE: When they do handstands, do their ribs pop out?

REBECCA: Yes.

JOE: Do you want to look like that?

REBECCA: Not that skinny, but the other girls think of me as a cow.

JOE: If a farmer had a cow as skinny as you, do you know what he would do to that cow?

REBECCA: No.

JOE: He would blow its brains out. The cow's no good to anyone that skinny. You get my point?

REBECCA: No.

JOE: Just eat something; you can start by drinking this iced tea. *(Holds it out to her)*

REBECCA: That will make you feel better.

JOE: Yeah, I think I'll feel a whole lot better.

REBECCA: Joe, you don't understand.

JOE: I do understand. Look, if you don't eat you'll become sick. Some women's hair fall out; they can't menstruate properly.

REBECCA: Menstruate? Since when do guys say *menstruate*?

JOE: All right, your moody monthly friend might stop visiting! And worst of all, and I say this in all seriousness, anorexia is a killer. So stop. All you got to do is drink. *(Raises bottle)*

REBECCA: That's it?

JOE: It's do or die.

REBECCA: Do or die?

JOE: Do or die. You drink or die, it's that simple.

REBECCA: But—

JOE: I'm about to smack you.

REBECCA: What?!

JOE: Do you understand how frustrating this is? All I want you to do is drink sixteen fluid ounces of iced tea—it's not that hard.

REBECCA: What's the big deal?

JOE: The big deal is I care. There, I said it. I hate you for making me say that. The really frustrating thing is that you don't care about yourself and that skinny piece of flesh you used to call a body. And if you don't care for yourself, we're going to have to do it for you.

REBECCA: What does that mean?

JOE: That means that we'll have to make sure you eat, and if we can't, a hospital might have to.

REBECCA: Hospital?

JOE: Did you lose your hearing? Yeah, I said hospital. And make no mistake, Mom's talking Bellevue.

REBECCA: I won't go to Bellevue.

JOE: Then drink the iced tea. This is the starting point. *(Pushes bottle toward her)*

REBECCA: But—

JOE: Shut up. Drink it.

REBECCA: *(Staring at the bottle)* You want me to drink this?

JOE: Rebecca. Look at me. Don't just drink, drink to life.

REBECCA: *(Staring at the bottle)* You want me to drink *this*?

JOE: *(Louder)* No, I want you to chug it.

REBECCA: *(Louder than JOE)* You want me to chug it?

JOE: *(Screaming)* Chug it, chug it down. Now.

REBECCA: *(Rising to the challenge, screaming)* All right.

JOE: *(Jumping on the chair to cheer her on)* Chug chug chug—

REBECCA: *(Opening the bottle)* Fine, here we go! *(She chugs it down without stopping.)*

JOE: *(Jumping up and down)* Go, go, go, go. Girl, see you did it!

REBECCA: *(She finishes.)* Yeah. That's right.

JOE: Now, smash the bottle, smash the freaking bottle.

REBECCA: No. *(She sits.)*

JOE: *(Sitting back down)* Oh well, can't win them all. But don't you feel better?

REBECCA: Yeah, I do.

JOE: So, are we going to eat Christmas dinner?

REBECCA: Oh, we're going to eat.

JOE: *(A little louder)* What was that?

REBECCA: *(A little louder)* We're going to eat.

JOE: *(Louder)* One for the road.

REBECCA: *(Louder)* We're going to eat.

JOE: *(Screaming)* What are we going to eat?

REBECCA: *(Jumping up on her seat)* Ham.

JOE: *(Jumping on his seat)* What are we going to eat?

REBECCA: *(Shouting in his face)* Christmas goose.

JOE: *(Shouting in her face)* What are we going to eat, Rebecca?

REBECCA: *(Shouting in his face)* Possibly the meat loaf.

JOE: *(Shouting in her face)* What are we going to drink?

REBECCA: *(Shouting in his face)* Eggnog.

JOE: *(Shouting in her face)* And who are we going to embarrass?

REBECCA: *(Shouting in his face)* Mom and Dad.

JOE: *(Screaming)* Word!

REBECCA: Yeah.

JOE: *(Throws out his arms and screams)* Ode to Joy!!

REBECCA: Huh?

JOE: Nothing.

VOICE: Flight 204 now boarding.

REBECCA: Oh God!

JOE: Let's go. Life is sweet.

BLACKOUT

Afterword

The process of compiling the material in this collection, some of which was on fraying, yellowed, hand-written paper from decades ago, was like time spent perusing a beloved family album.

What made all the effort worthwhile for me, as midwife to these works, was not just the applause and accolades of the audiences, but the relationships with the writers. I am in touch with each and every one of these remarkable people, and I remember vividly the agonies and ecstasies of the process of creation. You can't deliver a baby without falling in love with the mother—the miracle of birth inspires that—and delivering a well-crafted work of art is no different. As I read their reflections about the works they gave permission for me to include, I was transported back to the experience of shaping the piece of theatre that audiences encountered with us. More importantly, I was also transported back to the bond that we shared as a result of that. I have watched the younger *student* writers whose works are included flower into adults, some with families of their own now—all of whom have powerful voices that they bring to their particular fields, whether as ministers, lyricists, physical therapists, or teachers. I was particularly struck by how many of my young students, both represented in this collection and beyond, are still writing or helping others to write, so many years later. It is proof indeed that when you provide a valuable tool, with love, it is a tool that will be used for life. Many have taught beside me in my workshops, helped to administer FYV with me, watched my children for me, and sat on my board. Some I hear from regularly, others every couple of years, but when there is contact, it is with full engagement.

Find Your Voice was a twenty-year experiment in the creation and true sharing of dialogue between people ... all kinds of people. The fulfillment of this experiment inspired me to return to school for a third master's degree, this one in clinical social work. I had stumbled accidentally onto a process that helped scores of people to define and redefine themselves over the years; now I understand exactly why it was so effective. It is no longer an accident that when you find your voice, you find your self. I now offer the core tenets of this approach to self rediscovery as a one-on-one, private exploration, and it continues to be offered within group settings as a publicly social one. It is my great hope that readers of this collection will be inspired to reenact the dramatic material herein, or recreate the process of developing the products of this approach. (Please read *Find Your Voice* for a fuller guide to doing so; the book and the film can be ordered through our website: www. findyourvoice.us.) But equally as important, it is my hope that you will be inspired to honor authentic and connected dialogue with another person *wherever* you find it, whether there is an ocean between you, a footlight, or a candle.